Catharina Raudvere is Professor of the History of Religions at the University of Copenhagen. Her previous books include *The Book and the Roses: Sufi Women, Visibility and Zikir in Contemporary Istanbul* (I.B.Tauris, 2003) and *Sufism Today: Heritage and Tradition in the Global Community* (I.B.Tauris, 2008, co-edited with Leif Stenberg).

'Writing an introduction to such a vast, complex and disputed topic as Islam is to say the least a challenge. But Catharina Raudvere has executed this task with great imaginativeness, while displaying due sensitivity to detail and diversity. Descriptions and analyses creatively alternate between abstract notions of theology, jurisprudence and ethics, on the one hand, and details of daily life, rituals and experiences, on the other hand. Past and present are here ingeniously knitted together, so that the long continuities of Islam as a civilization are underlined. The author succeeds in representing Islam as a living tradition: a tradition in the making right now. Though her book is written for undergraduates, it provides a level of discourse challenging enough to pique the intellectual curiosity of a wider public of academics and educated lay people. A sound balance is struck between the pedagogical objective of conveying the basic aspects of Islam and of providing critical insight into various popular narratives and research agendas related to Islam. It is one of the great merits of the book that the author's proficiency in women's studies compensates for the lack of such perspectives in much of the scholarly literature about Islam. Of particular benefit is the emphasis given to quotations from the Quran. This approach literally and tangibly conveys the importance to Muslims of the holy book. In sum, Raudvere offers an unusually comprehensive, richly illustrated, up-to-date and enjoyable introduction to Islam. It is easy to grasp, without being simplistic, and represents instructive reading for students and rewarding teaching material for instructors.' – *Elisabeth Özdalga, Professor of Political Science, Bilkent University, author of* **The Veiling Issue: Official Secularism and Popular Islam in Modern Turkey**

I.B.TAURIS INTRODUCTIONS TO RELIGION

In recent years there has been a surge of interest in religion and in the motivations behind religious belief and commitment. Avoiding over-simplification, jargon or unhelpful stereotypes, I.B.Tauris Introductions to Religion embraces the opportunity to explore religious tradition in a sensitive, objective and nuanced manner. A specially commissioned series for undergraduate students, it offers concise, clearly written overviews, by leading experts in the field, of the world's major religious faiths, and of the challenges posed to all the religions by progress, globalization and diaspora. Covering the fundamentals of history, theology, ritual and worship, these books place an emphasis above all on the modern world, and on the lived faiths of contemporary believers. They explore, in a way that will engage followers and non-believers alike, the fascinating and sometimes difficult contradictions or reconciling ancient tradition with headlong cultural and technological change.

'I.B.Tauris Introductions to Religion offers students of religion something fresh, intelligent and accessible. Without dumbing down the issues, or making complex matters seem more simple than they need to be, the series manages to be both conceptually challenging while also providing beginning undergraduates with the complete portfolio of books that they need to grasp the fundamentals of each tradition. To be religious is in the end to be human. The I.B.Tauris series looks to be an ideal starting point for anyone interested in this vital and often elusive component of all our societies and cultures.' – *John M. Hull, Emeritus Professor of Religious Education, University of Birmingham*

'The I.B.Tauris Introductions to Religion series promises to be just what busy teachers and students need: a batch of high-quality, highly accessible books by leading scholars that are thoroughly geared towards pedagogical needs and student course use. Achieving a proper understanding of the role of religion in the world is, more than ever, an urgent necessity. This attractive-looking series will contribute towards that vital task.' – *Christopher Partridge, Professor of Religious Studies, Lancaster University*

'The I.B.Tauris series promises to offer more than the usual kind of humdrum introduction. The volumes will seek to explain and not merely to describe religions, will consider religions as ways of life and not merely as sets of beliefs and practices, and will explore differences as well as similarities among specific communities of adherents worldwide. Strongly recommended.' – *Robert A. Segal, Professor of Religious Studies, University of Aberdeen*

Please see the back of the book for the full series list

Islam

An Introduction

by

Catharina Raudvere

I.B. TAURIS

LONDON · NEW YORK

Published in 2015 by I.B.Tauris & Co. Ltd
6 Salem Road, London W2 4BU
175 Fifth Avenue, New York NY 10010
www.ibtauris.com

Distributed in the United States and Canada Exclusively by Palgrave Macmillan
175 Fifth Avenue, New York NY 10010

I.B.Tauris Introductions to Religion

ISBN: 978 1 84885 083 5 (HB)
ISBN: 978 1 84885 084 2 (PB)
eSBN: 978 0 85773 826 4

A full CIP record for this book is available from the British Library
A full CIP record is available from the Library of Congress

Library of Congress Catalog Card Number: available

Typeset by Data Standards Ltd, Frome, Somerset
Printed and bound in Great Britain by TJ International Ltd, Padstow, Cornwall

Contents

List of Maps and Figures   vii

Chapter I: The Muslim World: Past and Present   1

Chapter II: The Early History of Islam and Muhammad as a
                  Historical Person   29

Chapter III: The Canonical Texts of Islam: Historical
                  Documents and Personal Piety   59

Chapter IV: Sharia: The Law of Allah and Human Free Will   83

Chapter V: The Festivals of the Muslim Year and Lifecycle
                  Rituals: Community and Celebration   107

Chapter VI: Between Canonical Obligations and Devotional
                  Practices: Everyday Religiosity   133

Chapter VII: Shi'i Islam: Religious Authority and
                  Remembered Martyrdom   167

Chapter VIII: Muslim Ethics: Ideals, Responsibilities and the
                  Challenges of Modern Life   185

Chapter IX: Political Islam: Visions and Nightmares   213

Epilogue   239

Notes   245

Sources and References   249

Index   253

List of Maps and Figures

Maps

1. The Arabian Peninsula at the time of Muhammad's appearance as a prophet — 32

2. The early expansion of Islam — 52

3. The major Shi'i communities of the world — 169

Figures

1. The tomb of the granddaughter of Muhammad, Sayyida Zaynab, Damascus, Syria. *(Source: Umbertod [public domain], via Wikimedia Commons)* — 11

2. Pilgrims gathered around the Kaaba. *(Source: Aiman Titi [public domain], via Wikimedia Commons)* — 34

3. Buraq, the animal on which Muhammad was transported to the heavens. *(Source: Brooklyn Museum [public domain], via Wikimedia Commons)* — 46

4. A nineteenth-century *qibla* compass with an image of the Kaaba and the names of cities in the Muslim world, from Tunis to Samarkand. *(Courtesy of the David Collection, Copenhagen, photo: Pernille Klemp)* — 53

5. The Qur'an as a sacred object. *(Getty Images)* — 61

6. A woman signing a marriage contract (*nikah*). *(Getty Images)* — 96

7. A prayer rug (*sajjada*). *(Source: Walters Art Museum [public domain], via Wikimedia Commons)* — 145

8. The basic spatial structure of a mosque. *(Author)*   147

9. A sixteenth-century ceramic tile from Iznik indicating the
    direction of prayer. *(Courtesy of the David Collection,
    Copenhagen, photo: Pernille Klemp)*   148

10. Members of a Sufi order in Pakistan in ritual garb. *(Getty
    Images)*   155

11. The turning ceremony *(sema)* practised by the Mevlevi
    order. *(Source: Tomas Maltby [public domain], via Wikimedia
    Commons)*   161

12. A young man in Baghdad holding a poster of Ali, martyr,
    mystic and knight. *(Getty Images)*   171

13. *Turbah,* a clay tablet that connects the Shi'i fellowship
    over time and space. *(Courtesy of the David Collection,
    Copenhagen, photo: Pernille Klemp)*   180

14. Muslim women in Oxford Street, London. *(Source: Alfredo
    Borba [public domain], via Wikimedia Commons)*   200

15. A Halal counter in a modern supermarket. *(Getty Images)*   210

Chapter I

The Muslim World: Past and Present

This introduction to Islam is mainly intended to be a guide to the study of contemporary Muslim life in its many (and sometimes contradictory) forms, although the relevant historical background will be provided when necessary. Diversity and transformation will therefore be recurring themes throughout the volume, and several diverging answers to the question 'What is Islam?' will be presented. Examples from canonical literature such as the Qur'an and the narratives referring to the time of Muhammad (sing. *hadith*) will be quoted to give a sense of the character of the Islamic scriptures and to indicate how many possible interpretations the individual texts open up.

Today, there are approximately 1.5 billion Muslims across the world. Nevertheless, the conventional stereotype of a Muslim is an Arab, despite the fact that only 20 per cent of the world's Muslims live in the Arabic-speaking parts of the Middle East and North Africa. This fact should also be a reminder that all parts of the Middle East are not Arabic-speaking; Iran and Turkey, with Muslim majority populations, represent other cultural traditions and historical developments in the region. Of the 1.5 billion Muslims is it impossible to know how many practise Islam, to how many Islam is an issue of ethnic identity or family and community belonging, rather than personal faith, or how many regard themselves as secularized with a Muslim cultural background with or without personal piety. The problems of producing statistics on religious belonging are many. The methodology cuts through the private and the public spaces an individual dwells in, and does not grasp the identity shifts of individuals in various contexts or over time in different phases of life. Only 20 per cent of the world's Muslims live in one of the 30 countries where Islam is the denomination of the majority, which means that encounters with non-Muslims are part of everyday life (and not necessarily without

conflict) for the vast majority and not a particularity exclusive to
Muslims in Europe. The Muslim world is therefore hard to define,
and has been so for a long time.

1.5 billion Muslims in the world

There are significant differences between countries where Muslims
constitute a dominant portion of the population (in some countries in
the Middle East and North Africa over 95 per cent) and countries that
have the largest numbers of Muslims but are nevertheless multi-
religious (such as Indonesia, India and Nigeria) in terms of how local
life is lived. The four countries with the largest Muslim populations in
the world (all of them outside the Middle East) are:

- Indonesia: 210 million
- India: 170 million (12–15 per cent of the population)
- Pakistan: 160 million
- Bangladesh: 130 million
  followed by
- Egypt 82 million
- Turkey 74 million
- Iran 74 million
- Nigeria 40 million (50 per cent of the population).

These figures are drawn from Pew Forum's *Mapping the Global
Muslim Population*, 2009. The institute is known to give conservative
figures rather than over-estimations. Larger numbers for the statistics
of the world's Muslim population are therefore to be found in other
sources.[1]

In various ways, the countries all represent cultural and religious
amalgamations that have taken place over the centuries. Furthermore,
they have extensive diaspora populations all over the world with
transnational links at all levels of societal life, which adds to the
picture of a majority of Muslims in regular contact with people of
other faiths or living in countries with anti-religious traditions.
Muslims in China are estimated to constitute 1.6 per cent of the
population, which means 22 million people; and Muslims in countries
of the former Soviet Union number approximately 76 million, 16
million of them living in Russia today.

Both 'the Muslim world' and 'the West' are highly ideological concepts – disputed not only in the wake of the Orientalism debate, but also from the perspective of contemporary identity politics and diaspora culture. They are not the names of any distinct geographical places. Instead, the two terms carry an implicit dichotomy between 'Christian' and 'Muslim' and ignore the fact that many Muslims throughout history, as well as today, live in close contact with people of other denominations; neither do 'Muslims' constitute a homogeneous category, considering how theology and rituals have developed over time – not to mention differences of gender, generation and social status within communities. Not only are the diaspora groups in countries with traditionally few Muslims increasing in numbers, but new living conditions are also having a steadily growing global impact, bringing about all kinds of identity alternatives and producing cultural blends that may, or may not, be regarded as a provocative alteration of Islam's original message. These milieus are the breeding ground for pronounced reactions against traditionalism as well as for the construction of identities that integrate the local and the global, while retaining a link to Muslim history and the canonical texts. Although references to diaspora will be made frequently in this book, there are good reasons to question the underlining of diaspora when analysing Muslims in Europe and North America. There is segregation, prejudice and conflict, but there are also many examples of well integrated everyday religious life; perhaps most importantly, the Muslim presence in these regions now has a long-term history covering several generations and the members of the communities are in many cases not looking back to any homeland, but are citizens in their own right, no longer meriting a 'diaspora' label.

The mosque is traditionally a prime location for Muslim community life as the local site for canonical worship. It has by tradition also been an important locus for the execution of local religious authority (in most cases performed by the imam) and it has long served as a meeting place for its regular visitors and constituted a nexus for local (male) networks. The question is whether the mosque and its premises will remain the most important place of Muslim community and, if so, on what conditions. The mosque is still an important site for Muslim religious practice – for prayer, education, social networking and political mobilization – in what is conventionally recognized as the Muslim world as well as in the Muslim

Diaspora

The term diaspora refers to the dispersion or migration of a specific group and was originally used to describe the Jewish exile. The term further implies not only a geographical spread, but also a notion of homeland and/or a shared origin that keeps the dispersed from being absorbed in other environments. Fellowship in a diaspora group can be based on the recognition of a common denominator, an identity, which is founded on a conception of a shared geographical origin, a spatial belonging. When it comes to the relationship between identity and belonging, Benedict Anderson's *Imagined Communities* (1983) was influential in its discussion of how fellowships are based on narratives that construct collective memory. The book's focus on nationalism could easily be applied to religious narratives too.

diaspora. But the mosque has started to lose some of its local dominance in many Muslim contexts, especially since there are so many new forums in which take part in teaching, debates and socio-religious activities. The absence of women in traditional mosques must also be noted as something that is changing – in some places rapidly. This does not mean that the spatial separation between men and women is being eroded, but that alternative interpretive spaces are emerging. Today, Islam is practised, discussed and interpreted by agents and in settings that do not fit with the conventional image of 'Muslims'.

Orientalism

After the publication of Edward Said's *Orientalism* in 1978, a long critical debate took place about what power structures academic writing reproduce in their representations of Islam and Muslims and how many images of Middle Eastern and Asian cultures were rooted in European colonialism. Following Foucault, Said's work paved the way for a greater emphasis in Islamic studies on local expressions and individual voices that articulate contradictions rather than confirming the image of 'Islam'. The ideological side of Said's study soon became part not only of academic analyses but also of political discourse and merged with post-colonial perspectives and cultural studies.

Orientalism is nowadays mostly a pejorative term pointing at the uses of stereotypes and dichotomies in the production of knowledge – often formulated from a post-colonial perspective or a self-reflective criticism of Eurocentrism in analytical concepts. The contrasting term occidentalism, 'the Eastern' view of 'the West', is not so much the label of a counter discourse to orientalism but has rather come to connote 'anti-Westernism' in a broad, but not necessarily academic, sense.

Robert Irwin's *For the Lust of Knowing: The Orientalists and Their Enemies* (2006), like many other criticisms of Said, pointed to his lack of understanding of the academic contributions made over the centuries despite colonial power relations between Western scholarship and its objects of investigation.

As pointed out by Said, and others before him, Islam cannot be referred to as an idealized, homogeneous system,[2] a standpoint that has far-reaching consequences for the study of religion in general and certainly not only religions from the Orient. Leif Manger in *Muslim Diversity* (1999) stresses that differences and what appear to be inconsistencies can be useful tools for identifying variation in terms of historical and regional background and social and ecological structures. Local and regional traditions (*ada*) are determinants for ethics, rituals and social practice.

The world in which Islam emerged

Islam grew out of a specific context on the Arabian Peninsula in the seventh century, which had various distant cultural influences, and the presence of Jewish and Christian communities is apparent in the canonical texts. Even though most Christians and Jews left after World War II, the Middle East has for a very long time been multi-religious. The current situation in Iraq and Syria, and the encounter with the refugees from the area have made the general public in the receiving countries aware of the long history of many different Christian churches in the Middle East. Muslims in other regions have for centuries lived close to communities of other faiths. The devotional traditions of Muslims in Southeast Asia and on the Indian subcontinent are clearly a consequence of long-term interaction with Hindu communities. Sharing pilgrim sites and visiting saints' graves are not uncommon practices in this region – though attacked

The Muslim majority and the status of the Arabic language

Arabic has a special status among Muslims as a sacred language. The Qur'an refers to itself as a book in Arabic and the language of the daily prayers is Arabic. The beginning of the 12th section or chapter (*sura*) states:

Those are the signs of the Manifest Book.
We have sent it down as an Arabic Koran;
haply you will understand.

Even if only 20 per cent of the Muslims of the world are Arabs, the ideals of proper behaviour and a just society are based on the narratives of the early Muslim communities on the Arabian Peninsula during the time of Muhammad and the four generations after him.

Basic Islamic education in local Qur'an schools provides proficiency in reciting a few *suras*, some of them embedded in canonical and local prayer genres. This training does not necessarily provide discursive access to the holy text. Reciting the Qur'an in Arabic can be as much a mode of prayer as it is a way of extracting religious knowledge from the text.

by radical elements – as was the case in the Balkans before the war in the 1990s, after which such encounters became impossible.

Early Muslim concepts make a distinction between Muslim and other domains. The term for the non-Muslim world 'the house of war' (*dar al-harb*) was formulated in relation to the territorial expansion of early Islam but later received a wider meaning, indicating cultural struggle and contrasted to 'the house of Islam' (*dar al-islam*). A decisive factor in Muslim/non-Muslim contacts throughout history is the un-centralized way in which Muslim communities are organized. There is no central authority with jurisdiction on legal or theological matters. It is obvious throughout history how empires and states (or dominating clans, for that matter) have tried by various means to organize, and thereby control, religion in public life. It was crucial from the early days of Islam to establish clear definitions to indicate who is a member of the Muslim community (*umma*) and to state what the believer is expected to submit to its moral codex and ritual practices. Who should be defined as a sectarian or heretic and on what terms has been controversial, and the various positions indicate diverging self-definitions.

The traditional theological concept for a tolerated non-Muslim person is a *dhimmi*, meaning 'protected', and hence the expression 'the protected peoples' (*ahl al-dhimma*). The differentiation between monotheists with a holy scripture and followers of other religions has had an enormous historical impact on how Muslim rulers have related to their non-Muslim subjects. Being a tolerated monotheist implied a juridical status that made some non-Muslim communities pay a special tax (*jizya*), but it also rendered a certain civil autonomy. This categorization carries a distinction between Muslims – the followers of the completed religion Islam – and the tolerated religions whose followers are monotheists and accept a revealed book, and the broad category of unacceptable groups of pagans, polytheists, unbelievers and heretics; in short, followers of what is not included in the genealogy of true revelation. The Qur'an claims:

> But had the People of the Book believed
> and been godfearing, We would have acquitted
> them of their evil deeds, and admitted them
> to Gardens of Bliss.
> Had they performed
> the Torah and the Gospel, and what was
> sent down to them from their Lord, they would
> have eaten both what was above them, and
> what was beneath their feet. Some of them are
> a just nation; but many of them – evil are
> the things they do.[3] (5:65–66)

The People of the Book (*ahl al-kitab*) are identified in history through a line of earlier prophets (*al-anbiya*), of whom 28 are mentioned in the Qur'an. The third *sura* says: 'People of the Book! Why do you disbelieve in God's signs, which you yourselves witness?' (3:70). The People of the Book constitute a category separated from local and distant pagans. On the one hand, these are clearly non-Muslims; on the other, is there a similar shared genealogy indicated by the definition of the People of the Book as monotheists with a canonical script; that is, Jews, Christians and, to some extent, Zoroastrians. The Qur'an refers to itself as 'the Book' or 'the Script'.

By tradition, the People of the Book have been granted limited freedom of religion and autonomy, as long as the minorities did not challenge Islamic law. Muslim tradition has not accepted revelations more recent than Islam, which would go against the fundamental definitions. The Zoroastrians of Persia constitute a source of dispute, as they fulfil the criteria of being followers of a canonical text but their monotheism is disputable and their rituals are rejected. Hindus and Buddhists have never qualified, as they are considered polytheists. Groups considered Muslim apostates, such as Ahmadiya and Bahai, have likewise never received protection (*dhimma*).

The *millet* system

The Ottoman Empire developed an administrative structure for the governance of religious minorities. As early as the fall of Constantinople in 1453, non-Sunni minorities were given the status of 'nations', in which each nation (*millet*) in the meaning religious community in the empire to some extent carried out its own jurisdiction (at least in civil matters). The minorities occupied particular blocks (sing. *mahalle*) and therefore to a large extent led their lives in restricted urban areas, specializing in certain trades and handicrafts. The internal autonomy of the group could be consider-able, but individual autonomy was limited to what was considered customary. Membership of a religious community was therefore of greater importance to a subject of the sultan than individual citizenship. To some extent, this understanding of identity lives on in large parts of the old Ottoman Empire, where only religious (not ethnic) communities are officially recognized as minorities (in Greece, Turkey and Bosnia-Herzegovina, for example).

In Ottoman times, outward signs were demanded of the different groups (such as special clothes, colours and headgear) and restrictions were placed on the economic and civic interaction between *millet*s. The appearance in public of non-Muslim signs such as crosses was also regulated.

In many ways the *millet* system provides a historical mirror for the discussions of multiculturalism and power relations between majority and minorities today: similar questions, different living conditions.

Umma: a mode of living in the local and the worldwide community

The concept of *umma* has always had a double meaning, indicating the worldwide, unified fellowship of Muslims as well as the immediate local congregation. The idea in both understandings of the term mirrors the image of the community established by Muhammad as the moral norm. In the contemporary world, *umma* has acquired a broader meaning of Muslim diversity, visible in everyday encounters as a consequence of national and international migration. Migration and media reporting have made variations between Muslim groups more visible, a fact Islamic leaders must relate to irrespective of whether appreciating or rejecting these cultural differences. Since the early expansion of Islam, *umma* has been an inclusive worldwide concept. *Umma* tends to have another global meaning nowadays, offering other modes of being Muslim than the customs of the local community. In many respects – politically, socially, artistically, to mention but a few areas besides the obvious communicative and economic as well as lifestyles – the impact of globalization has been a parallel process of smoothing out differences as well as strengthening local identity.

A *virtual* umma

Social media not only offers websites and debate forums of various Muslim groups and organizations, it also provides new modes of piety. The combination of text, imagery and sound is an effective tool for communication. Also in alternative worlds, congregations are formed and prayers performed. Virtual daily prayers are offered on the web as a way of building community irrespective of distance and redefines the *umma* when the internet is not only a tool for education, mission or debate.

Today, the traditional *umma* is contested, or at least facing competition. Modern living conditions, new lifestyles and changing authority structures, as new groups have access to religious knowledge, have an effect on young people and gender relations. These could be argued to be processes that have had a worldwide impact since the second half of the nineteenth century, and are now spreading globally with increasing speed. Their impact on Muslim social practices and Islamic theology is considerable and lessens the importance of regional and ethnic diversity in favour of difference in terms of social and virtual networks, education and political orientation.

Traditionally, local and regional leadership has been conducted by the imams, in most cases sharing a background with the community, fulfilling the expectations of the role and following the given paths of authority.

On the one hand, these changes have a tendency to make the imam a more pronounced community leader with more formalized ties to his community (the congregation, often community-based) and a particular place (the local mosque). One the other hand, the position of the local imam is being challenged by new professional groups.

World migration and transnational lives is not only an issue of the contemporary Muslim diaspora in Europe. The Islamic world has always been characterized by mobility and long-distance communication between groups, though the impact on large groups of Muslims of increasing world migration over the last three or four decades cannot be overestimated. Some of the larger communities of refugees with Muslim backgrounds are to be found in Pakistan, Iran, Sudan and Jordan as a consequence of the long conflicts in the Afghanistan-Pakistan, Palestine and Sudan-Somalia regions. The conflicts in these areas have been the breeding ground of violent radicalism, with a worldwide impact, and the conflicts have been iconic in arguments relating to other debates and disputes.

Along with urbanization, which has caused major changes in demography, new lifestyles and labour patterns have been decisive factors in the construction of alternative Muslim identities. Mobility is a key concept in this context, as it indicates both mobilization within movements and that of humans and ideas over national and other borders. Transnational individual lives are in many cases lived between several places called home, and family and community might well be connected to yet other sites that are of importance to identity and belonging. A Lebanese Shi'i family in London might have links through travel and social media to certain blocks in Beirut that they recognize as home, but also to sites of worship in Syria, Iraq and Iran that confirm their religious affiliation. A special condition for life in diaspora is that these places are often difficult or impossible to visit (for political or economic reasons). Nevertheless, emotional links are maintained through narratives, rituals and artwork – and by political discourse.

At the mausoleum of Sayyida Zaynab, (see Figure 1 next page) the granddaughter of Muhammad, just south of Damascus, thousands of pilgrims gather each day to pray and touch the latticework in front of

Fig. 1   The tomb of the granddaughter of Muhammad, Sayyida Zaynab, Damascus,
Syria. *(Source: Umbertod [public domain], via Wikimedia Commons)*

her coffin. They come here to perform the ceremonies that provide a
tactile link with the Muslim genealogy and transmit a blessing to the
visitor. Groups of pilgrims listen to recitations of the tragic legend of
the descendants of the prophet.

The mausoleum is heavily decorated; imagery, sounds and
architecture create an intense atmosphere and strong emotions
connect past and present, places of devotion and families scattered as
a consequence of regional and international politics during the last
decades.

The establishment of new Muslim spaces under novel conditions,
and the links to what is conceived as the 'homeland' (sometimes even
by the third generation of migrants), should not only be interpreted in
negative terms – in terms of loss – although this can be a fundamental
sentiment in individual lives. Transnational living conditions can very
well constitute openness to creative spaces of hybridity – not always
appreciated by the older generation – and have influences in both
directions. The French Sufi rapper Abd al Malik uses contemporary
performance forms to depict alienation in the *banlieues* as well

as classical Sufi thinking about love and the ultimate unity of everything.

> Everything is mixed-up confusion between the
> important and the futile
> Everything has a meaning to be understood; it is a
> question of opening its heart
> Do not surrender to horror, get back on your feet after
> making a mistake
> When I am scared of not being at my best I hear
> A voice telling me I am loved and the lover
> Love my only vestment like the robe of the Prophet. (Malik,
> 2009: 154)

This text voices flux and confusion, but also refers to the protection afforded by the mantle of Muhammad, an old and much loved metaphor for the protecting qualities of belief and divine support in the life of the individual.

Hybridity

Hybridity has been a term frequently used in cultural studies to analyse the domains where cultural and religious expressive forms mix and merge. The observed cultural fusions are often controversial, as religious communities (and certainly not only Muslim ones) define themselves as the keepers of heritage and tradition. The generational conflicts are apparent in terms of both form and content.

In Muslim hip hop the pious intentions of the singers cannot be denied. Nevertheless, the songs have stirred controversy, as has the film *The Taqwacores* (2010), which depicts a fictitious Muslim punk collective in Buffalo, NY. This artistic expression is regarded by some as ill-willed blasphemy, but by others as an honest attempt to represent the many faces of Muslim life in North America.

The local *umma* in diaspora, often with an emphasis on ethnic belonging, appears to be important to newly arrived and first-generation Muslims (work migrants, war refugees and other victims of forced migration), as is the case in all migrant environments. At this point, the ethnic and religious aspects of the life of the local *umma* are inseparable, as local communities offer a much-needed network and maintain what their members conceive as tradition while many factors push for the establishment of new identities in new environments. Attempts to balance the conflict between the two can cause discord for both individuals and communities. Furthermore, a local community offers children and youths access to tradition and a Muslim identity that is not always welcomed; neither the ethnic nor the religious identity is always attractive to the second generation. Muslim congregations across ethnicities sometimes compete by means of the theological orientation of a mosque and/or its social activities, and the new local vernacular becomes the shared idiom in conversations and sermons. The encounters in new congregational constellations open up to knowledge about other Muslim ways of living, in areas where Muslims constitute the majority as well as in the diaspora. They also open up new spaces of authority and processes of establishing legitimacy to interpret tradition and the scriptures.

The concepts of religion as expressed in beliefs, practices and ideals

There is a general tendency in the study of religion to limit the theological processes of change to the world of learning. In the Muslim world, this means to imams and scholars, who have traditionally had socially established authority to provide interpretations, judgement and advice. In the wake of globalization and the eruption of new media, religious institutions worldwide are witnessing an apparent shift in authority, which is often beyond the reach of local leadership. This shift has been criticized by more conservative forces, but the changes have already taken place.

Emphasizing the new Muslim voices is important, but it can also hinder the view of the alternatives to local hierarchies that have been posited throughout Islamic history. Eleanor Doumato's study *Getting God's Ear* (2000) provides a long-term analysis of women's religious knowledge in an environment dominated by Sunni orthodoxy, where women had (and still have) limited access to Islamic learning. Drawing on written accounts produced by Christian missionaries in the Gulf region (in both Sunni and Shi'i communities) and travellers' accounts about women in charge of the holy words and with full legitimacy to take leading positions from the late nineteenth century onward, Doumato is able to discuss alternative ritual practices. These archive documents shed new light on how Sunni and Shi'i Muslims have lived together in everyday encounters characterized by both conflict and cooperation. Perhaps the most important conclusion to be drawn from Doumato's study is that ritual space is not only a question of gender, as is often assumed in the case of Islam; it is also to a large extent an issue of the choice of ritual forms and textual genres. Women's engagement in mourning ceremonies, prayers at gravesites, celebrations of the prophet's birthday or healing rituals by means of reciting the Qur'an indicates that alternative spaces such as shrines, burial grounds and private premises are neglected in overviews of where religion takes place.

Religion has always been given interpretations at the local level by individuals who are not in general regarded as authorities, interpretations which in many ways contradict conventional theological views of religion (views often reproduced in academic writing without any further reflection on whose image of Islam is being reflected). No doubt, processes like globalization, world migration, transnational lifestyles and the development of social media have had an impact on groups that have not been particularly visible when it comes to theological interpretation. Among them are women, but also young people and in general those with no formal religious education, who nowadays by means of other professional skills come to grasp the canonical texts from their own points of departure and introduce other spiritual experiences. New people accessing the canonical texts mean that conventional categories in the study of Islamic theology need complementary tools, from comparative literature, art and semiotics. These challenges to the old interpretative domains are certainly not something unique to the Muslim world; they can be observed in all world religions today.

The early history of Islam will be presented in Chapter 2, with a special emphasis on how the new teaching defined itself in relation to Judaism and Christianity. This is, however, not only an interesting historical fact with an impact on the theological development of the Muslim tradition; it is also highly visible in the canonical literature, where an understanding of what 'Muslim' indicated was formed in relation to the competing religious identities. Islam's particular features were to be visible in social life, in order to make a difference in a multicultural environment; fasting during Ramadan, the mosque as a communal prayer hall for the (male) community and rules for moral conduct (sharia) were established during Islam's formative period. These public practices manifested the presence of the new religion. The *hadiths* provided images of collective identity for the early community. The following example from one of the collections draws a scene where coherent ritual behaviour is emphasized.

> Once Allah's Apostle fell off a horse and his leg or shoulder got injured. He swore that he would not go to his wives for one month and he stayed in a Mashruba (attic room) having stairs made of date palm trunks. So his companions came to visit him, and he led them in prayer sitting, whereas his companions were standing. When he finished the prayer, he said, 'Imam is meant to be followed, so when he says "Allahu Akbar," say "Allahu Akbar" and when he bows, bow and when he prostrates, prostrate and if he prays standing pray, stand.' (Sahih Bukhari 1:8:375)

The canonical texts of Islam show a great cognizance of other religions and define the only God in relation to other faiths that surrounded the early *umma* (see Chapter 2). The message brought by Muhammad is depicted in relation to other religions present when Islam developed as a specific community in terms of teaching, rituals and institutions. It positioned itself by means of reflection over other religions and moral stands in the early formative texts.

Islam grew in an environment of trans-regional contacts and influences, introduced by trading in many directions; Islamic normative literature often defines the position of the *umma* through its encounters with other religious groups – a situation that is not so different from the living conditions many Muslims in the diaspora experience today. From its outset, Islam was conceptualized as a religion with universal claims, not knowing any regional or ethnic limits, and as a fulfilment of earlier messages delivered to mankind. The universality of the message goes beyond ethnic borders, embracing the followers of the final revelation and sets the limits for encounters with other denominations.

Both Adam and Abraham have iconic status in Islam, the former as the father of mankind and the latter as the founder of monotheistic religion and the first believer, as the Qur'an recounts in 2:124–40 and 3:65ff. They shared the role of forebearers of the new religion. The Qur'an does not provide longer mythical narratives, but the second *sura* tells of Adam, with references to the Judeo-Christian myth: the fundamental split between Allah and his creation, which both theology and rituals seek to bridge in order to bring back a closeness between the Creator and his creation.

> And We said, 'Adam, dwell thou, and thy wife, in the Garden, and eat thereof easefully where you desire; but draw not nigh this tree, lest you be evildoers.' Then Satan caused them to slip therefrom and brought them out of that they were in; and We said, 'Get you all down, each of you an enemy of each; and in the earth a sojourn shall be yours, and enjoyment for a time.' Thereafter Adam received certain words from his Lord, and He turned towards him; truly He turns, and is All-compassionate. (2:35–37)

As in the other two Abrahamic religions, the fall of Adam constitutes the beginning of the master narrative of humankind in search of salvation and its endeavour to return to the primordial order.

The concept of religion is always difficult to translate between cultures. The term *din*, literally 'way of life, custom or behaviour' and conventionally translated as 'religion', implies a definition of Islam as primordial, unaffected by time and space. From this perspective other religions are thought to be misunderstandings or corruptions of the original religion. The canonical texts formulate requirements to be fulfilled by the believer, while institutional structures and rituals each provide their interpretation of how religion should be practised and what legitimizes certain behaviour. Islam is defined in the Qur'an as 'the religion of God' (3:19) and the text is at many points self-reflective over the role the Book holds in the process of transmission of the will of God, but it does not always prescribe in detail how Islam is to be lived; there is always space for interpretation.

The way religions define themselves in their sacred scriptures is not always comparable to the actual organization of religious activities and claims of legitimacy. The anthropologist Talal Asad provided a conceptual view of religion in the wake of the discussions following Edward Said's *Orientalism* (1978) when he wrote: 'If religious symbols are understood, on the analogy with words, as vehicles of meaning, can such meanings be established independently from the form of life in which they are used?', and he continued: 'can we say much about them without considering how they come to be authorized?' (Asad, 1993: 53). The history of Islam and Muslim life is therefore also to a large extent the story of how authority is claimed for leadership, scriptural interpretation and moral standards. The Islamic concept *din* involves a set of beliefs and ritual practices that function as the basis of a distinct community (*umma*). These doctrines of faith and ritual do not distinguish between private and public matters. The legal standards for this amalgamation of law and morality are referred to as *sharia*, which is not a written codex, but legal traditions argued from cases in the Qur'an and the *hadiths* in a form not so different from common law, which is based on precedent.

The frequently recited 'Throne Verse' in the second *sura* (2:255) summarizes the theological basis of Islam: its absolutely monotheistic belief in the eternal and incomparable God. It offers a popular outline of Allah's qualities and underlines at the same time how incomprehensible he is in his greatness:

> God there is no god but He, the Living, the Everlasting.
> Slumber seizes Him not, neither sleep;
> to Him belongs all that is in the heavens and the earth.
> Who is there that shall intercede with Him save by His leave?
> He knows what lies before them and what is after them,
> and they comprehend not anything of His knowledge save such
> He wills.
> His Throne comprises the heavens and the earth;
> the preserving of them oppresses Him not;
> His is the All-high, the All-glorious. (2:255)

The verse explicates the qualities of Allah and the linear timeline of earthly life in relation to eternity.

The following is a brief outline of some of the basic concepts in the Muslim faith. All the concepts mentioned above and below have been interpreted and discussed throughout history; they have constituted the glue of communities and fellowships as well as being the source of conflicts.

Al-Fatiha is the *sura* of the Qur'an and is regarded by many Muslims as a synthesis of the Muslim faith, pointing to its essential elements, such as the characterization of Allah (compassionate and still the judge), the relation of humans to Allah (servants in need of help) and the path that leads to Allah as well as the destiny of those who turn their backs on him. It would, however, be wrong to label it a creed, since the Christian equivalents were formally accepted at Councils of the Church and no such interregional institution to confirm dogma has ever existed among the Muslims. Authority to claim the correct

Fatihat al-Kitab

Fatihat al-Kitab, 'The Opening of the Book', is a chapter acting as the introduction to the Qur'an and spoken as a prayer. The chapter, referred to as 'The Opening' (al-Fatiha), is often treated as a statement of faith:

> In the Name of Allah, the Merciful, the Compassionate.
> Praise belongs to Allah, the Lord of the worlds,
> The Merciful, the Compassionate,
> Wielder of the Day of Judgement.
> Thee do we serve, and on Thee do we call for help;
> Guide us in the straight path,
> The path of those upon whom Thou hast bestowed good,

interpretation of religion has been either local or connected with the state apparatus of an empire. The direction of communication here is different from the rest of the Qur'an, which represents the voice of Allah; in this opening *sura* it is mankind speaking to Allah. The *basmala* phrase 'In the Name of Allah, the Merciful, the Compassionate' (*bismilllah-al-rahman-al-rahim*) is not only an introduction to this *sura* and prayer, but also the introductory statement to all but one chapter of the Qur'an and is used as vocation when beginning recitations and during prayer meetings.

The introductory *sura* constitutes a vital part of the five mandatory daily prayers and is repeated several times during each prayer session. Al-Fatiha, with its invocatory character, is frequently used during all kinds of prayer meetings, not only the mandatory, often indicating the opening or the closing of a section of prayers, blessing or praise. It is a prayer for the individual as well as the collective. Pronounced or inscribed on artefacts, the words are perceived to be protective. One of the *hadith* collections, Sahih Bukhari, relates the following: 'Allah's Apostle said, "Whoever does not recite al-Fatiha in his prayer, his prayer is invalid"' (1:12:723). Al-Fatiha is therefore often claimed to be the minimum of Islamic and Arabic knowledge required of a Muslim.

The essence of Islam is contained in the concept of 'the five pillars'. These provide the common denominators of Islam and combine faith and practice in the claim of unity, but they have also served as excluding arguments, rejecting diversity. The 'pillars' are obligatory (*fard*) according to sharia and go back to a saying of Muhammad that five things in religion are compulsory.

The five pillars of Islam

The five pillars of Islam (*arkan al-islam*) present the core of the Islamic faith, but with more emphasis on religious practice than al-Fatiha, quoted above. Both the pillars and the opening *sura* can be regarded as an indication of how Islam was profiled in relation to Judaism and Christianity, and it can also be noted that several of the demands imply social practice in one way or another that underline Muslim practice as public identity marker.

The five pillars of Islam are:

- Bear witness to the Muslim belief (*shahada*) that 'There is no god but God, and Muhammad is his messenger' (*la ilaha illa Allah wa-Muhammad rasul Allah*), a sort of creed;
- Perform the five daily *salat* prayers and the accompanying intention and purification;
- Give alms (*zakat*);
- Fast during the month of Ramadan (*sawm*);
- If possible, conduct a pilgrimage to Mecca (*hajj*) once in your lifetime.

These five imperatives are not made explicit by any formal act or institution, but are based on customary practice – as is sharia as a whole. The canonical literature of Islam does not include any doctrinal thesis. The Qur'an provides some distinct rules and prohibitions; the *hadiths* supply narratives about the judgements and choices made by the prophet and his first followers in the community. Efforts to codify the religion for pedagogical purposes are based on local tradition. Most Muslims would agree that the pillars constitute the basis of Islam, but when it comes to how to practise them, customs diverge. It should be noted that this traditional list starts with the declaration of faith and its conceptual framework, followed by the four other pillars, which are rituals and/or social practices. Islam, seen from this perspective, is a matter of practices and literally means 'surrender to Allah'. A Muslim is, according to the Qur'an and the pillars, principally defined as a person whose belief in the origin of the world implies a certain ritual and social conduct as a community member.

There is a long tradition in Muslim theology of systematizing the fundamentals of the faith (pl. *aqaid*) as extracted from the Qur'an and the *hadiths*, mostly with a pedagogical purpose. Local understandings of how to live according to these demands are consequences of living conditions and of the conventions of the four schools of law and regional diversity (see Chapter 4).

A common understanding makes the following division in the organization of theological knowledge: belief (*iman*), practice (*islam*) and virtue (*ihsan*).

Belief (*iman*), the conceptual content of religion, has its basis in an understanding of Allah's unity (*tawhid*) and in the revelation in the Book, through Muhammad. A Muslim is one who falls down, and believer (*mumin*) literally means 'faithful'. Much exegesis is made from the translation of Muslim: 'one who submits' or 'one who surrenders' – both being dogmatic statements accepting the sovereignty of Allah and acted out in the ritual performance of the daily prostrations.

The following six fundamental beliefs (*aqaid*) are often put forward as the essential parts of *iman* and part of the absolute doctrines a Muslim must accept:

- the monotheistic belief in the unity of Allah (*tawhid*) and
- belief in his angels (*malaika*, sing. *malak*), created from divine light;
- acceptance of the revelation (*tanzil*) in the books (the 104 divine books revealed to earlier prophets and the angel Gabriel (Jibril) and the final revelation, the Qur'an, through Muhammad);
- recognition of Muhammad as God's messenger (*rasul*) and prophet (*nabi*) and
- recognition of the Final Judgement (*yawm Al-hisab*, lit. 'The Day of Reckoning') and the following resurrection, and finally
- belief in divine predestination (*jabr*) or providence (*qadar*) as recorded on 'the well preserved tablet', a metaphor for the Qur'an, which is assumed to be eternal, spotless and flawless.

The first of these doctrines, the indisputable monotheism, is the same as the first pillar of Islam, and is represented in al-Fatiha, al-Ikhlas and other prayer-like formulas. In the witness of faith (*shahada*) from the Qur'an (37:35), which can be said to be the common denominator of the Islamic faith, 'I testify, there is no god but Allah, and

al-Ikhlas

The short *sura* 112, al-Ikhlas, is referred to as 'The Pure Faith' (or 'Sincere Religion' in Arberry's translation) and also formulates the pronouncement of the fundamental truths:

Say: 'He is God, One,
God, the Everlasting Refuge,
who has not begotten, and has not been begotten,
and equal to Him is not any one.'

Muhammad is Allah's messenger' (*ashhadu an la ilaha illa Allah wa-Muhammad rasul Allah*). The pronounced testimony constitutes the Qur'anic identification of those who believe and accept the message (*al-muminun*), a category that most often equates to practising Muslims in a broad sense.

The absolute monotheism and the concept of God are illuminated in the name Allah, meaning simply 'the God' – in the definite singular. Not only is this a linguistic note, but it carries a whole theology. The One God does not need a name, as he is the only one of his kind. There is a general reluctance in Islam to give Allah anthropomorphic traits, even in the metaphoric language. Traditionally his transcendence is rather identified through characteristics that underline his essence as incomprehensible in every respect.

The absolute character of Allah stands out in the following *sura*:

That then is God your Lord;
there is no god but He,
the Creator of everything.
So serve Him,
for He is Guardian over everything.
The eyes attain Him not, but He attains the eyes;
He is the All-subtle, the All-aware.
Clear proofs have come to you from your Lord.
Whoso sees clearly, it is to his own gain,
and whoso is blind, it is to his own loss;
I am not a watcher over you. (6:102–104)

The image of Allah in the Qur'an has many reflections. It is the image of a loving god, close to people's hearts, who is still an avenger of disbelief and apostasy. The concept *taqwa* implies that God is to be feared as well believed in, and covers the all-embracing aspects of Allah. The theological basis of the reasoning around the nature of Allah is the concept of unity (*tawhid*, literally to unify). It refers not only to the character of the Utmost Being, but also to the very intention with his creation as coherent and harmonious at existential, social and political levels and therefore an important concept in political Islamism. *Tawhid* could therefore be said to be the essence of Islamic monotheism, although with wider connotations. As the Qur'an states: 'like Him there is naught' (42:11). Further, *tawhid* implies the greatness of Allah, his absolute transcendence over human deficiency, as he is absolute in power. The often-heard call: 'God is greater' (*Allahu akbar*), the phrase from the Qur'an known as *takbir* (greater), is in itself both a prayer and a creed, and is used in a number of situations. The act of pronouncing *takbir* summarizes the notion that nothing can be greater than Allah (not even as a conceptual speculation) and nothing should be placed at his side; Allah can therefore not have any offspring.

Closely connected to the concept of unity is the role of Allah as the creator (the very reason behind history and individual destinies), the judge and the redeemer as represented in holy scriptures, prayer and theology. Eschatological concepts are very much part of early Islam and combine the image of Allah's sovereignty and compassion.

In Sufi tradition, which has developed elaborate rituals reiterating the various names, attributes and characteristics of Allah, the ritual repetition of the 'names' is connected with a theological viewpoint that both stresses the distance, described as a veil, between Allah and his creation and provides ritual means for believers to get closer to him. Only Muhammad is believed to have experienced the full presence of Allah – and that only through his mystical experience during his Night Journey, discussed in Chapter 2. God is beyond description and is by tradition given 'the 99 most beautiful names' (*al-asma al-husna*). The figure 99 indicates that the names, or rather characteristics, are 'innumerable', as the limited human mind cannot fully comprehend the greatness of God. It is only possible – by means of these verbal indications of essence and qualities – to grasp aspects of God and use them when contemplating him. Names, often nouns and adjectives, appearing in the Qur'an, such as the Truth (*al-Haqq*), the Living (*al-Hayy*), the Merciful (*al-Rahman*) or the Compassionate (*al-Rahim*), are used as repetitive parts of prayers. The hundredth name, the completion of the description of the absolute transcendental being, is reserved for Allah himself.

This unquestionable unity is linked to the understanding of the message delivered by Muhammad as the final revelation, which is not regarded as accumulated progression of the previous prophets, but complete from the beginning. Islam is therefore thought of as the religion of the natural order (*din al-fitra*), in contrast to temptation or trial of faith (*fitna*), which creates a world of social and moral disorder. But Muhammad is not a redeemer comparable to Christ in Christianity. Muhammad is human; he is good and *the* infallible example, but not divine. 'The Light of Muhammad' (*nur Muhammadi*) could be of comfort to the believer, but it can never replace the relationship to Allah.

A human (*insan*) is different from other created beings, like angels and demons (sing. *jinn*), that inhabit the cosmos: intelligence, free will and strength provide the ability to choose, but also the predicament of being held responsible for acts and beliefs. A human is a servant (*abd*) in relation to Allah, and serves as keeper of the creation; in every respect subordinated to the will and grace of Allah. The very last *sura* of the Qur'an (114, al-Nas, 'The Humans', or in Arberry's translation 'Men') has the character of a protective prayer and expresses a fundamentally caring god, strong but at the same time unbending. Humans are safe with the Almighty:

> Say 'I take refuge with the Lord of men,
> the King of men,
> the God of men,
> from the evil of the slinking whisper
> who [Satan] whispers in the breast of men
> of jinn and men'. (114)

There is no specific narrative of creation (*khalk*) in the Qur'an comparable to the Genesis story in the Bible or similar myths in other religions. The Qur'an simply states that Allah made the world in six days (3:59; 57:4). 'Be!' is Allah's performative phrase to give life to his creation by means of the spoken word (36:82). The Qur'an differs in its information on what substance humankind is made of. It is said to be mud (38:76), dust or water (3:59; 25:54) and, in another *sura*, clotted blood (96:2). Allah is the sole creator and gives man spirit (2:30–33). He has also set the measured time for an individual (*dahr*).

Predestination is described as a parallel to the eternal nature of the Book. Therefore, the celebration of Allah's sending down the Qur'an at the end of Ramadan is associated with the fated events of the coming year. Defence for this view on the fates of the coming year being established this night is found in the second *sura* of the Qur'an:

> The Messenger believes in what was sent down to him from his Lord,
> and the believers; each one believes in God and His angels,
> and in His Books and His Messengers; we make no division between any one of His Messengers. They say, 'We hear, and obey.
> Our Lord, grant us Thy forgiveness; unto Thee is homecoming'.
> (2:285)

Various rituals of divination and fortune-reading are popular but controversial and are often condemned in traditional theology.

In opposition to all that Allah stands for are the vices. Polytheism (*shirk*, 'to assign Allah a partner') is the absolute contrast to the prime characteristic of Allah, *tawhid*. The godless and therefore immoral are also to be counted among those who are excluded from the category 'Muslim'; without Islam as their moral compass, people are evil.

Heretic, freethinker or atheist (*zindiq*) is not a Qur'anic term, but was used to define unwanted Manichean and Gnostic tendencies in early Islam, dualism in general and later some Sufis and other groups were considered heterodox. These distinctions are not only historical features of the early days of Islam; the concepts are frequently used when Islamic history is used as a mirror to the contemporary world, as they serve as a useful political tool. To declare a fellow Muslim an infidel (*kafir*) is an act called *takfir*, a de facto excommunication from the *umma*. Historically, *takfir* served as a warning against intra-Islamic sects and against conversion to other denominations. As will be apparent in the coming chapters, formal theology has had difficulty in relating to piety established in local custom as expressions of acceptable rituals. Today, *takfir* can be a political strategy used by radical Islamists to dismiss unwanted opinions by defining them as un-Islamic and the people holding them as unbelievers, which puts them in a complicated situation in relation to sharia.

The last four components of the five pillars (*arkan al-islam*), after the emphasis on belief (*iman*), point more directly to the correct practice of religion (*ibadat*) and will be dealt with in Chapters 5 and 6. The transactions between humans, or conduct (*muamalat*) of a legal, moral and economic character, can, outside the sharia system, be compared to civil codes.

These ritual obligations and observances could be summarized as what defines a Muslim in social practice:

- perform the five daily *salat* prayers and the accompanying intention and purification;
- give alms (*zakat*);
- fast during Ramadan (*sawm*);
- go on the pilgrimage to Mecca (*hajj*) at least once in a lifetime, if possible.

Belief and practice form the basis of moral judgements: good deeds and manners, including rules of conduct (*adab*) as well as a personal moral code and ethics (*akhlaq*). The status of Muhammad, represented in the *hadith* literature as the example to follow, forms the basis of the concept *sunna*.

Being Muslim

This chapter has dealt with some significant concepts in the Muslim faith and how the canonical texts and traditions present Islam as a religion distinct from other faiths, yet with a relation to Judaism and Christianity. Reference to unity are common in traditional discourse and are used in many metaphors when explaining belief and practice. Irrespective of this diversity and a long and complex history of interpretation, as well as the influx of local customs worldwide, there is a nexus most Muslims relate to. Islam is regarded as the ultimate religion, which conveys the eternal message from the only god, Allah; and his message is pronounced in the Qur'an as transmitted to Muhammad through the revelations he received, the last in a chain of prophets, by the angel Jibril. Even if varied over time and over vast areas, the unquestionable monotheism and the status of the sacred scripture constitute fundamental features in Muslim belief along with the conception of Islam as the ultimate message.

Novel conditions in the modern world have brought new parameters for belonging and new identities to alternate between in relation to what it means to be a Muslim. Today, many define themselves as Muslims in terms of cultural background, but are not necessarily practising Muslims. This development can be taken in many rhetorical directions: as indicating cultural richness or an impending split. As the following chapters will show, references to a shared cultural history and collective memories are today as complicated an issue as ever. History, when used as a mirror, gives Muhammad's Medina community a particular status. It is regarded as the embodiment of virtues and the model to follow in the endeavours to create a just society today. But from this vastly diverging conclusions can be drawn.

In line with Talal Asad's (1993) argument that religion is always a discursive tradition, Islam must be regarded from a contextualized perspective as a conceptual framework that can be given a multitude of interpretative and performative meanings in human interaction, and focus must then be directed towards how Muslims represent Islam through discourse and practice. John Bowen's (1993) comment on how to analytically balance a focus on local custom with an open eye for the impact of the scriptural traditions epitomizes a view where the norms of scriptures and theology are not in conflict with the study of local multiplicity: 'Muslims shape their rituals to local cultural concerns and to universalistic scriptural imperatives. Islamic rituals thus fit comfortably neither in an ethnographic discourse of bounded wholes nor in an Islamicist discourse of a scripture-based normative Islam' (Bowen, 1993: 656). To get a view of contemporary Islam in its many facets, canonical texts, theology, performative practices and material representations must be taken into consideration as well as the consequences of changing living conditions for many Muslims in the world in terms of education, civil liberties, claims to authority and access to knowledge. The varieties of being Muslim in the world today are striking.

Further reading

Anderson, Benedict, *Imagined Communities* (London: Verso, 1983).
Asad, Talal, *Genealogies of Religion. Discipline and Reasons of Power in Christianity and Islam* (Baltimore, MD: Johns Hopkins University Press, 1993).
Bowen, John, *Muslims through Discourse. Religion and Ritual in Gayo Society* (Princeton: Princeton University Press, 1993).

——, *A New Anthropology of Islam* (Cambridge: Cambridge University Press, 2012).

Doumato, Eleanor, *Getting God's Ear. Women, Islam, and Healing in Saudi Arabia and the Gulf* (New York: Columbia University Press, 2000).

Irwin, Robert, *For the Lust of Knowing: The Orientalists and Their Enemies* (London: Allen Lane, 2006).

Lugo, Luis et al., *Mapping the Global Muslim Population: A Report on the Size and the Distribution of the World's Muslim Population* (Washington, DC: Pew Forum, 2009).

Malik, Abd al, *Sufi Rapper: The Spiritual Journey of Abd al Malik* (Rochester, VT: Inner Traditions, 2009).

Rippin, Andrew, *The Islamic World* (London: Routledge, 2008).

Said, Edward, *Orientalism* (New York: Pantheon, 1978).

Sajoo, Amyn B. (ed.), *A Companion to Muslim Cultures* (London: I.B.Tauris, 2012).

Chapter II

The Early History of Islam and Muhammad as a Historical Person

Muhammad is often described in sweeping terms as 'the founder of Islam'. The historical individual active on the Arabian Peninsula during the seventh century did, of course, establish a strong and expanding community – and is hailed for this in Muslim tradition and historical writing – but the role of Muhammad in legendary narratives is quite different from that of the central characters in other world religions, such as Jesus or Buddha. To a pious Muslim the term 'founder' does not best characterize his activities. From a theological point of view, it is one of the central conceptions in the Muslim faith that Muhammad was a human being and strictly without any transcendental qualities. This is also why Muslims consider 'Muhammadanism' a less proper term for their religion. The strict monotheism of Islam does not place anything at the side of Allah; 'Allah has no companions', it is often stated, and no family-related metaphors are used to describe the relation between Allah and mankind, such as humans being the 'children' of God or God being depicted as a heavenly 'father'. Despite this fundamental doctrine, Muhammad is the focus of much local piety, which will be discussed in the second part of this chapter. A tension is apparent throughout Muslim history between, on the one hand, the theological concept of Muhammad as solely a messenger and, on the other, the practise of veneration that expresses a personal closeness to the prophet (and sometimes to members of his family) – a custom not always appreciated by more orthodox Muslims.

One point of departure in order to clarify the position of Muhammad in the Muslim faith is to place him in relation to the Qur'an, which is regarded to be in essence both eternal and unwordly, perfect and existing before Allah's creation of the world. Muhammad's historical mission was to be the bringer of this message (rather as Mary brought Christ, God's gift, into the world in the Christian tradition).

Muhammad's life is not accounted for in the Qur'an through a chronological sequence of events and he is not the main agent of the text. Muhammad in Islamic faith and in the Qur'an could not be paralleled with Jesus, who appears as an acting character as well as a saviour and mediator in the Gospels of the New Testament throughout a developing storyline. Muhammad is mentioned by name only four times in the Qur'an (and once under the name Ahmad, 'the most praised'). Although his persona is embedded in the subtext as the prime receiver, he does not appear in any of the longer narratives.[4] The 47th *sura* bears Muhammad's name and the second verse defines the divine message sent down to him, marking the distance between eternity and earthly life. The Qur'an is not regarded by Muslims as the recorded words of Muhammad, but as a complete message directly from Allah. In Islamic tradition the words of the Qur'an are a verbatim transmission of the voice of Allah. Muhammad is the one who transmits the eternal, unchangeable words from Allah. He is therefore referred to in the Qur'an as the prophet (*al-nabi*), the messenger (*al-rasul*) and the seal of the prophets (*khatam al-anbiya*), the various aspects of his being the channel chosen by Allah to deliver the final message.

The link between Muhammad and the Book is close. Nevertheless, there is no doubt about the origin of the text. This is one of the four passages in the Qur'an where Muhammad's name is mentioned directly alongside a definition of his obligations and the origin of the message:

> It is He who has sent His Messenger with the guidance and the religion of truth, that He may uplift it above every religion. God suffices as a witness.
> Muhammad is the Messenger of God, and those who are with him are hard against unbelievers, merciful one to another.
> (48:28–29)

The Qur'an makes frequent references to itself as the final revelation (*wahy*) and in the following two verses the text assures believers that it is the correct version that has been brought by the messenger, who can be trusted in his guidance.

The diverse stands on Muhammad as a historical individual, as a prophet and the channel through which the Qur'an was delivered to mankind, and as a model for mankind and the focal point of piety have promoted conflicting lines in Islamic theology throughout history and in legal and ritual practice: how ritualized can the devotion of Muhammad be without being in conflict with the concept of *tawhid*? This chapter will deal first with the historical milieu in which Muhammad emerged with his visions and claims of providing the fundamental elements of the fulfilled religion. It will then discuss what can be known about the person and in what respects the community he established constituted a radical change with pre-Islamic societal order. Finally, it will raise the question of the piety surrounding Muhammad as a model and guide, and the narratives about this ideal in legendary narratives and history writing.[5]

The pre-Islamic world and the Arabian Peninsula at the time of Muhammad

The pre-Islamic world on the Arabian Peninsula is conventionally characterized as a nomadic tribal society, although substantial changes took place from the fifth century onward that deepened the social differences between the desert area of the north and the thriving trading areas in the south. The south was far poorer in terms of natural resources than the areas close to 'the fertile crescent' of the Near East, as it was dependent on oases to maintain productive communities. Nevertheless, it was, through trade, a prosperous area, situated between two struggling empires: in the west, the East Roman Byzantine empire and in the east, the Persian (with Zoroastrianism as its official religion), but societal power was not organized in any state formation in contrast to those of the surrounding empires and kingdoms. Rather than through an administrative structure, control was exercised through small mobile units – the tribes.

The developing trading centres of the south and the growing importance of urban settlements that could handle the long-distance transmission of commodities were also instrumental in the introduction of new ideas. The tribe Muhammad was born into, the Quraysh, played an important role in this development. With its caravans to Syria trading in silver and leather, it became an active part of the transit operations in the region. The Quraysh controlled the area of southern Hijaz, where the settlement called Mecca was situated. The site was not a fertile oasis but, typically for the southern area, dependent on supplies from the outside. Most importantly, the Quraysh was part of a regional

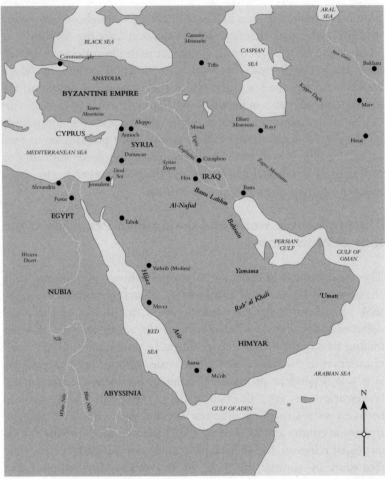

Map 1   The Arabian Peninsula at the time of Muhammad's appearance as a prophet.

web of alliances and conflicts, and Mecca started to serve as a transit point between east and west in terms of trade and cultural contacts.

Mecca is the indisputable focal point of the Islamic world: it is the direction for *salat*, *qibla*, and it is the destination of the mandatory pilgrimage. Since 1932, Mecca has been part of Saudi Arabia, but for many centuries before that it was part of the Ottoman Empire. It has remained, beside its religious importance, a meeting point and a centre for trade. The shrine at Mecca, the Kaaba, is a pre-Islamic construction, but today the grand *hajj* mosque includes the ancient Kaaba as part of its premises.

Mecca was not only a commercial centre. The local shrine, the Kaaba (meaning 'cube'), attracted crowds of pilgrims, and even Christian Arabs found their way to the sanctuary. In pre-Islamic times, it was most likely dedicated to the god Hubal, who is said to have had a large statue erected at its centre. By the time of Muhammad, however, it had become the site of worship of a multitude of local deities, foremost among them being the highest god, Allah (al-Lah, the God). This god was of high importance, but he did not necessarily stand in opposition to other, lesser divine powers that were worshipped here. The area around the sanctuary was proclaimed a safe area (haram, literally forbidden or secluded) demanding certain behaviour, and the peace was to be protected, an honorary duty taken on by the Quraysh clan. The religious alliances of the tribe added to the success of the Quraysh's trade as the commerce around the pilgrim site grew. Already before Muhammad, circumambulation (tawaf) of the Kaaba monument was an essential ritual at the location. The pagan gods were closely linked to the tribes and specific places, and Muhammad's categorical rejection of polytheism was therefore an attack on the very nexus of the old power relations when faith in the one god was the fundament of fellowship.

The sanctuary is known as 'the holy house' (bayt al-haram) and has been a place of worship since pre-Islamic times. It is a cubic structure, about 15 metres high and 12 metres wide. Today, the structure around the Kaaba is part of the grand mosque of Mecca. The cube is covered with a black cloth (kiswa), which is embroidered with quotations from the Qur'an and the shahada. The cloth is replaced every year and pilgrims cherish a piece of it as a treasured memento to bring back from the hajj. The eastern wall of the Kaaba features a silver-framed black stone (al-hajar al-aswad) of unknown but definitely pre-Islamic origin. An important moment of the obligatory circumambulation ritual during the hajj is the touching of the stone. This ritual goes far back in history. In the Qur'an, the Kaaba is spoken of as 'the House' (al-bayt) and as 'the protected house of prayers' (al-masjid al-haram). It is unquestionably the focal point of Islam, despite its pre-Islamic background.

Ancient Arabian religion shared many features with other Near Eastern religions. The deities were connected with astral phenomena. Gods and goddesses were linked to specific tribes and special cultic sites for offerings, worship, divination and oracles. Although the Qur'an

Fig. 2   Pilgrims gathered around the Kaaba. Following the model of Muhammad,
millions of Muslims go to Mecca every year. *(Source: Aiman Titi [public domain], via
Wikimedia Commons)*

warns 'Bow not yourselves to the sun and the moon' (41:37), three of
the goddesses, al-Lat, al-Uzza and Manat, are mentioned in the Qur'an
(53:19–20.); they are depicted as names to which hopes are attached,
but having no influence.[6] To Muslims, polytheism (*shirk*) represents
the prime vice, as it contradicts the concept of *tawhid* in every respect.

The core message of Muhammad's preaching was from the very
beginning that monotheism is unquestionable. However, features of
the pre-Islamic worldview remained important conceptions in the
new religion. The emphasis on providence in Muhammad's early
revelations is one such reminiscence of the beliefs and divinatory
rituals connected with the concept of destiny or measured time (*dahr*)
in ancient Arabic religion. Pagans are accused of being fatalistic, and
Allah is all-knowing and has a path laid out for every human being. A
second lingering feature is the belief in the djinns. These are spirits
shaped by fire (in contrast to the angels, who are eternal) and
associated with Iblis, the devil, who is capable of assaulting human
beings and causing illness and distress. One of the *suras* in the Qur'an
(72) even takes its name from these demons, 'The Jinn'. It states that

some of the spirits have surrendered to Allah, and entered on the straight path, while some are on their way to Hell. Third, the role of poetry and trust in the spoken word are often emphasized as pre-Islamic characteristics. Whether the Qur'anic text is poetic has, however, been contested. Although some parts of the Qur'an rhyme, the poetic qualities should not be mistaken for a work of poetry (shir).

The performance of the spoken word was cherished and the status of the speaker high. Thus, the call to attention in the Qur'an and the imperative tone of a strong speaker are reminiscences of an oral cultural background; the strong pre-Islamic poetic traditions lingered on and complex odes with a pre-Islamic background were written down in the ninth century. Both the Qur'an itself and Islamic tradition emphasize the importance of the spoken word: this was the medium chosen by Allah for communication with humankind.

Muhammad's skill in highlighting features familiar from the old religion, as well as references to Judaism and Christianity, and combining them with new religious and social ideas is an important reason for the early success of Islam. The ancient Arabic heritage is a complicated element in Islamic historiography. On the one hand, it is something that serves to define or distinguish Islam; on the other hand, the origin of Arabic culture is cherished.

Similarly, the term *jahiliyya* has a dual meaning. It has a chronological dimension, as it refers to the pre-Islamic state/world of ignorance, and it relates to the arrogance of unbelievers in general. *Jahiliyya* is in both historical writing and theology depicted as the very antithesis of Islamic culture and its iconic vice is *shirk*, usually translated as polytheism or idolatry. The concept *jahiliyya* also has a general meaning of associating other beings with Allah. The use of the term has re-emerged in modern political Islam not only as a metaphor for contemporary ignorance of religion, but also as a rallying cry in the combat against godlessness and immoral lifestyles. In the eighth-century *Book of Idols*, Hisham Ibn al-Kalbi (d. 819) compiled an overview of pre-Islamic religion, including a catalogue of the old gods and a depiction of the activities surrounding the Kaaba: the ancient circumambulation and the worship of stone idols. The peak of the narration is, of course, when Muhammad clears the sanctuary, attacks the idols and 'start[s] to pierce their eyes with the point of his arrow saying, "Truth is come and falsehood is vanished. Verily, falsehood is a thing that vanisheth [sura 17:81]". He then ordered that they be knocked down, after which they were taken out and burned' (Ibn al-Kalbi, ed. Faris, 1952: 27). After this both symbolic and forceful action, the Kaaba served the one God. It thus confirms the link to Arab culture as well as the construction of the centre of the new religion.

Muhammad as a historical person

From a source-critical point of view, the accounts of the life of Muhammad are intertwined with the early history of Islam. The time of the prophet Muhammad and his deeds were central topics for the Muslim historians whose chronicles were written from a hagiographical point of view, underlining the qualities of the creed and the person.[7] No written biographical records exist from the time of Muhammad. Systematic histories began to be written only a full century later. Parallel with this, early theological doctrines were developed around the character of Muhammad and his roles as messenger, last prophet, leader and model man.

Two traditional sources other than the Qur'an should be mentioned in relation to the life of Muhammad. In the *hadith* literature, the collections of 'traditions' from the early Muslim community in Medina, Muhammad stands out as a distinct character who speaks and acts.[8] These texts focus on the deeds and judgements of Muhammad as a community leader rather than on theological doctrines; in other words, on the implementation of Islam in everyday life. Chains of orally transmitted knowledge constitute the authority of these guiding accounts, which are fundamental to the construction of arguments in Islamic theology and jurisprudence. Distinct sayings are attributed to Muhammad and chains of witnesses are presented. The Qur'an and the *hadith* collections constitute the textual ground for *sunna*. This abstract concept is based on the conception of Muhammad as a human who provides the matrix of belief and behaviour. The Qur'an repeatedly asserts the authority of the messenger and the trust to be put in him as the transmitter of the final message.

There is an early biographical literature (*sira*) from some centuries after the death of Muhammad that compiles narratives of the life of the prophet and puts them into a chronological sequence. The structure of chains of authority is the same as in the *hadiths*, indicating who transmitted what to whom. *Sira* means 'biography' and refers to a genre of literature telling the life of Muhammad as a historical person and as a prophet that has been produced in the centuries after Muhammad's death. From a source-critical perspective, the coherence of Muhammad's life as presented in legendary history writing is doubtful. Rather, this literature brings forward emblematic situations that form the ideal of a prophet and his message. The reading of them is very different from that of the Qur'an. In the *sira* literature, longer direct speech is attributed to Muhammad, such as his sermon during the final pilgrimage to Mecca, whereas the *hadith* collections provide only a few short sentences. These biographies also emphasize the choices made by the early Muslim community and the major events during its expansion. A second meaning of *sira* is 'conduct', and this genre, as well as the *hadith* literature, constitutes the basis of the abstract concept of *sunna*, which indicates proper behaviour and choices. The *hadith* literature are edited text collections, whereas what is considered *sunna* is always a matter of interpretation and reasoning. *Sira* texts can also include comments on Qur'an verses that relate them to the acts of Muhammad or the early Muslims, or present the circumstances surrounding a specific revelation. The *sira* literature – a vast and heterogeneous genre – is part of the corpus of historical writing that grew into the pious canon. Many modern *sira* accounts are to a great extent compilations of the classics in terms of content, but contemporary in form, and they may be presented as computer games, graphic narratives or summarizing booklets.

The most famous biography of Muhammad is the *sira* by Muhammad Ibn Ishaq (d. 767). It is only preserved in a later adaptation, but it is generally considered one of the earliest biographies of Muhammad. It narrates all the important events in the life of Muhammad in detail, the construction of the community and its successes and failures, with references to the Qur'an to confirm the authority of the presentation. It must, however, be remembered that Ibn Ishaq lived more the a hundred years after the death of Muhammad, and the text has provided the master narrative for many pious narrations about the prophet rather than being a historical source in its details. The outline of a *sira* is similar to that of the *hadiths*, as can be seen in the examples given in the text boxes below; this genre makes frequent use of quotations from the Qur'an and provides interpretations and supplementary narratives that strengthen the moral argument. But where the *hadith* expositions are thematically arranged, the *sira* literature follows the chronological sequences in the life of Muhammad.

The early life of Muhammad

Muhammad was born in Mecca around CE 570, which is sometimes referred to as 'the year of the elephant', as legendary history tells us that in this year the leading elephant of the attacking Abyssinian army stopped its march towards Mecca and peacefully knelt down in front of the Kaaba, thus preventing the intruders from destroying the holy site. The event is alluded to in *sura* 105, 'The Elephant', and is sometimes interpreted as indicating that the whole of Allah's creation knelt in front of the Messenger and that his birth is therefore to be considered a matter of world importance. Many details in the theological literature on the life of Muhammad are of a hagiographical character, and therefore uncertain. The positions taken on the sources can serve as examples of the potential conflicting perspectives between cherished pious narratives and source criticism when it comes to outlining early Islamic history, including the life of Muhammad.

However, *sura* 93 provides a hint as to Muhammad's childhood and the hardships he had to face, and it shows how Muhammad is present in the text in relation to the demanding explicit speaker as the trustful implicit receiver of the message.

> Did He not find thee an orphan, and shelter thee?
> Did He not find thee erring, and guide thee?
> Did He not find thee needy, and suffice thee? (93:6–8)

There are considerable difficulties in establishing a genealogy or a chronological biography of Muhammad, although some historical details from the scriptural tradition seem to be trustworthy. Muhammad was a member of a branch of the Quraysh tribe. Parts of the Quraysh tribe were very wealthy, thanks to their influence over the commercial routes that had developed in southern parts of the Arabian Peninsula, and they had also gained status as defenders of the shrine in Mecca, the Kaaba. Muhammad's father died before the child was born and, despite the apparently patriarchal structure of Quraysh society, he is not a significant character in the stories about Muhammad's background. A greater emphasis in the legendary texts

Muhammad's life on film

Local piety has always produced vivid imagery of the life of Muhammad in narratives, songs and pictures. The use of modern media is a far from surprising development along this line. Two commercially successful examples of 'biopics' to present the life of Muhammad are the action film *The Message* (1977), directed by Mustafa Akkad, and the animated *Muhammad: The Last Prophet* (2004) by Richard Rich. Both are aimed at Muslim as well as non-Muslim audiences.

Depicting the prophet is, however, controversial. Neither film shows Muhammad or lets us hear his voice, and the directors have chosen two very different strategies in order to reach a contemporary audience. In the first, Hollywood star Anthony Quinn played Muhammad's uncle Hamsa (who was mistaken by some audiences for Muhammad himself), while the second used cartoon imagery in order to combine the ambitions of a popular movie with respect for Islamic tradition.

The world of computer games and virtual worlds has created new ways of spreading the Islamic message to the younger generation, but the old problem of depiction remains.

is put on the influence of the two women closest to him in his early life: his mother, Amina, and his wet nurse, Halima.

Amina, however, died when Muhammad was six years old. From then on the orphan was raised by his paternal uncle, Abu Talib (the head of the Hashim family), who would play a major role in the early days of the Muslim community. So would Abu Talib's son, Muhammad's cousin Ali. The status of 'The People of the House' (*ahl al-bayt*), Muhammad's immediate family, is the root of the conflicting theological positions of Sunni and Shi'i Muslims. The latter regard *ahl al-bayt* to be exemplary in conduct and include them in veneration practices while the former see these characters as humans who played important roles in the early history of Islam.

The fact that Muhammad was an orphan has been pointed to as a possible explanation for the emphasis in the Qur'an and the *hadith* literature on care for the vulnerable as well as for the fact that Muhammad was free to establish a community based on a fellowship of faith rather than family lines.

At the age of 25, Muhammad married a wealthy widow active in merchandise, Khadija. She was 15 years his senior and had hired him for her business. She is an important voice in the chain of witnesses in the *hadith* and *sira* narratives, which portray her as loyal and supportive. She was the very first to accept the message Muhammad brought and thus became the very first Muslim. Ibn Ishaq's *sira* tells how Muhammad confided to her his first shaking experiences of hearing Allah's voice, and that she exclaimed at once: 'Verily, by him whose hand is in Khadija's soul, I have hope that thou wilt be the prophet of this people' (155). The one son (or, according to some texts, two) she bore him died young, but the daughters from this marriage – Zaynab, Ruqayya, Umm Kulthum and Fatima – have their part in early Islamic history. Muhammad established himself as an affluent tradesman in Mecca, took his cousin Ali into his household and offered him Fatima for a wife.

It is said that as long as Khadija lived, Muhammad did not take another wife, but after that he married several women. Muslim men can, according to the Qur'an (4:3), take more than one wife, even though social practices have varied. This custom has coloured the perception of Islam in the West since the Middle Ages, when knowledge about Islam began to spread. 'Muhammad and his harem' has been used as a theme to ridicule Muslims and Islam. The issue about the wives has caught disproportional attention and became a trope in anti-Muslim discourse. In the Muslim narrations of the life of Muhammad, these marriages are often depicted as a way of establishing alliances with other tribes, and the portraits of the wives are illustrations of virtues rather than actual biographies.

The first period of Muhammad's public activities, 610–622

Not only was Muhammad a successful man in terms of improving his social position and wealth before his public appearance as a religious leader, but he was also, according to legendary history, generally known to be a pious and righteous man. The biographies underline that Muhammad's interests were always other than worldly and that he sought solitude for contemplation in a cave on the mountain Hira (known as 'the mountain of Light').

Tradition tells that in 610, during the month of Ramadan, Muhammad, in retreat at Hira, began to have visions in which he encountered the angel Jibril and received messages from Allah. The image of the man in solitude ready to reconsider established truths forms an emblematic image of Islam as the final message.

Islamic history considers the first lines of *sura* 96 to be an account of Muhammad's first revelation (*wahy*), when he was instructed to recite (*iqra*) what he heard from Allah, although he was illiterate:

> Recite: In the Name of thy Lord who created,
> created Man of a blood clot.
> Recite: And thy Lord is the Most Generous,
> who taught by the Pen,
> taught Man what he knew not. (96:1–5)

The verbatim recitation of the Qur'an has remained a core virtue, a sign of devotion and endeavour. The theological interpretation of this scene has been that it confirms that the Qur'an is solely the words of Allah, without any interference by any human scribe.

There is, however, a certain ambiguity in the tradition of delivery of the Qur'an. On the one hand, the Qur'an is regarded as a complete entity sent down at a specific moment in history – as in the quotation below – and this unique event is celebrated at the end of Ramadan every year. The strong speaking voice in the Qur'an declares:

> By the Clear Book.
> We have sent it down in a blessed night
> (We are ever warning)
> therein every wise bidding determined
> as a bidding from Us,
> (We are ever sending)
> as a mercy from thy Lord
> (surely He is the All-hearing, the All-knowing)
> Lord of the heavens and earth, and all that between them is,
> if you have faith. (44:1–7)

The key term when describing the transmission of the message to Muhammad via the angel Jibril is the sending down (*tanzil*, 'to send or bring down'). On the other hand, the individual *suras* include a comment after their titles indicating that they are 'From Mecca' or 'From Medina', and thus the very structuring of the Qur'anic text argues in favour of a progressive delivery.

In his biography of Muhammad, Ibn Ishaq describes the time of the first revelation as one of hardship:

> The revelation came fully to the apostle [prophet] while he was believing in Him and in the truth of His message. He received it willingly, and took upon himself what it entailed, whether of man's goodwill or anger. Prophecy is a troublesome burden – only strong, resolute messengers can bear it by God's help and grace, because of the opposition which they meet from men in conveying God's message. The apostle [prophet] carried out God's orders in spite of the opposition and ill treatment which he met with. (Ibn Ishaq: 157, trans. Guillaume 1955: 111)

This quotation indicates an ambiguity that can be found in the many narratives about the prophet: his willingness to execute the demands of Allah and his simultaneous realization that the path to that execution would be stony. Although human, Muhammad is faultless (*isma*), and he serves as the example to follow (33:21).

The angel (malak) *Jibril and the transmission of the message*

Angels (*malaika*) play an important part in the fundamental beliefs of Islam. They appear as individual characters as well as part of a collective. There is no such concept in Islam as 'archangel', but the angel Jibril plays a particularly important role; it is he who brings the Qur'an to Muhammad. Jibril's name is mentioned in three verses in the Qur'an. One of them says:

> Say: 'Whosoever is an enemy to Gabriel – he it was that brought it down upon thy heart by the leave of God, confirming what was before it, and for a guidance and good tidings to the believers. Whosoever is an enemy to God and His angels and His Messengers, and Gabriel, and Michael – surely God is an enemy to the unbelievers.' And We have sent down unto thee signs, clear signs, and none disbelieves in them except the ungodly. (2:97–99)

Jibril is said to have come to Muhammad in the shape of a man, and he appears in other narratives as a helper to the earlier prophets. Jibril is the tool by which the Qur'an was sent to Muhammad's heart.

It is not uncommon that the structure of the Qur'an is used as an outline in order to depict phases in the public appearance of Muhammad. The revelations are identified as having taken place in an early phase not only by their subheadings 'From Mecca' in the standard editions of the Qur'an (a chronology that is contested by modern scholarship), but also by their content and themes. This group of *suras* is focused on what are usually regarded as the central themes of the young Muhammad: the warnings and signs of the times that the Judgement is approaching, the acceptance of monotheism as the path to be taken and surrender to Allah, the creator and judge of the universe; emphasized by the apocalyptical intensity in the language of the Qur'anic text. The eschatological themes – the approaching Day of Judgement and the fundamental distinction between believers and unbelievers – are expressed in glowing metaphors.

Some scenes stand out in the *hadith* and *sira* literature as significant for the new teachings, which were formulated as a radical break while also connecting to a distinctly Arabic heritage. Muhammad turned his back on the local polytheistic religion and gradually marked his teaching as distinctively new in relation to Judaism and Christianity.

The social and ritual obligations of the Muslims are emphasized in the canonical literature. Most important of them are the daily prayers to the only God, with permission to ask for Allah's forgiveness. Moral conduct and social responsibility were at the forefront of what was expected from new adherents. Initially, were there three daily prayers, conducted facing Jerusalem. It was Muhammad's experience of the Night Journey to the heavens that established the rule of the five *salat* prayers, conducted facing Mecca. The required prostrations were as much a sign of personal piety as a public manifestation of belonging to the new Muslim fellowship, one who surrenders to Islam. Gradually, a community (*umma*) based on ritual fellowship and shared beliefs started to grow, irrespective of tribal connections and social status. The old security for individuals provided by the strength of the group was gradually replaced by trust in Allah's protection.

In 612, Muhammad's public appearance began; his preaching was based on the revelations he successively had received in solitude. Khadija's immediate support and trust in the truth of the message delivered is emphasized in Muslim history, as is the role of other early followers, such as Muhammad's cousin Ali (son of his uncle Abu Talib and later his son-in-law), Abu Bakr (the father of Aisha) and Uthman ibn Affan of the Umayyad family. These three would all play an important part of the formative period of Islam after Muhammad's death.

For a period of ten years, 612–622, Muhammad preached in his home town, Mecca, trying to convince people to turn to a belief in a single God and to build up a small community. But he met with opponents, and strong ones. The conflicts were apparently not only over the religious context of his message, but also due to the fact that Muhammad was challenging the establishment in terms of social cohesion and authority. Some thought that his claims of being the messenger of the only God were outrageous, that he was insane or even possessed by djinns; others realized that his emphasis on a fellowship based on faith rather than blood lineage was a threat to the established power relations between the tribes.

Consequently, by 617, Muhammad was in open conflict with his opponents in Mecca. Some extraordinary events in the life of Muhammad are related to this period, which emphasize it as a turning point. The legendary history of Muhammad especially emphasizes the miraculous events in the life of Muhammad. Two of them are hinted at in the Qur'an: 'Muhammad's Night Journey to Heaven' (17:1) and 'The Splitting of the Moon' as a proof of Muhammad's extraordinary capacities (54:1). The third, 'The Opening of the Breast' and the cleansing of Muhammad's heart, has been narrated throughout Muslim history and the transmitters have often been accused of spreading controversial beliefs. Still, these stories are deeply embedded in tradition.

Of all the miraculous narratives told about Muhammad, the first story of the Night Journey (isra) and the prophet's ascent (miraj) to the heavens is the most significant, as it has influenced both theological concepts and ritual expression. The Night Journey and the ascent are commemorated during a Muslim festival, laylat al-isra wa-l-miraj (see Chapter 5).

The Qur'an gives only a hint of this extraordinary nocturnal experience in one single verse, but the whole sura is given the name 'The Night Journey' from al-Masjid al-Haram to al-Masjid al-Aqsa.

If the Qur'an is brief, Ibn Ishaq relates several versions of the story in his sira, which is based on several witnesses' varying accounts of the event. Muhammad was sleeping next to the Kaaba during Ramadan when the angel Jibril took him on a heavenly winged creature named Buraq through the skies to Jerusalem. The animal is said to have been

From the Holy Mosque (Mecca) to the Furthest Mosque (Jerusalem)

The opaque introductory verse to the *sura* 'The Night Journey' relates the following:

> Glory be to Him who carried His servant by night from the Holy Mosque to the Furthest Mosque, the precincts of which We have blessed, that We might show him some of Our signs. He is the All-hearing, the All-seeing. (17:1)

The formulations are traditionally interpreted to be a description of a journey from the Kaaba (the Holy Mosque) to the temple in Jerusalem (the Furthest Mosque).

smaller than a mule but larger than an ass, or sometimes to have been half mule, half donkey, to have had a woman's face and a peacock's tail. At the site of Solomon's temple, Muhammad is said to have prayed with Abraham, Moses and Jesus; and the prophets of the past accepted Muhammad as imam. There are two – if not diverging, at least different – ways of interpreting the story. One is more concrete: that prayer is the fundamental act of indicating Muslim belonging in public. The followers of this interpretation often dispute whether it is correct to emphasize the narrative as a blueprint of a spiritual experience based on a particular historical event. This is, however, what is done by the more mystical and symbolic interpretation, which sees the stages in the journey as a metaphor for the development of the soul.

The second part of the narrative tells of the ascent to the seven heavens, of which nothing is mentioned in *sura* 17:1. A ladder (*miraj*, later the name for the ascent) is brought down for Muhammad and he starts his journey up to the heavens. In the lowest heaven, Muhammad witnesses how sinners are punished in accordance with their crime, which Ibn Ishaq in his *sira* conveys in a first-person narrative:

> Then I saw men with lips like camels; in their hands were pieces of fire like stones, which they thrust into their mouths, and they would come out of their posteriors. I was told that these [men] were those who sinfully devoured the wealth of orphans. (Ibn Ishaq: 269, trans. Guillaume 1955: 185)

The apparent similarities between this story and Dante's *Divina Commedia* have been pointed out, and the story is thought to have reached the Florentine author through traders, travellers and learned

Fig. 3   Buraq, the animal on which Muhammad was transported to the heavens, according to the narratives about his Nightly Journey. *(Source: Brooklyn Museum [public domain], via Wikimedia Commons)*

men of his time who knew of Islamic philosophy. In the seventh heaven, Muhammad encounters Abraham, Moses and Jesus, and acts as imam in their joint prayer at what is traditionally identified as the al-Aqsa mosque. This is traditionally interpreted as the earlier prophets' acceptance of Muhammad as the final messenger. Due to the intervention of Moses, the number of daily prayers was reduced from 50 to 5, which is often interpreted as humans' limited capacity to meet the praise that befits Allah. The last man Muhammad encounters is Abraham, 'sitting on a throne at the gate of the immortal mansion' (270), who takes him into Paradise.

The deaths in 619 of Abu Talib, who had protected Muhammad, and his wife Khadija were two blows to his social position. Beside their personal support in accepting him as a prophet, they had both provided him with a strong social network.

In 620, a peace agreement was made with representatives of Yatrib, known in Muslim history as Medina (literally 'the City'). This town was quite different from Mecca. Medina had developed around an oasis and was a mixed settlement, with a substantial Jewish community, that had extensive trade connections. In this setting, Muhammad's teachings functioned not only as eschatological warnings of the consequences of the broad road, but also a basis for long-term social cohesion. The vision of a different and just society was presented and was further emphasized after 622, when many adherents followed Muhammad to be part of the new community – known as the migration (*hijra*) from Mecca to Medina. It is from this point that the *umma*, a community where claims of blood lineage were downplayed in favour of loyalty within the congregation, can be identified.

AH – *anno Hegirae*

The Islamic calendar starts with the migration (*hijra*) to Medina in CE 622 and each year thereafter was sometimes in early Western literature on Islam labelled 'anno Hegirae' (AH) in its Latinized form, in analogy with the Christian concept anno Domini (AD). The *hijra* calendar is used to mark all important Islamic events and to distinguish them from secular history and contemporary matters.

The religious dimension of the new constellation of Medina is obvious, but the social aspects of its success, breaking up from the network of tribes, should not be underestimated. It is difficult to get an impartial view of the life of the early *umma*, as its history is inscribed in the editing process of the corpus of canonical texts that reproduce the norms and regulations of societal life, such as the Qur'an and the *hadith* literature.

Muhammad as a religious, communal and military leader in Medina, 622–632

Surrounded by – and in contact with – other religious communities to which the concept of and use of canonical scriptures played a major self-defining role in how Islamic theology and ritual had a significant impact on Islam. Zoroastrianism, Judaism and Christianity all cherish their canon as something more than a source of doctrinal information. These canonical texts provide a historical mirror for their followers, and this view of holy scriptures was to make its mark on Islamic theology.

The age of ignorance (*jahiliyya*) is not only a reference to the period before the appearance of Muhammad with the final message, but also an attitude to religious and moral matters. The first followers are identified in the canonical texts with distinctive characterizations, such as 'one who surrenders' (*muslim*), 'monotheist' (*hanif*) and 'believer' (*mumin*). The 'Supporters' (literally 'helpers', or *ansar*) is an honorary name given to the group in Medina who supported Muhammad and his *umma* after the migration, and backed the early community. The first companions of the prophet (*sahaba* – a concept that can also refer to the first generation of Muslims, especially in their capacity as transmitters of *sunna*) are iconic characters in the narratives about early Islam.

Medina, in pre-Islamic time called Yathrib

Medina, literally 'the City', was the town where Muhammad established and developed a community after the migration (*hijra*) in CE 622. The Mosque of the Prophet traces its history back to the time of Muhammad, and today it includes his house and his grave. It is an area restricted to Muslims and is visited by many pilgrims on their way to Mecca.

The establishment of an *umma* of believers and the migration to Medina indicate the strength of Muhammad's religious, social and military leadership. The historical person had not only the charisma and authority to make people accept him as the deliverer of the words of God, but also the legitimacy to organize social and religious life according to new standards. 'The Medina model', as represented in the *hadith* literature, is the narratives describing Muhammad's visions of how to create the ideal community – ideal for humans as individuals and members of collectives as well as for society. This model has throughout history been the basis of various visions of social order and cohesion. The requested individual conduct (in religious observance, morals, diet, etc.) plays a major part as the platform for further social relations and the authority of an individual. A form of tax or mandatory alms (*zakat*) was introduced early on for the poor and needy; the payment was a token of belonging and a statement of ethics.

The concept of Muslim community, *umma*

The early Muslim community is hardly depicted in the Qur'an (cf. the letters of the New Testament). Rather, it is the *hadith* literature, with its narratives about the sayings and deeds of Muhammad, that provides detailed imagery of his social visions. For this reason, they are used today for both Islamist and more liberal projects.

In times of change, Muhammad's visions of a good and just society based on a community of monotheists with a discursive base in terms of theological conceptions and a strong relation to the holy scriptures, regulated social conduct and ritual fellowship. Muhammad not only reshaped local society but also established the basis for a rapid and extensive expansion of the new religion.

In Medina, several features were established that definitively distinguished the faith of the Muslim community as a religion separated from the other, surrounding, monotheistic faiths. There the mosque became a specific building for prayers and sermons, and communal Friday prayer became the principal gathering of the week. The indication of the direction of prayer (*qibla*) was changed in 624 from Jerusalem to Mecca, a decision interpreted in Islamic (as well as Jewish and Christian) historiography as the definitive break with the two other religions and the establishment of Islam as an independent monotheistic religion with its own points of reference. The *umma* related its version of the Abrahamic genealogy of Genesis by claiming Arabic ancestry for Hagar and her son Ishmael. Pious history says that Abraham and Ishmael established the Kaaba as a site of pilgrimage and worship.

It is also during the period in Medina that the expansion of Islam by means of military action begins. A war with Mecca, which had rejected Muhammad and the *umma*, was eventually successful. The battle of Badr in 624 between the people of Mecca and the Muslim troops from Medina was the first successful campaign for Muhammad and his followers. The victory at Badr is commemorated one night during Ramadan and is often evoked as an imperative to fight for the Islamic cause, despite hostility and antagonism. Muhammad here confirmed his role as a leader fighting with Allah on his side. Several other battles have become significant events in Muslim historiography. At the battle of Uhud in 625 the Muslims from Medina made an alliance with Muslims from Mecca and thus took the first step towards the unification of the two cities, but the battle against the enemies of the *umma* itself was a defeat. Several early followers died, among them Muhammad's uncle Hamza, and their graves received visits for centuries. In 627, at 'the battle of Trench' (as it is known in Islamic history writing), the Muslims defended themselves successfully against an attack from Mecca thanks to the skilful strategy of 'besieging themselves' and avoiding direct confrontation. The armed conflicts continued, with both victories and defeats for the Muslims, but on the whole they established the Muslims as a major force in the area.

As underlined above, the acts and behaviour in problematic situations relating to Muhammad have, since the beginning of Islam, been regarded as normative and his visit in a white garment to Mecca in 628 reinstated the old pilgrimage tradition. As the Kaaba was a protected area (haram), no weapons could be used and the pilgrimage was a provocation to the Quraysh, who were the defenders of the shrine. In 628–30, negotiations were conducted that led to a peace treaty, though this was soon broken by the Quraysh. In 630, Muhammad and his army finally entered Mecca and cleared the Kaaba of its idols, making it the most significant place of worship of the only God, Allah. Polytheism (shirk) was definitively thrown out. Once Mecca was conquered, its interests were made the Muslims', and the two old enemies fought the city's remaining enemies together. Muhammad's final hajj to Mecca, now part of a larger area unified under the Muslims, settled the rules of conduct and ritual behaviour for the pilgrimage: kissing the black stone and circumambulating the cube anti-clockwise

Muhammad died in 632, and legendary history has it that he, when given the possibility, chose the keys to Paradise before eternal life on earth. Muhammad was buried in the cemetery of the mosque of Medina and the prophet's grave is now part of the immense complex. A visit here is an additional part of many hajj tours, although rejected by radical reformers. In the nineteenth century, some wahhabis even tried to demolish the grave.

After the death of Muhammad, no hierarchical clergy or centralized institutions developed. There were, however, schisms; regional dynasties established themselves and, over time, different caliphates competed for power and influence. Nevertheless, Islam was definitively established as a world religion within a few centuries. The message of monotheism was forwarded and addressed to mankind at large in contrast to the previous religions of the region, most of them based on ethnic fellowship. The social organization of Islam and the military success of the Muslims helped to consolidate the role of the new religion.

No rules for governance were established during Muhammad's time and there were differing views on the position of the family of the prophet (*ahl al-bayt*). Fatima (605–33), the daughter of Muhammad and Khadija, married Ali, Muhammad's cousin and the son of Abu Talib, Muhammad's uncle and his protector during the early years in Mecca. Fatima and Ali had the two sons Hasan and Husayn, who were therefore the grandchildren of the prophet. From the beginning, there were those who claimed that the family line carried legitimate authority to lead the community. The majority of Muslims, however, claimed – and still claim – that there is a line of four rightly guided (*rashidun*) caliphs whose behaviour and decisions, along with Muhammad's, constitute *sunna*. The first four caliphs stood by his side when the community struggled and have thus earned special status as reliable witnesses in Muslim history.

The early expansion of Islam

The seventh and eighth centuries are characterized by the early expansion of Islam; 634–732 is the period of the great Muslim conquests. As Muhammad, according to Shi'i Muslims, had not appointed any successor as the leader of the community, the early political leaders took it upon themselves to serve as successors (sing. *khalifa*, pl. *khulafa*) in Muhammad's absence. The first four caliphs were all from the Quraysh tribe and, even though the first three were not directly related to Muhammad, there were still family connections. The caliphs not only had religious supremacy, but also carried the title 'Commander of the Faithful', which indicates their military importance.

Abu Bakr, caliph from 632 to 634, had already served as a leader of the community during Muhammad's last period. There was no direct blood link, but he was Muhammad's father-in-law, being the father of Aisha. He is generally considered to have been the first companion (*sahib*) of Muhammad, even among the first to accept Islam, and he migrated with him from Mecca and thus was influential in the development of the *umma*. Abu Bakr managed to unite several tribes which had previously been in conflict and conquered Yemen.

Umar, caliph from 634 to 644, was also one of Muhammad's fathers-in-law. He organized the consolidation of many social and religious institutions that were to be essential for the growing empire in the region. Umar was the head of the Arab expansion, which had been initiated during Muhammad's lifetime, and under his reign

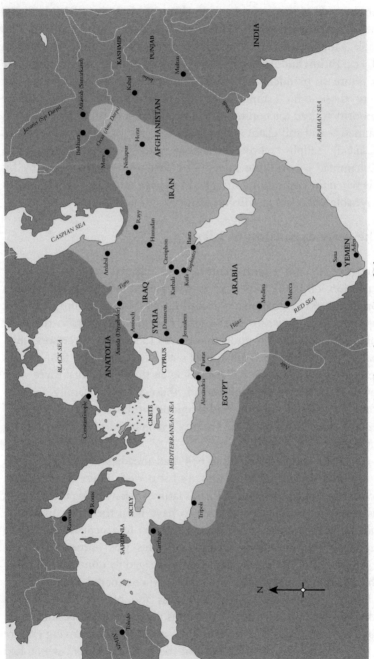

Map 2   The early expansion of Islam.

Fig. 4 A nineteenth-centry *qibla* compass with an image of the Kaaba and the names of cities in the Muslim world, from Tunis to Samarkand. *(Courtesy of the David Collection, Copenhagen; photo: Pernille Klemp)*

Palestine, Egypt, Syria, Iraq and Persia were conquered. This was the dawn of the Muslim empire.

Uthman, caliph from 644 to 656, could also draw his authority from having been an early follower of Muhammad and from being a son-in-law to him. Uthman was not a strong political leader, but from his side grew the later influential Umayyad line that was to be essential for the development of Sunni Islam. It is said in traditional history that the Qur'an was collected in its final version and established as a canonical text under Uthman's reign.

The Umayyad caliphate, 661–750, was a formative period for Islamic theology, aesthetics and intellectual life in general, with its capital and cultural centre in Damascus.

Ali, caliph from 656 to 661, was the fourth of the *rashidun* accepted by the Sunni Muslims, but to the Shi'i Muslims is the first legitimate leader after Muhammad because of his blood lineage to Muhammad – Shi'i Muslims claim that Muhammad named Ali his successor in his last sermon. This is denied by the Umayyad line of the first three caliphs and the clash was inevitable. Regarded by Shi'i Muslims as a martyr, as he was murdered in Kufa, which remained the centre of 'Ali's party' (Shiat Ali), Ali was married to Fatima, the daughter of Muhammad. Their son Husayn was also martyred, at Karbala. The fate of the many martyrs in Ali's family is held in great respect among Shi'is through commemoration and veneration.

The four rightly guided caliphs (rashidun)

The four first caliphs are seen as guided by Allah, and therefore their judgements and sayings are included in *sunna* and they are known as *rashidun*, the rightly guided.

The role of deputy to Allah's messenger was contested and the caliphs stood in the midst of political power struggles. All but the first were assassinated.

Abu Bakr, caliph 632–34
Umar, caliph 634–44
Uthman, caliph 644–56
Ali, caliph 656–61

Though contested by what later would develop into Shi'ism, the Umayyad caliphate, 661–750, dominated the expansion of Islam and with its 14 caliphs established the Arabic character of Islam despite its trans-regional ambitions, with Damascus at its centre. The appearance of the Abbasids meant the decline of the Umayyads, but in 710 the latter had entered Andalusia, where the title caliph was held by a member of the dynasty in the caliphate of Córdoba.

The Abbasid uprising against the Umayyads meant that Baghdad became the centre for the caliphate between 750 and 1258, although a political decline is noticeable from the middle of the ninth century. Conflicts with the Shi'i Muslims were many during this period, when a distinct Shi'i theology was formulated. In 1258, the Mongol conquest put an end to Baghdad's influence and made a new family dominate the eastern realms of the Muslim world. Timur Leng (or Tamerlane) and his descendants had an enormous impact on the development of Islam in India and China, with Samarkand as their centre. In the twelfth century, Turks from Central Asia settled permanently in what is known as Turkey today and, after the fall of Constantinople in 1453 and the conquest of the Balkans, Islam became an influential religion in south-eastern Europe. After Damascus and Baghdad as power centres, the Ottoman Empire became the dominating Muslim power and they established Istanbul as the site of the caliphate from 1517 until 1924, when it was abolished by the republican government in Turkey. In the Persian region, the Safavids resisted Arabic, Turkic and Mongol influences and made Shi'i Islam the state religion in Iran. During the period 1500–1700, three great empires dominated the Muslim world: the Safavid, the Mughal and the Ottoman.

The position of Muhammad in Muslim piety

The story of Muhammad and the Medina model as the ideal for man and society as well as for various visions of social order and cohesion run right through the Muslim tradition. Muhammad's human nature is indisputable in Islamic theology and philosophy, and the distinction between Allah and his creation absolute. In local practice, however, Muhammad is addressed and ritually approached in modes that have caught the attention of conservative theologians throughout history and been deemed questionable. Being sinless or infallible (*isma*) is a quality sometimes attributed to Muhammad and even transmitted to his daughter Fatima. The evil powers did not have any influence on him and, when he made mistakes, they were corrected during his lifetime so that he was not to be punished for them in his afterlife. Muhammad, although human, even preceded Adam; he is considered to be 'the trustworthy', a quality he had even before he received the revelations.

When uttered in pious conversation, Muhammad's name is followed by the phrase 'may Allah's blessings and peace be upon him' (*salla Allahu alayhi wa sallam*) and the blessing on the prophet is repeated in the daily *salat* prayers. Muhammad – and saints and other commemorated people – are, more controversially, approached for supplications, a practice that comes close to what theologians reject as mediation between Allah and humans. Piety speaks of traces Muhammad being left: footprints, hair from his beard, even a tooth after the battle of Uhud, where he was wounded. Muhammad's grave in Medina became a much-visited site during the pilgrimage to Mecca but also a point of conflict. It was attacked by radical purist reformers in the nineteenth century, and later restored.

____

To all Muslims, Muhammad is the perfect human being (*insan kamil*) and the canonical texts underline Muhammad as a guide and as the example to follow. Some Islamic theology speaks of his light of guidance (*nur al-huda*) emanating from him and the Qur'an calls Muhammad a 'light-giving lamp' (33:46; 5:15–16). When Muhammad's qualities and character is spoken of metaphors of light are frequent; it is an edifying way of representing him that has no earthly or tangible references that could diminish his status as sinless. The Qur'an states: 'O Prophet, We have sent thee as a witness, and good tidings to bear and warning, calling unto God by His leave, and as a light-giving lamp' (33:45–46). Qur'anic passages like this have been a source of esoteric speculation, not only in Sufi tradition, and a major question for theological debate has been whether the light connected with Muhammad is to be regarded as 'pre-eternal'; that is, not created, but existing with Allah before the beginning.

The role Muhammad is given in piety is sometimes controversial. From an orthodox perspective the emphasis on the prophet can be regarded as a challenge to absolute monotheism. On the other hand, many Muslims are convinced of the blessings that come from the light of Muhammad (*nur Muhammadi*) through supplications and petitions for intermission.

Like all prophets, Muhammad is thought to have been able to perform miracles (*mujizat*), and the birth of Muhammad was accompanied by marvellous signs and blessings that were transmitted to the child's surroundings. The legendary history of the infant Muhammad show many similarities with the narratives of significant individuals in other religions: Moses, Jesus, Buddha, Krishna.

Süleyman Çelebi's long and much-esteemed poem from the early fifteenth century tells the following of the birth of Muhammad:

> The miracles his eyes displayed are many;
> Attend while I recount these blessed marvels.
> /—/
> On earth his [the angel Jibril's] scent would fill the Prophet's nostrils,
> Who waited then with joy the coming message.
> Those glorious lips had but to quiver faintly,
> And lo, the sun with all his train would tremble.
> When winds of dawn about his head played lightly,
> The scent of musk and amber filled their eddies.

By night his pearly teeth so brightly glittered,
Lost needles by that light might be recovered.
His breast poured forth a light by which his comrades
Through darkest night could walk the path of safety.
The Friend of God in twain the moon divided,
Though he but gestured towards it with his finger.
The Ruler of the World would oft plant palm-trees,
And pluck the honeyed fruit within the hour. (trans. MacCallum
1943: 28f.)

Other fantastic events are hinted at in the Qur'an and developed in pious narratives. As an infant living with his wet nurse Halima, Muhammad was approached by angels, who opened his breast, took out something black, cleansed his interior with snow and sealed the body with light. There are several versions of this narrative and some of them end with the young Muhammad being weighted so that the infant outweighed the people around him. The traditions around 'the splitting of the moon' take as their point of departure the beginning of *sura* 54 'The Moon', which opens with two cryptic verses: 'The hour has drawn nigh: the moon is split. Yet if they see a sign they turn away, and they say "A continuous sorcery!"'

The status of Muhammad in Muslim tradition

Even if the process of early Islamic history writing was very much established as part of the formation of the new religion's identity, it is beyond doubt that Muhammad was a historical person who was active on the Arabian Peninsula and established a community of adherents who accepted his claims to be the final link in a chain of prophecy starting with Adam. Hence is he known as the seal of the prophets.

The prime role of Muhammad in the Islamic faith is as the channel for the words of Allah as he heard them being recited for him on the mountain Hira; he is the tool, not the message itself. Muhammad is not a saviour, but the model human. The theological emphasis on Muhammad's human nature has caused tension between (conservative) clergy and local piety, in which emotional bonds with the prophet are expressed. His normative sayings, choices and actions constitute *sunna*, which is recorded in narratives of the *hadith* collections. The Qur'an is not a direct source of facts about the life of the historical Muhammad or his teaching activities in the way the gospels in the Bible represents Jesus. The 'I' or 'We' that speak(s) in the Qur'an is Allah himself, and Muhammad is the implicit receiver of and listener to the text brought down, the 'Him' or 'You' spoken to. Muhammad has from the early days of Islam, however, constituted the foundation for piety, ritual behaviour and social conduct. Alongside the Qur'an, which represents the words of Allah, Muhammad's words and deeds are the canonical basis for sharia. The *sunna* of Muhammad is primarily represented in the *hadith* collections as quoted sayings, depicted actions and judgements made in complicated situations.

Further reading

Bennett, Clinton, *In Search of Muhammad* (London and New York: Cassell, 1998).

Berg, Herbert (ed.), *Method and Theory in the Study of Islamic Origins* (Leiden: Brill, 2003).

Brown, Jonathan, *Muhammad: A Very Short Introduction* (Oxford: Oxford University Press, 2011).

Cook, Michael, *Muhammad* (Oxford: Oxford University Press, 1983, and later editions).

Humphreys, Stephen, *Islamic History: A Framework for Inquiry* (rev. edn., London: I.B.Tauris, 1999).

Knysh, Alexander, *Islam in Historical Perspective* (Upper Saddle River, NJ: Pearson Prentice Hall, 2009).

Motzki, Harald, *The Biography of Muhammad: The Issue of the Sources* (Leiden: Brill, 2000).

Robinson, Chase, *Islamic Historiography* (Cambridge: Cambridge University Press, 2003).

Rubin, Uri, *The Eye of the Beholder: The Life of Muhammad as Viewed by the Early Muslims* (Princeton, NJ: Darwin Press, 1995).

Schimmel, Annemarie, *And Muhammad is His Messenger: The Veneration of the Prophet in Islamic Piety* (Chapel Hill, NC: University of North Carolina Press, 1985).

Chapter III

The Canonical Texts of Islam: Historical Documents and Personal Piety

The Qur'an is the supreme canonical text of Islam, influencing in one way or another the world's 1.5 billion Muslims.[9] As a holy book, the scripture is conceived as Allah's direct message to humanity and it has been subject to various interpretations and local constructions of authority throughout Muslim history. But the Qur'an is much more than a source of solutions to moral and legal questions. It serves as a historical and literary document, a devotional manual and a sacred object that should be treated with the utmost respect, and it transmits blessing as a tangible artefact. The text of the Qur'an is a fundamental part of the daily Muslim rituals, especially the five daily prayers, where the opening *sura* of the Qur'an (al-Fatiha) is given a particular position, which it has in other genres of prayer too, as a marker of the opening and closure of sequences in the cermony.

Listening to the recitation of the Qur'an is an essential part of prayer gatherings in both mosques and domestic settings. There is a special relationship between the sound of the text and the Arabic language, even for the vast majority of Muslims, who have other mother tongues. According to the Qur'an, Arabic is the language of Allah. The pronounced text is believed to have the power to protect and is considered to be full of blessing. Recent major changes in the worldwide mediascape have made listening to the Qur'an a more individual activity, more independent of community arrangements. The recited text is available on cassettes and CDs and via the internet, and there is the choice of radio and TV stations providing different modes of recitation as well as different interpretations of the content. In societies with an increasing level of education, growing numbers of people have access to the Arabic text and translations that contribute to individual understanding of the holy text, independent of local men of learning. It is hard to underestimate the importance of the changes in media and communications. New groups of Muslims are steadily becoming familiar with the Qur'an, but not necessarily through conventional guidance within the community; they therefore develop their own relationship with the text.

The Qur'an is more than a text – oral or written; it is also a sacred object. By tradition, Qur'an recitation is accompanied by a certain decorum among both reciter and audience. It is essential that the place where a copy of the Qur'an may be kept is pure. In private homes, the stand supporting the Qur'an is often in the space of the house where the daily prayers are performed and other pious prints are often kept: pictures of the Kaaba, framed calligraphic verses from the Qur'an and pilgrimage memorabilia.

The Qur'an states about itself:

> it is surely a noble Koran
> in a hidden Book
> none but the purified shall touch,
> a sending down from the Lord of all Beings. (56:77–80)

Here, some fundamental conceptions of the character of the holy book are summarized in a few lines, with the focus on its sender and how humans should receive it.

When not in use, the holy scripture is often accompanied by images of Mecca and calligraphic plates with Qur'anic quotes and blessing formulas.

In this chapter, the canonical texts of Islam will be discussed and the various directions Qur'anic traditional exegesis or explanation (tafsir) have taken will be touched upon, as well as the biographical literature on the life of the prophet Muhammad (sira). The historical background, transmission and role of theological schools, with their different positions on the principles of how to interpret the texts and the Islamic tradition, will be discussed. Second to the Qur'an in importance in terms of legal and moral judgement are the collected narrations from the time of Muhammad (hadith). The structural differences and the hierarchical order between them will be discussed. Both the Qur'an and the hadith literature serve as the foundation for juridical and theological interpretive arguments, based on an ambition to reach the authentic normative behaviour of Muhammad (sunna) applicable to a contemporary issue.

Fig. 5 The Qur'an as a sacred object. When not in use, a copy of the Qur'an should rest on a stand or otherwise be kept properly, so that it does not touch a table or the floor, where it could be contaminated by substances that are not ritually pure.

(Getty Images)

The final book

The Qur'an is actually not the title of a book in the strict sense of the term, and the script can be referred to in several ways. It is traditionally called the Recitation (*al-Qur'an*) or the Book (*al-Kitab*); these and other names the book gives itself point to the importance of scripture as the ultimate confirmation of the eternal principles and doctrines of faith.

The message of the Qur'an has been given to mankind before, but it has, according to Muslim tradition, been misunderstood or corrupted. Previously sent revelations are not only referred to in general in the Qur'an; they are also identified with the specific names of the books and connected to the religious groups in question.[10] Three other scriptures are thought to have preceded the Qur'an: the Torah (*tawrat*) or 'the Book of Moses (Musa)', the Psalms (*zabur*) – often referred to as 'the Book of David (Dawut)' and the Gospel (*injil*), the original book given to Jesus or 'the book of Jesus (Isa)'. With regard to the last, the use of the singular should be noted. The Christian view that there were four evangelists (i.e. humans) as witnesses and authors is not

62 Islam: An Introduction

> **The status of the Arabic language of the Qur'an**
>
> The Qur'an speaks of itself in the following way in one of several self-referential statements:
>
>> Truly is the revelation of the Lord of all Being, brought down by the Faithful Spirit upon thy heart, that thou mayest be one of the warners, in a clear, Arabic tongue. Truly it is in the Scriptures of the ancients. (26:193–196)
>
> The strong emphasis on the Arabic language and the eternal quality of the script are the basis of the often pronounced Islamic opinion that it is impossible to translate the Qur'an.

accepted. The original message of Isa was as much founded of *tawhid* as the others. All three are mentioned at several points and, when the Qur'an speaks of Wisdom (*hikma*) in relation to these three scriptures, is it referring to the collected wisdom given to the prophets by Allah, although spoken of in a tone as if it were a book of its own.

The link between the three religions is a recurring theme and is emphasized at several points that indicate a certain familiarity with the Jewish tradition:

> Children of Israel, remember My Blessing
> wherewith I blessed you, and that I
> have preferred you above all beings. (2:47)

or:

> He has laid down for you as religion
> that He charged Noah with, and that
> We have revealed to thee, and that We
> charged Abraham with, Moses and Jesus:
> 'Perform the religion, and scatter not
> regarding it' /—/
> And say: 'I believe in whatever Book God has sent down'
> (42:13–15).

However, it is not an uncomplicated relationship between the religions that is depicted in the Qur'an; harsh words about the corruption (*tahrif*) and deformation of the previously sent messages occur too. The Jewish and Christian traditions are regarded as misreadings of the original message, out of ignorance or malevolence, and the cause of this distortion. Diverging views can be noted on what blame is to be put on non-Muslim communities for turning their backs on the message, or whether such behaviour is thought to be characteristic of humanity in general. Traditional theology usually interprets the evolution of revelation to be the chain leading up to Muhammad. The prophets have delivered an unchanged message that has been with Allah since before creation; 'it is a glorious Qur'an in a tablet preserved' (*lawh mahfuz*), as the Qur'an says (85:21–22). Another reference to this 'well-preserved (or guarded) tablet' is the recurring phrase 'the mother of the Book' (*umm al-kitab*) (3:7; 13:37–39; 43:4), which means that the heavenly Qur'an is *the* matrix. It is a poetic imagery that indicates the relationship between the one original, that represents both the eternal message in an abstract sense and the perfect text, and the earthly copies, which may contain errors as a result of the process of copying.

The structure of the Qur'an

A chapter in the Qur'an is called *sura* and a verse *aya* (literally 'sign'; pl. *ayat*). There are some 6,200 verses (depending on the editorial principles) organized in 114 *suras*. The differing suggested numberings of the verses, which represent a fairly recent phenomenon, have been greatly disputed, but the wording of the text itself is largely the same in all the Arabic editions. The *suras* are not directly related, like conventional chapters, but are structurally independent units. Every *sura*, except the ninth, begins with the invocation *bismillah al-rahman al-rahim*, 'In the Name of Allah, the Merciful, the Compassionate', thus indicating the origin of the text (this prayer formula is known as *basmala*). The *suras* are given names (or titles) that in some cases give an indication of the content (*sura* 4, for example, is called 'Women' and is partly dedicated to themes related to females), but in others they constitute something of an intriguing code. At the beginning of 29 of the *suras* is a combination of letters (or one letter) placed after the vocative *basmala* formula, but before the Qur'anic text itself. These 'mystic letters' have prompted many readings in exegetic tradition and attempts to read them as words with a message or comments on the *sura* in question. Not least the esoteric and mystic traditions of Islam have paid the introductory letters particular interest. Both the names

and the order of the *suras* are thought to be God-given, not an
addition made by humans.

With the exception of the first *sura*, al-Fatiha (consistently called
'the Opening'), the *suras* are organized according to length, with the
longest first, which breaks with any coherent chronological and
thematic structure. A reader not familiar with the text cannot expect
to find longer narratives in the biblical mode in the Qur'an, but rather
vocative speech, condensed statements and to some extent poetic
expressions. The Qur'an is partly poetic in its representation of the
message, but is not poetry in the literary sense. By tradition, the *suras*
are characterized as 'from Mecca' or 'from Medina', thus placing them
roughly on a timeline, although modern scholarship questions these
chronological indications. A classic debate in Islamic theology centres
on the issue of whether the Qur'an is to be regarded as identical with
(or part of) Allah himself, or if the text is to be seen as a part of Allah's
creation. The Qur'an itself gives arguments for both lines of reasoning.

> A sending down from the Merciful, the Compassionate,
> A Book whose signs have been distinguished as
> an Arabic Koran for a people having knowledge,
> good tidings to bear, and warning, but
> most of them have turned away, and do not give ear. (41:2–4)

Sending down (*tanzil*) is the key concept for describing the origin of
the eternal Qur'an and the process of reaching mankind through
Muhammad's revelations and recitations. Reading the Qur'an
nevertheless gives a sense of chronology, as the *suras* are indicated as
being Meccan or Medinan at the very beginning (after the title, but
before the *basmala* and the eventual letters). These two groups of *suras*
differ in terms of both content and themes. The first (indicated to
come from Meccan period) have an intense tone with a distinct
message of moral revival and expectations of the approaching
Judgement. In these supposedly early *suras*, the end of time is
approaching and the relation between Allah and the individual is a
central theme. Salvation lies in the acceptance of the consequent
monotheism and its internalization. The one who surrenders, *muslim*,
is on the straight path and will escape eternal punishment. The
eschatological and apocalyptical themes are phrased as in the following
quotation that formulates a warning of the approaching judgement
and the judge that will strike like a bolt of lightning:

The Clatterer! What is the Clatterer?
And what shall teach thee what is the Clatterer?
The day that men shall be like scattered moths,
and the mountains shall be like plucked wool-tufts.
Then he whose deeds weigh heavy in the Balance
shall inherit a pleasing life,
but he whose deeds weigh light in the Balance
shall plunge in the womb of the Pit.
And what shall teach thee what is the Pit?
A blazing Fire! (101:6–11)

The second group of *suras* ('From Medina') conveys an image of a religious community under construction, where social commitment and relations between individuals and groups play a central part. The instructive tone sounds as follows:

O believers, the testimony between you
when any of you is visited by death,
at the bequeathing, shall be two men
of equity among you; or two others from
another folk, if you are journeying in the land
and the affliction of death befalls you.
Them you shall detain after the prayer, and
they shall swear by God, if you are doubtful,
'We will not sell it for a price, even though
it were a near kinsman, nor will we hide the
testimony of God, for then we would surely be among the
sinful'. (5:106)

The instructions are on the one hand practical and general, but on the other the application of the commands on concrete issues calls for consultation in other genres of literature that are deemed by Islamic tradition to transmit authentic tradition. The image of Medina and the community founded by Muhammad, with its strong place in Islamic thinking, is depicted in more detail in the *hadith* narratives.

Irrespective of whether the Qur'an is believed to have been sent down as a complete unit or as a stream of revelations to Muhammad on several occasions, some Qur'anic verses can be seen to annul previous verses; so-called abrogations, in which a formulation in a verse is declared to have been modified or an opinion in an earlier revelation is taken back. 'God blots out, and He establishes whatsoever He will; and with Him is the Essence of the Book' states the Qur'an

(13:39). The best-known example is the so-called Satanic verses. Islamic history claims that Satan succeeded in influencing Muhammad to pronounce an acceptance of the old gods. Verses 19–23 in *sura* 53 are said to replace this sinister attempt to blur the correct message. These explicit replacements speak in favour of a processual formation of the Qur'an, also from a pious view.

The way the structure of the Qur'an is conceived is highly dependent on the view of how the Qur'an was received, its heavenly background and eternal qualities.

> Lo, We have sent it [the Qur'an] down on the Night of Power.
> What has let thee know what is the Night of Power?
> The Night of Power is better than a thousand months; (97:1–3)

According to legendary history, Muhammad was at the mountain Hira ('the mountain of light') when he was approached by the angel Jibril. The voice at the beginning of *sura* 97 is apparently the sender of the book.

The *sura* that precedes the quote provides a key scene in which a voice pronounces the injunction to read: 'Recite!' (*iqra*), as quoted in Chapter 2. Hearing is characteristic of how the revelations were delivered to Muhammad and the sound of the script has kept its status in the Muslim world. According to the Qur'an, Muhammad recited the revelations he received (17:106), but they were also recited to him (75:18; 28:3). The emphasis in legendary history that Muhammad was illiterate has served to indicate that the Qur'an was not written by a human, but was received verbatim by Muhammad, serving as the tool of a divine will. The conception of the Arabic text as the words of Allah, even among the vast majority of Muslims who have other mother tongues, is well established. The words themselves are therefore to be regarded as a divine manifestation (theophany).

> By the Clear Book.
> We have sent it down in a blessed night
> (We are ever warning)
> therein every wise bidding determined
> as a bidding from Us,
> (We are ever sending)
> as a mercy from thy Lord. (44:1–6)

These verses express the firm relationship between the warnings at the centre of Muhammad's revelations and the sending-down of the complete scripture with instructions to follow it in order to avoid the approaching Day of Judgement – the relationship between the message of salvation in the Qur'an and the method for Allah's plan, sending the Book.

> **The story of how revelations came to Muhammad according to pious tradition are described in Ibn Ishaq's biography (sira) of Muhammad**
>
> This passage indicates how the other normative genres relate to the Qur'anic text, in this case with a direct quote and a reference: 'The apostle began to receive revelations in the month of Ramadan. In the words of God, "The month of Ramadan in which the Qur'an was brought down as a guidance to men, and proofs of guidance and a decisive criterion"' ([sura 2:185] Ibn Ishaq: 155, trans. Guillaume, 1955: 111).
>
> The sira text fills out what is only hinted at in the Qur'an and continues: 'Prophecy is a troublesome burden – only strong, resolute messengers can bear it by God's help and grace, because of the opposition which they meet from men in conveying God's message. The apostle carried out God's orders in spite of the opposition and ill treatment which he was met with'.

The Qur'anic text itself comprises both intense injunctions for repentance from a god who will avenge sin but have mercy on those who fall down and regret before the approaching end, and instructions for an emerging community that needs identity and structure for its development.

The redaction of the Qur'an

There are standard versions of the Qur'an with some variations, but in general the Qur'anic text itself is not controversial from a theological or redactional point of view. It is more the history of the editorial process and the interpretations of the content of the text that are the subject of debate.

The process of writing down the words of Allah is inscribed in the most profound beliefs in Islam and emphasizes the role of Muhammad as the channel – not the author – and Allah's tool. The history of the early days of the *umma* is used to provide guidance to individuals and groups (*sunna*). Here the compilation of the Qur'an plays a significant role. The pious perspective of the Qur'an differs from the more academic source-critical approaches, which emphasize context and process. The period of the first four righteous caliphs (632–61), who are thought to be guided by Allah, was formative for the Muslim community, but also the period when the split between Sunni and Shi'i, which would later develop into distinct theologies, began to show. According to theological history writing, the Qur'an was completed as a coherent text ca. 650 under the reign of the third caliph, Uthman (644–56), and even that he himself took part in the redaction of it. The texts known today as the *suras* of the Qur'an were memorized and probably to some extent written down already during Muhammad's lifetime. After Muhammad's death, the first caliph is said already to have started the collection of the *suras* and the compilation of what would become the standard version of the Qur'an. In 1972, a large number of very old Qur'anic manuscripts were found in Sana, Yemen. Some of them were dated to the second half of the seventh century, which confirms an early textualization of the Qur'an. The oldest known copy of a complete Qur'an, however, dates from the eighth century.

The traditional authorities on the interpretation of the Qur'an – in exegesis and in preaching – are men of learning. A broad term for these learned experts is *ulama* (sing. *alim*), which refers to a certain authority rather than to a specific post within a community. Both reading methods and interpretive results have been scrutinized by opponents in theological discourse throughout history and at the Islamic centres of learning generations of students have graduated after acquiring the skills of not only reading the holy text, but also the local conventions of how to apply it to everyday life. The concept of explanation (*tafsir*) is preferred to interpretation, while *tawil* is the term for the more symbolic or esoteric ways of interpreting the Qur'an and is sometimes contrasted to *tafsir*.

It is reasonable to assume that there was a divergence of views on the editing of the canonical literature as well as on the interpretation of its content, although early documentation is scarce. The very structure of the narratives of the *hadith* literature implies varying positions – on detail as well as on more profound issues. Reflective legal reasoning (*ijtihad*), which has the same root as *jihad* (which also means 'effort' or 'struggle'), was never considered to be possible to achieve without intellectual endeavour. In the eighth to tenth centuries, the Mutazilites (or 'rationalists') gave reason priority over tradition. Even if the immediate impact was limited, the two positions marked fundamentally different positions on the principles of theological interpretation. The position taken by the Mutazilites was a consequence of Islam's expansion and encounter with Aristotelianism and Neoplatonism. These influences became an important part of early Islamic theology, especially after the translations of Aristotle into Arabic and the emphasis on the systematization of theological knowledge. The trust in reason implied a necessity to interpret the holy scriptures in order to provide answers relevant for a particular context. A central theme was the justice of Allah in relation to the free will of humans. With rational arguments and the potential of human reason it is possible, according to the Mutazilite position, to reach the truth about the nature of God and the meanings of the Qur'an. The Mutazilites came to some controversial conclusions when separating the eternal words of Allah from the historically constructed Qur'an. The Mutazilite movement was also drawn into political conflicts, beside the theological opposition they met from traditionalists, who emphasized the rightly guided transmitted knowledge within the *umma*.

The Mutazilites' significant opponents during the ninth and tenth centuries were the more orthodox Asharites, who tried to find a balance between traditionalism and rationalism. Some debates circled around the question of whether the Qur'an could be created but still be conceived as eternal. Other diverging interpretations appeared during the Middle Ages. One important divide was between explicit and implicit readings of the Qur'an. Mystical or symbolic interpretations of the Qur'an flourished in more esoteric Sufi traditions as well as in Shi'i theology. These methods of understanding the Qur'an were condemned by orthodox theologians and traditionalists alike.

Traditions from the time of Muhammad

An important aspect of the legitimacy of Islamic jurisprudence is its claim to reach back to the time of Muhammad and its references to the developing community in Medina, where a structure for a God-

The Qur'anic Jesus – Isa and his mother Maryam

In the Qur'an and later Muslim tradition, Isa is an important part of the succession of prophets, but he is not the son of God: 'And He will teach him [Isa] the Book, the Wisdom, the Torah, the Gospel to be a Messenger to the Children of Israel', it is stated in the Qur'an (3:48–49).

According to the Qur'an, Isa was not crucified and he does not play any role as a saviour in Muslim tradition. The Christian dogma of incarnation is anathema to Islamic theology and regarded as an offence against the concept of absolute monotheism, as is the Christian trinity. Instead, Isa predicts the coming of the final message in the Qur'an (4:155–159). In principle, the prophets all received the same message, but they were rejected and no umma was built around them; the scriptures that were produced in the wake of their appearance did not contain the complete truth because the message was misunderstood and corrupted.

As in the Bible, Maryam, the mother of Isa, plays an important role in the Qur'an. Although a virgin, she gives birth to a child, who in his swaddling clothes proclaims: 'I am God's servant; God has given me the Book, and made me a Prophet' (19:30). Maryam speaks directly to Allah and is answered, even comforted in her labour pains. Sura 19, 'Maryam', is given her name and verses 9 to 33 tell her story and relate motifs known from the Gospels in the Christian Bible.

The devotion to Mary in the Catholic and Orthodox traditions has its equivalent in the role of Fatima, Muhammad's daughter and only surviving child, in Shi'i piety – and to some extent in local Sufism.

Both Isa's and Maryam's names are mentioned several more times in the Qur'an than Muhammad's, though it must be remembered that Muhammad is the implicit receiver in the scenes of the Qur'anic texts without always being present or referred to by name or by an epithet like the prophet, the praised, the warner or simply the 'you' the speaker is addressing.

fearing life was built up. The Qur'an itself gives few details on such matters, but another genre delivers a clear image. A hadiths is a report in the form of narratives that relate the sunna of Muhammad and the early community; it is a story upon which model behaviour and parallel cases can be argued. Nothing is more important than the Qur'an, as it reproduces the words of Allah, but the hadiths are regarded as representing human deeds and sayings, based on divine guidance. The canonical status of the *hadith* narratives as second in importance to the Qur'an constitutes the basis of the use of the texts in legal practice. In theological and juridical reasoning, these texts represent and confirm the authenticity of the *sunna*: they bring forward the exemplary life of Muhammad, the pious companions (*sahaba*) who migrated to Medina (*muhajirun*) and the first (four) generations (*salaf*), whose actions and judgements are recounted in the *hadith* literature. Muhammad is the main character in the *hadith* literature, as it is his behaviour and judgements that the narratives point to. His example is primary to the followers and the ideal beginning of the narrative lineage.

The word *hadith* itself means 'narrative' or 'discourse' (the term can refer to both the genre as well as to a particular narrative). It is a witness story and represents actions, statements and decisions from the time of Muhammad and his immediate community. The term *hadith* is sometimes more loosely translated as 'the sayings of Muhammad', which is true to some extent, as Muhammad's words are referred to in the form of direct speech in a way that is not used in the Qur'an. Sometimes this corpus is referred to as *al-hadith* in the sense that these narratives transmit the unquestionable tradition in every respect. Though it certainly has some significant features. It is a compact narrative that transmits a 'chain' (*isnad*) of testimonies in the beginning that confirms the authentic tradition, followed by narrative (*matn*), which establishes a scene where a conflict or an issue is to be solved. The list of names in the *isnad* shows the primary transmitters and is generally thought of as the strongest part of a *hadith* in terms of building arguments, as it tells how close the transmitters were to the original *umma*. Muhammad himself or the people close to him are, of course, the most trustworthy beginning of such a chain. The short example below from one of the most used *hadith* collections depicts a case from which conclusions can be drawn.

> Narrated by Aisha:
> The wife of Rifa'a Al-Qurazi came to Allah's Apostle while I was sitting, and Abu Bakr was also there. She said, 'O Allah's Apostle! I was the wife of Rifa'a and he divorced me irrevocably. Then I married Abdur Rahman bin Az-Zubair who, by Allah, O Allah's Apostle, has only something like a fringe of a garment, showing the fringe of her veil.' Khalid bin Said, who was

standing at the door, for he had not been admitted, heard her statement and said, 'O Abu Bakr! Why do you not stop this lady from saying such things openly before Allah's Apostle?' No, by Allah, Allah's Apostle did nothing but smile. Then he said to the lady, 'Perhaps you want to return to Rifa'a? That is impossible unless Abdur Rahman consummates his marriage with you.' That became the tradition after him. (Sahih Bukhari 7:72:684)

As in many other *hadith* narratives, the plot presents alternatives of behaviour and points to the straight path. After the chain of transmitters, which indicates people close to Muhammad, comes the identification of a problem, followed by a suggested solution that includes a direct quotation from Muhammad. The last sentence functions as a confirmation. As in the Qur'an, the social background of a trading community is highly visible in the cases and concerns of the narratives. The texts discuss explicit rules, individual and inter-personal relations, even contracts and agreements, as well as the violation of them and consequential punishments. Correct deeds are as important as the beliefs. The identities of the individuals bringing the testimony, in this case the wife of Muhammad, are well known from the history of the early days of the *umma*. The conclusion cannot, however, be drawn from this that the *hadith* collections can be used as historical sources.

The third century of Islamic history was formative for the collection of narratives of what Muhammad had said and done, which was in many respects parallel to the redaction of the Qur'an. The very number of *hadith* narratives on the same theme open up for moral and legal judgements that are in opposition to each other, as various solutions to problems and issues can be read into them. The fact that the *hadith* stories are material collected and validated as normative about Muhammad and his first four successors as leaders of the *umma* implies that there is considerable space for theological differences. The process by which the *hadith* collections were recognized as authoritative in many respects comprises the formative period of Islam in the eighth and ninth centuries. The framework of the narratives is the near history of the early Medina community; that is, no myths about the creation, the fall of Adam or the like. No central institution with the authority to canonize or reject has ever been part of Muslim life. Instead, the process of formalization runs parallel with the development of centres of learning and education, and the political development of the Muslim empire. The *hadith* traditions therefore became influential, though with regional variation.

Six collections of *hadith* texts (all of which are referred to by the names of their compilers) are traditionally recognized as authoritative. They are regarded as second to the Qur'an as a reliable basis for understanding the *sunna* of the prophet in that they are about or from Muhammad. The two generally regarded as the most authoritative are Bukhari (named after Muhammad Ibn Ishmael al-Bukhari, d. 870), in six volumes comprising over 7,000 narratives, and Muslim (Abul Husayn Muslim ibn al-Hajjaj, d. 875).

The six classical collections of hadith narratives

The six most commonly used collections, which took precedence in the Sunni tradition from the tenth century, are compiled by the following and are referred to by their names:

- Muhammad ibn Ismail al-Bukhari (d. 870)
- Muslim ibn al-Hajjaj (d. 875)
- Abu Abdillah ibn Maja (d. 886)
- Abu Dawud (d. 889)
- Abu Isa al-Tirmidhi (d. 892)
- Ahmad al-Nasai (d. 915)

The *hadith* collections use various methods of organizing the narratives. The most common is a classification by theme – quite different from the outline of the Qur'an, but useful when seeking advice on what stand to take on a particular issue. In Bukhari and Muslim, for example, there are sections on prayer, marriage, oaths and repentance.

A special group of reports are referred to as the Holy Tradition (*hadith qudsi*). These contain direct statements by Allah, but are distinct from the Qur'an. This group is also divided into collections, some large and some small. The difference in tone between the *hadith qudsi* on the one hand and the Qur'an and the other *hadith* narratives on the other handcan be noted in this example from one of the *hadith qudsi*, where the word of Allah promises a reward to those who are faithful believers:

> On the authority of Abu Hurayrah (may Allah be pleased with him), who said that the Messenger of Allah (PBUH) said: Allah

(mighty and sublime be He) says: 'My faithful servant's reward
from Me, if I have taken to Me his best friend from amongst the
inhabitants of the world and he has then borne it patiently for
My sake, shall be nothing less than Paradise'. (*Hadith Qudsi* 29)

The quotation indicates the hierarchy of voices, which move in
several steps before a direct quote from Allah is provided. Like the
Qur'an and the *hadith* literature, the *isnad*s in the *hadith qudsi* open up
space for discussions on the transmission and approval of tradition.

The question of whether the *hadith*s can be used as historical sources for
the life of Muhammad and the early Muslim community is debatable.
Criticism and assessment of the traditions became an important part of
Islamic theology, not source-critical in the academic sense, nevertheless it
followed certain criteria of religious authority when the Islamic centres of
learning developed technical terms and methodologies for defining and
classifying the the transmitted texts. These theological arguments were part
of the process of establishing early Muslim history by claiming legitimacy
for the narratives of the early community. The question of whether a *hadith*
is sound or weak has both theological and source-critical aspects. The
method is built around a discussion of the number and character of the
transmitters and the *isnad* in order to be able to recognize the line and the
content as genuine. A lot of intellectual energy has been invested in
theological debates on which *hadith* narratives are authentic and valid
(*sahih*). For example, the references Sahih al-Bukhari and Sahih al-Muslim
are generally regarded as representing reliable lines of testimony.
Depending on their chain of transmission, the individual *hadith* reports
are also ranked according to a theological classification based on how close
to Muhammad and his immediate circle the narrator is. There is a long and
detailed tradition of the study of the transmission of *hadith* within Islamic
theology. As there are many *hadith*s on most issues, a central part of Islamic
theological interpretation is to evaluate what *hadith* texts can present the
most trustworthy (*thiqa*) transmitter to base a verdict on.

The Qur'an and *hadith* collections constitute the main sources for
Islamic theology (*kalam*) and jurisprudence (*fiqh*), which try to explain
and interpret the meaning and application of the holy scriptures. The
methodologies of *fiqh* as the basis of sharia verdicts will be discussed in
Chapter 4. Jurisprudence, that is, the reflection on or the understanding of sharia, has produced a vast literature on legal matters, often
related to philosophy (*falsafa*) or *kalam*.

The formalization of the hadith collections

Formalization of the collections constituted the basis for new genres of explanation and interpretation. Muhammad al-Tabari (d. 923) collected and systematized *hadiths* referring to Qur'anic verses and his work became a standard point of departure for future *tafsirs* well into contemporary times. His detailed commentaries (now edited in 30 volumes) were based on his teaching and contained large amounts of previous exegetical work that connected *hadiths* to individual verses in the Qur'an. Thereby, Tabari gave an overview of the different possible interpretations and supplemented these with his own comments on the Qur'anic text.

Born in the Tabriz region, Tabari devoted his long life to scholarly work and spent most of it in Baghdad, the intellectual centre of the period. Tabari diverged from the Hanbali school (*madhhab*), which had initially inspired him, and established his own, which, however, did not survive him for long. In many respects, he can be said to be a traditionalist; he was not in favour of the Mutazilites' rationalist interpretations of the Qur'an or Islamic history. Tabari's argumentation is founded on the narratives of the *hadiths* and the status of the transmitters, rather than interpretations of the possible application of the scenes recounted in the narratives. His commentaries became a standard reference for future interpreters of the Qur'an.

In his youth, Tabari travelled widely, which probably inspired him to write a history of the world even more extensive than his *tafsir*, called *The History of Prophets and Kings*. This encyclopedic work starts with the creation and is brought into the author's own time.

The closest translation of *kalam* is 'theology', and the fact that the term also means 'debate' reflects the nature of the Islamic normative literature: the cases given in the *hadith* collections, the line back to the sources and how they can be related to the Qur'an as well as to local custom open up varying discourses. Theology in the conventional Christian understanding is the study of God and God's attributes, and it implies a certain amount of systematization of interrelated concepts. The wider concept of *kalam* includes both argumentative reasoning on dogmatic issues and more speculative philosophy of a somewhat spiritual nature.

The history of *kalam* is the history of the efforts to find structures for
the reasoning and the identification and assessment of the claimed lines
of authority. The science of theology (*ilm al-kalam*), or theological
discourse, is a discipline practised at Islamic institutions of learning that
is expressed in both theoretical and literary genres. *Kalam*, understood
as systematized theological knowledge, is traditionally expressed in
philosophical tracts, *tafsir* and collections of sermons as well as
jurisprudence, political reflection and history writing. This is all part of
Islam's intellectual history, but it should not overshadow the fact that
other genres such as oral literature, songs and visual representations
have been, and still are, bearers of theological thinking outside the
world of Islamic scholars (*ulama*).

The recitation of the Qur'an

The revelations are said to have come to Muhammad as heard words,
and the vocalization of the holy text has always had a special status in
Muslim life as a duty to make the sacred words accessible to those with
little or no understanding of Arabic, as well as the illiterate. The
reception of the words is equally important. Public recitation of the
Qur'an has been a vital part of the celebration of Muslim festivals. If
theology and philosophy represent the discursive approaches to the
Qur'an, then the art of reciting points to the qualities embedded in the
sound of the sacred text, along with the status of the Arabic language,
which follows from how the Qur'an speaks of itself. The *kalam*, *fiqh*
and *falsafa* have by tradition been a part of the world of learning, while
recitation has always had a prominent position in the practice of
religion in everyday life with its prayers, songs and oral traditions. The
importance of the spoken word in piety practices comes from some
significant features of certain themes of the Qur'an that emphasize the
words of Allah as spoken. The narrative structure of the Qur'anic text
with a strong – implicit or explicit – voice, Allah, implies an audience
or listener who is clearly in the receiving position.

Traditionally, the Qur'an is divided into 30 or 60 parts (sing. *juz*, pl.
ajza) for the purpose of systematic recitation (*tilawa* or *qiraa*) of the
whole text over a specified period, and often during Ramadan.
Sometimes the Qur'an is divided into seven parts in order for the
whole of it to be read in a week – pious training for both reciter and
listeners, who sometimes follow with their own copies of the Qur'an

or leaflets containing single *suras*. The division of the Qur'an into parts is one of several mnemotechnical tools for those who want to learn the art of reciting, and it creates a rhythm of social activity. Being a reciter or training in recitation and devoting time as a listener are considered virtuous activities. Ritualized reading plays a special role during Ramadan, when the whole of the Qur'an is frequently recited at mosques by a chain of reciters (pl. *qurra*). Large crowds often attend before and after the last two daily prayers. The collective recitations unify individual and collective piety practices during the Ramadan celebrations: the joining of the circles around the reciter in a mosque courtyard links personal observance during the month of fasting to a larger scheme of recitals. In large parts of the Muslim world, women have their own gatherings in the vicinities of mosques during Ramadan for recitations and commemorative celebrations with female leaders.

Reciting the Qur'an is a highly appreciated skill (not an art in the sense of aesthetics but a skill behind which there is endeavour and spiritual ambition), but it also something every Muslim should learn to do to some extent – even if the recitation is only of a short *sura*. Selected short *suras* or parts of the Qur'an are conventionally regarded as the minimum for a suitable Islamic education. The status of the Arabic language has been touched upon in an earlier chapter, but is a crucial matter when it comes to popular education among the vast majority of Muslims, who have other native tongues.

The imperative *iqra* ('Recite!') was the injunction Muhammad heard when he received his first revelation and, ever since, this has been the emblematic scene when the importance of hearing the words of Allah is emphasized in Islamic tradition. A reciter who knows the Qur'an by heart is called *hafiz*. It is an honorary title that confers respect, but does not imply a position within a community. Both men and women can qualify for this title and serve as local instructors for boys and girls, as well as in adult education. The task of reciting the Qur'an at gatherings outside the mosque often comes with commenting on the recited texts and both men and women can give a sermonlike interpretation.

The method of reciting the Qur'an (*hifz al-quran*) is taught in Qur'anic schools (sing. *madrasa*) as part of a traditional Islamic education. But it is not necessarily combined with instructions on interpretation. A recitation always starts with a *basmala* as an invocation for full attention. The shorter *suras* at the end of the Qur'an are traditionally used as prayers, some of them integrated in the daily prayers: *salat* and voluntary prayers. Many know the wording in Arabic and how to pronounce it, but perhaps not the precise content. In Islamic learned tradition a more philosophic and theological access to the techniques of reciting the Qur'an developed and there are now seven classical methods and modes of reading the Qur'an. These various 'readings' (*qiraat*) are taught with variations in *madrasa* schools around the world.

The Qur'an is both a text and an object with assumed qualities to heal and protect. A widely spread custom throughout Muslim history is the production of amulets with verses from the Qur'an (sing. *tamima*), with reference to the Qur'anic phrase 'putting oneself under Allah's protection'. Situated at the crossroads between verbal and ritual practices, it is as contested as it is popular. Nevertheless, amulets are much cherished for protection against djinns, illness and the evil eye. In its own right, this tactile manifestation of faith indicates a strong relationship to the written holy texts; verses in the Qur'an that includes appreciation of the discursive message of the text as well as a wish to keep the blessing that comes from the closeness to the words of Allah.

The multitude of contemporary readings of the Qur'an

As in all religious traditions, there are conflicting answers to be found in the Qur'an, depending as much on the formulation of the question as on the preconceptions of the interpreter. Today, many more Islamic institutions of learning in all parts of the Muslim world face competition from actors outside the *ulama* who make use of the Qur'an in their argumentation, are regarded as authorities by their sympathizers or simply claim the authenticity of their personal reading of the canonical texts.

Some moral aspects of interpretation have been debated in Islamic theology since the Middle Ages. Even today, there are controversies as to whether the door to interpretation of the message in the Qur'an is closed or if symbolic readings of the Qur'an are legitimate. The tension between the Qur'an as a historical document and as the words of Allah is therefore present not only in modern Islamic theology, but also in everyday practices that require interpretation. Paradoxically, the emphasis is on the search for a local, regional and national heritage combined with the ideals related to the more unified culture of the *umma*, conceived as independent of time and space, and mostly authoritarian in its insistence on purity and authenticity.

Source criticism and contextualized readings of the Qur'an and the *hadith* literature have found their way into contemporary interpretations and historicizing the understanding of the Qur'an has become a major tool in liberal interpretations. Complex relation to Islamic heritage can be interpreted in a number of ways, as well as how to link it to contemporary life. From an educational point of view, new voices are heard both within the Islamic sciences and outside the traditional institutions of learning following academic source-critical methods, as well as attempts to combine the two.

The theoretical points of departure in contemporary Qur'an interpretation are as varied as in any discipline. In *Modern Muslim Intellectuals and the Qur'an* (2004), the editor Suha Taji-Farouki puts forward a variety of theological positions adopted over the past century in relation to the challenges of modernity, such as those of Fazlur Rahman, Nurcholish Madjud and Mohammed Arkoun, who established positions as international public intellectuals in the last decades of the twentieth century. Among the best-known contemporary writers in English to take up the debate are:

- Amina Wadud (b. 1952) and Asma Barlas (b. 1950), who are both making re-readings of Islamic texts in search of arguments in favour of gender equality.
- Nasr Hamid Abu Zayd (d. 2010), who caused major controversy when he applied literary perspectives and semiotics to his reading of the Qur'an as a system of signs to be decoded in every individual reading.
- Mohamed Talbi (b. 1921), a Tunisian academic historian rather than an *alim*, who emphasizes pluralism and dialogues between religions and draws on European philosophical tradition to define the bridges.
- Abdol Karim Soroush (b. 1945), who in exile from Iran has published extensively on ethics and philosophy, and been acclaimed for his defence of human rights and democracy with reference to Islamic sources and underlining the importance of individual interpretation.

The holy scriptures of Islam

As the 'eternal scripture', the Qur'an stands out in Muslim belief as the concrete link between Allah and humanity – through Muhammad's revelations and the following scripturalization of the message. It serves as a source of moral guidance on how to organize earthly life and provides the fundamentals of Islamic beliefs as well as constituting a vital part of ritual life through recitations and prayers. The Qur'an provides few commandments as such. These are to be found in the collections of Muhammad's sayings and judgements, the *hadith* literature and 'the traditions', which include narratives relating to the first four generations of Muslims. The narrative structure of the latter texts opens up many possible interpretations within sharia and the implementation of law.

A notable feature of the Qur'an is its many self-referential statements, as expressed in the following verse:

> O believers, believe in God and His Messenger
> and the Book He has sent down on His Messenger
> and the Book which He sent down before.
> Whoso disbelieves in God and His angels
> and His Books, and His Messengers,
> and the Last Day, has surely gone astray into far error. (4:136)

The Messenger, Muhammad, and the Book – the Qur'an – are significant elements in the delivery of the final message, though not acting personas in a narrative sense. The main voice in the Qur'an belongs to Allah.

The introduction to this volume emphasized the variety and richness of the understanding of Islam to be found among Muslims all over the world. This chapter shows how the very character of the canonical scriptures is open to diverging interpretations and that Islamic tradition from the beginning has been multi-voiced. Qur'anic studies and the literature of comments and exegesis is part of a large intellectual contribution of more general principles of hermeneutics, philosophy and ethics.

The interpretative traditions are, however, but one element in an even larger web of representing Muslim faith. The Qur'an is also very concretely part of everyday prayer, lectures and preaching, and most practising Muslims have a personal relationship to the original Arabic text, although not necessary a discursive one.

The Qur'an can be regarded from three major angles: as a text with a discursive message, the value of the recitation of the text and the text as an artefact. The Qur'an is a text that historically has been transformed from oral to scriptural, and it still bears reminiscences of an oral text in style and modulation. Traditional Islamic history writing emphasizes both the importance of Muhammad's revelations as direct audio-visions and at the same time the significance of this voice of Allah as a book, a holy script. The many references in the Qur'an to other religions with a book are a reminder of the significant status it has in Islam. Equally importantly, the Qur'an is full of blessing and comfort, irrespective of whether it is recited or received. The material qualities of the Qur'an as a holy artefact – to be handled in a dignified way and as an object that transmits blessing (baraka) – are shown in the construction of the places set aside for the Qur'an in domestic spaces as well as mosques.

As there are no formal organizations to provide generic interpretations, traditionally local and regional learned institutions and religious authorities have been more or less part of the state administration – or executed by means of other forms of governance – and so consolidated generally accepted patterns of interpretation.

An image of the time of Muhammad, his sunna and the community he established in Medina is created in a more narrative way by the hadith literature. The concepts of umma and tawhid have been absolutely central in Muslim theology since the early formative period, and both are key concepts in understanding the status of the Qur'an. Even though the Qur'an is considered to be impossible to translate, as it was sent down to humankind in Arabic, access to the text has increased with the spread of education and modern media. These processes have resulted in more individual readings of the Qur'an and put the traditional institutions in new positions.

In contrast to most other religions, the Islamic tradition does not employ references to a mythic past. The narratives of early Muslim history are regarded as representations of a factual past and therefore a source of guidance as well as a timeless narrative to be internalized in personal piety. The Qur'an, which represents the words of Allah, and the hadith literature, providing narratives of how issues were solved by Muhammad and the first generations of Muslims, have formed the basis of the ways in which Islamic law has been locally and regionally interpreted.

Further reading

Burton, John, *An Introduction to the Hadith* (Edinburgh: Edinburgh University Press, 1994).

Cook, Michael, *The Koran: A Very Short Introduction* (Oxford: Oxford University Press, 2000).

Gade, Anna M., *Perfection makes Practice. Learning, Emotion, and the Recited Qur'an in Indonesia* (Honolulu: University of Hawaii Press, 2004).

——, *The Qur'an: An Introduction* (Oxford: Oneworld, 2010).

McAuliffe, Jane Dammen (ed.), *The Cambridge Companion to the Qur'an* (Cambridge: Cambridge University Press, 2006).

—— (ed.), *Encyclopaedia of the Qur'an* (Brill Online, 2008).

Rippin, Andrew (ed.), *The Blackwell Companion to the Qur'an* (Oxford: Blackwell, 2007).

—— (ed.), *Classical Islam: A Sourcebook of Religious Literature* (London: Routledge, 2012).

Taji-Farouki, Suha (ed.), *Modern Muslim Intellectuals and the Qur'an* (Oxford: Oxford University Press, 2004).

Chapter IV

Sharia: The Law of Allah and Human Free Will

Few things have set the image of Islam more in modern media than the concept of sharia. Related notions like *fatwa* and *hudud* along with debates on polygamy and whether human rights are applicable to an Islamic worldview have promoted a popular understanding that sharia is all about harsh punishments, death sentences and authoritarianism. It must therefore be stated from the beginning that the conventional translation of sharia as 'Islamic law' gives too narrow an understanding, which can pave the way to several misconceptions. Sharia is not a collection of books or a corpus of legal texts; it is an abstract umbrella term, used in many ways and with a wide impact on the contemporary world – from everyday life to international politics. It comprises the discussion and implementation of civil, religious, economic and penal regulations. Literally, the term means 'road', 'way' or 'path' (to the water pond) and it is only mentioned once in the Qur'an, which states: 'Then We set thee upon an open [determined] way [sharia] of the Command; therefore follow it, and follow not the caprices of those who do not know' (45:18). The term sharia also implies 'method', indicating a systematic approach to just verdicts in accordance with the will of Allah, which immediately brings up the complicated issue of different standpoints in Islamic interpretative tradition.

Sharia must therefore be given a broad definition as it has broad usages. It indicates not only regulation in the widest sense, but also the implementation of law. The frequent expression sharia law must therefore be considered a tautology. Following the basic conceptions of Islamic theology, sharia is regarded as eternal, as is Allah – its origin – and it is based on the revelations received by Muhammad and the traditions collected after him by the first generations of followers. Sharia can therefore not be instituted (as it is so already through the revelations) or be discussed in terms of formal legislation (as the law is already given); it can only be interpreted and applied. A central aspect of the conception of Allah is that he is the sole provider of law. In the very earliest *suras* of the Qur'an, Allah is already perceived as the judge and humans as under his jurisdiction, although he is also repeatedly said to be gracious, forgiving and just. To balance these two significant images of Allah has been a major endeavour in Islamic theology and in the discussions about what constitutes sharia.

There is an apparent rift in Islamic theology on the issue of whether knowledge (*ilm*) – or, more specifically, formal religious knowledge, founded in the testimony of the canonical literature (the Qur'an and the *hadith* reports) – should be distinguished from general knowledge based on human perception and experience. The limits of human knowledge in relation to the claims of absolute truth made in the canonical literature can be in conflict, especially when it comes to the estimation of reasoning as a method to reach a verdict in accordance with sharia and *sunna*. In Islamic theology, there is an apprehension that intellectual immodesty can lead people astray from the belief in Allah's superiority as well as a trust in the capability of the human mind as part of the intensions with Allah's creation. 'It is not for any believer, man or woman, when God and His Messenger have decreed a matter, to have the choice in the affair. Whosoever disobeys God and His Messenger has gone astray into manifest error' (33:36) states the Qur'an.

Even if sharia is an abstract term, as emphasized above, this does not mean that the discussions about the implementation of sharia have not resulted in any literature; quite the opposite. The applications of sharia, with all their juridical, theological, philosophical, political and practical implications, have generated a huge literature over the centuries, expressed in many genres and forms – and covering most aspects of life, from philosophical reasoning to everyday behaviour.

The first part of this chapter will discuss the sources and the principles of sharia, its features and methods, and the second part will present some aspects of its implementation, with a special focus on contemporary issues.

The straight path

Reasoning around sharia in a strict sense has throughout Islamic history been a matter for the learned elites and, more generally, those with a higher formal Islamic education. However, when expanding the discussion to norms and ethics in general, the role of regional or local tradition and custom (*urf*, *ada*) should not be underestimated – normative opinions that are rarely taken down as written texts but nevertheless guide behaviour and judgements in everyday life and social practice. Local ethics are transmitted by means of *madrasa* education, preaching and public debate, but also through socialization, aesthetic representation and rituals.

The sharia categories reflect the early Muslim community that got its local form in hierarchical societies in the full sense of the term: power structures based on gender and age, favouring male authority and the subordination of women. These are circumstances that some contemporary interpretations of sharia take into consideration and historicize, while on the other hand the examples from *sunna* are read as verbatim instructions in conservative interpretations.

Throughout the early history of Islam, an increasing formalization of sharia took place, although it was never unified institutionally. Rather than collections of regulations in the tradition of common law, regional traditions of interpretation of sharia were established. Sharing the normative sources, but giving space for local custom – the organization of courts, appointments of judges and administrators – has been an integrated part of the political structure at large, from tribal culture to the empires of sultans, and legal tradition has developed along varying lines.

In the nineteenth century and the first half of the twentieth century, colonial rule in large parts of the Muslim world introduced a separation of criminal law, family law and economic regulations. As a result, Islamic jurists and teachers lost a great deal of influence over politics as well as over everyday life. During the process of change (and Westernization), legal systems were influenced by European codes with their conceptions of the relation of the individual to the collective (such as family, religion or ethnic community), and the private sphere became separated from the public. In many Muslim countries today, it is primarily family law (marriage, divorce, inheritance) that remains under Islamic regulation and follows the local interpretation of sharia. Another challenge to the Islamic legal system was introduced by the decrees of the Ottoman sultans, who instituted a legislated law (*qanun*) for the elaborate administrative system of the empire. These administrative regulations were not explicitly based on sharia, but from a theological perspective they were referred to the *ulama* for approval. Nevertheless, they represented a significant shift in the early phases of modernity in the Muslim world, proposing other sources of legal authority and influencing in one way or another the conditions for marriage, divorce and inheritance. Still used today, *qanun*, a Greek loanword widely employed in the Muslim world, refers to legislation in a specific country or international law that is not based on sharia, but often at least formulated from a theological point of view.

Some basic legal concepts recur in the institutionalized interpretations of sharia made by its juridical officials, some of which are of an epistemological nature: knowledge (*ilm*), theology (*kalam*), exegesis (*tafsir*), ethics and norms (*akhlaq*) and jurisprudence (*fiqh*).

An established formal authority is a necessity in courts and for the organization of the application of justice, that is, jurisdiction, as well as for the action of judging and the administration of the justice system – judicature.

The sources of sharia

As stated above, Islamic law is not codified and does not provide sets of exact rules and regulations; nor does it make any distinction between private and public law. The canonical basis of sharia is the divine revelation of the will of Allah as represented by the normative sources discussed in the previous chapter; its practice is the history of interpretation and the consequences in the execution of verdicts.

In principle, and to some extent in practice, the validity ideals and norms can be declared directly after consultation of the Qur'an and the *hadith* literature, but for most issues the normative literature cannot provide direct answers. Further efforts to ascertaining the will of Allah in a demanding matter would consist a systematic exploration of the normative literature, weighing up the examples acquired on similar issues and consultation of theological treatises.

Islamic thinking has, over the centuries, developed several disciplines devoted to both the philosophical and the practical side of the law. To seek 'the roots of jurisprudence' (*usul al-fiqh*), that is, the methods of reaching a verdict in line with the will of Allah, is the term for the systematic investigation of the law, and it indicates the path in search of the models in Muhammad's Medina community. These methods must never be in conflict with the concept of *tawhid*. The primary source of Islamic law is, of course, the Qur'an, but it contains few explicit regulations. As such, specific quotations from the Qur'an are seldom directly applicable to modern issues. Instead interpretation is needed, and different words from the Qur'an are often used for very contrasting positions of arguing. Yet, no verdict can contradict what is stipulated in the Qur'an. The methods developed in Islamic science in order to reach a legitimate and authoritative verdict follow a specific pattern that classifies deeds and objects: from the mandatory to the forbidden. The relationship between the Qur'an and the *hadiths* was discussed in the previous chapter and the hierarchical relationship between these two texts remains the same in the implementation of sharia. The background to the concept of *sunna* is the vision of the righteous judgements stemming from the prophet and the first caliphs and the justice (*adl*) implemented in the Medina community at the time of Muhammad. *Sunna* is depicted in the *hadith* literature and *sira* narratives through the examples from the first (four) generations (*salaf*). The examples from the *hadith* literature are not to be understood as precedents, but as cases to reason from, and it is not correct to identify Islamic law as a variant of common law.

If no similar situations are to be found, it is possible to argue a verdict by analogy (*qiyas*), that is, to seek a similar problem and its solution in the holy scriptures and apply it to a contemporary situation – without contradicting the Qur'an or *sunna*. This method was proposed as early as the ninth century to determine how decisions could be made in accordance with *fiqh* in contexts with challenges and conditions different from the world described in the *hadith* narratives. To some extent, analogy has been a controversial method, as this way of reasoning to come to a verdict involves a dual problem. Its critics underline the risk of introducing novelties to belief and ritual that do not conform strictly to the original message and the very identification of the comparable case carries a large proportion of interpretation. In many Muslim societies, consensus (*ijma*), that is, general agreement on a matter among *ulama* in a certain context, has therefore been the favoured method of applying sharia. Consensus is itself, though, a point of disagreement between the leading Islamic schools of law, in terms of where to identify the consensus and whose articulation of consensus should be accepted. Some recognize only the *ijma* of the first four generations of Muslims, while others accept the necessity of applying rules from ancient texts to new contexts and hence consensus emerging after Medina.

This fundamental opposition between the two positions taken on the possibilities of interpretation reappear throughout the history of Islamic theology: to follow the examples in the normative sources (*taqlid*; literally 'imitation') or open up for interpretation (*ijtihad*) based on reasoning in relation to the context given to the case. The philosophical dichotomy between the concepts should be separated from legal practice, where both methods can be used at the same time.

A scholar who is qualified to conduct *ijtihad* is called a *mujtahid*, literally 'one who strives' – an *alim* who performs a systematic reflection on the few explicit rules stipulated in the Qur'an and the testimonies of the *hadith* collections and thereby acquires the authority to interpret sharia. It is a controversial term, or rather title, in the sense that there is a strong line in Sunni theology claiming that the 'gate of *ijtihad*' is closed; it was only the founders of the four dominating Sunni legal schools (not to be understood as educational institutions, but as major traits in the methodology for how to argue for a verdict in accordance with sharia) that could claim the title of *mujtahid* based on their knowledge and closeness to the time of Muhammad. Sunni tradition has instead advocated *taqlid* of the good example and compliance with the established practice of one of the legal schools to avoid making new interpretations that take in the conditions of the current situation and could blur the original message. This attitude to interpretation developed in the later Middle Ages, when so many verdicts were circulating to be tested for relevant guidance and in different versions with the intention of holding on to a unified tradition.

Sharia distinguishes between several main categories of deeds, materials, substances and attitudes, spanning what is lawful (*halal*) and what is forbidden (*haram*).

The five sharia qualifications

Traditional *fiqh* classifies human acts and activities into five categories (*al-ahkam al-khamsa*), also known as the five sharia values:

> *fard* – obligatory religious duty
> *mustahabb* – recommendable
> *jaiz* – passing (morally neutral)
> *makruh* – reprehensible, discouraged
> *haram* – forbidden, unlawful, restricted

The often-quoted Qur'anic phrase calling for every Muslim to 'promote the good and prohibit the evil', with its background in *sura* 3:104,[11] known as *hisba*, could, beside being a moral principle, refer to an institutional duty for an appointed person to oversee the extent to which sharia is observed within a community, but with no formal legal mandate. It has been used during the last decades to silence unconventional interpretations of Islam in the name of preventing apostasy.

The European Fatwa Council

The European Fatwa Council (formally The European Council for Fatwa and Research – ECFR) was founded in 1997. It is known for its conservative, not to say sometimes extreme, Sunni interpretations. The council is structured as a foundation and has no institutional position or juridical district. The controversial Islamic scholar Yusuf al-Qaradawi (b. 1926) has from the beginning been one of several conservative theologians voicing verdicts and judgements. The ECFR has global ambitions, but with a special emphasis on spreading advice to Muslims in Europe, the USA and elsewhere who are living as a minority and, in many cases, under new conditions where Islamic ethics are tested against new situations.

To Muslims of a liberal theological inclination this combination of global aspirations and hegemonic claims is unacceptable.

The fundamental conception is that Allah is the legislator and that the will of Allah is good and eternal; human interpretations of sharia can therefore always be the target of criticism and redefinition. Consequently, Islamic jurisprudence – or the philosophy of law as interpreted by men of learning and covering all areas of life (including religious observance) – *fiqh* (literally 'understanding', i.e. of the path, sharia) is based on reasoning; it is open-ended and not absolute. Therefore, sharia courts have no tradition of legal assistance or representation; nor are there prosecutors. In a conflict or disagreement, queries are raised by one party and each case is, ideally, scrutinized from different angles. A *qadi* is a judge, today often appointed by local or state administration. A jurist or jurisprudent, a scholar who interprets the law, is generally known as *faqih*, while *ulama* is a broad term for Islamic scholars in education, instruction, theology and jurisprudence. Scholars of law constitute one specialization among several in this group. An Islamic scholar trained to provide answers to concrete problems and recommendations (sing. *fatwa*) is called a *mufti*. A *fatwa* is guidance rather than a verdict and a *mufti* is not a member of a sharia court. The *fatwa* provided is formulated to have a general character – whereas a *qadi* makes a decision after court proceedings.

There are several different terms for the jurisprudents that traditionally have had the authority to interpret sharia in order to give advice, solve disputes and declare verdicts.

Sharia jurists

- *alim* (pl. *ulama*) – Islamic scholar in the broad sense of the word;
- *mufti* – Islamic scholar who provides recommendations for resolving formulated issues and may provide a *fatwa* on the theme; often referred to as a collective;
- *qadi* – judge at a court;
- *faqih* – jurist;
- *shaykh* – head of a Sufi order, who may also give advice to his disciples that can be of a binding, but not legal, character.

In modern times, several countries with Muslim majority populations have installed national grand *mufti*s – an institutionalized position that gives reinforced authority to the pronounced *fatwas*.

The implementation of sharia

A division-based regional variation of the implementation of sharia must always be approximate. The branches of the legal schools throughout history form a complex web, and the four Sunni *madhahib* (sing. *madhhab*, literally 'path' or 'direction') have dominated specific areas of the Muslim world. The term law school should be understood as an intellectual course in regard to legal matters, and is in development over time. The background to the appearance of formal law schools was a theological current in mid-eighth-century Basra. The *mutazila* ('rationalist') movement emphasized free will and the human capacity to distinguish between good and evil. The Mutazilites considered that the text of the Qur'an to be flavoured by the spirit of its time of edition and therefore called for an exegesis that took account of shifting conditions.

The Hanafi school is named after Abu Hanifa (d. 767) and has its historical roots in Kufa and Basra. It has over time been comparatively open to new interpretations and contextualization. The Hanafi school governed the interpretation of sharia through the long history of the Ottoman Empire and today dominates Central Asia and the Indian sub-continent, Iraq, Syria, Jordan, Palestine, Turkey and the Balkans.

The Hanbali school, named after Ahmad ibn Hanbal (d. 855), is known to be the strictest of the four law schools. The medieval theologian Ibn Taymiyya (d. 1328), who wanted to cleanse Islam by ridding it of any form of innovation (*bida*), has had a renaissance as a key thinker in the modern era among reform movements that strive for authentic religion. Though the least widely spread school, this line of what they conceived as thought is nevertheless influential as it constitutes the intellectual basis for various radical reform interpretations and is followed by *salafis* and other purist reformers. It is the official sharia school of Saudi Arabia and sharia constitutes the law of that country.

The Maliki school was founded by Malik ibn Anas (d. 795), who lived in Medina, and is therefore sometimes called the Medina school. It was the school of the Muslims in medieval Spain and today dominates North Africa and large parts of Western and Central Africa.

The Shafii school has its origins in Egypt and is named after Idris al-Shafii (d. 820), who opposed the Hanafi and Malik schools. Its *ulama* made efforts to develop the methodology of analogy (*qiya*) when interpreting the Qur'an. Today, the Shafii school is still influential in Egypt, but even more so in East Africa, Southeast Asia, Malaysia and Indonesia. The emphasis on analogy has made the school influential in Sufi theology.

Alongside the four Sunni *madhahib* must also be mentioned the major law school among Shi'i Muslims, Jafari. It was founded by Jafar as-Sadiq (d. 765), also a respected transmitter of the *hadith* narratives among Sunni Muslims. The canonical Shi'i collections of *hadith* differ from the Sunni and in Shi'i-dominated areas where the implementation of sharia in legal practice is highly dependent on clerical hierarchies who represent divine guidance in their verdicts. Since the Islamic revolution in 1979, the Jafari school has constituted the basis of the legal system in Iran.

In Islamic jurisprudence a fundamental distinction is made between two areas, sometimes regarded as a literal expression, sometimes as a question of distinct borders: the house of Islam (*dar al-islam*), where Islamic law and the rules of sharia are to be unconditionally implemented, and the house of war (*dar al-harb*), where disbelief rules. The position of non-Muslim communities living among a Muslim majority population has been an issue of varying theological stands, as have varying practices for organizing differences in civic life between Muslims and non-Muslims. In most cases, the regulation of non-Muslims' civil life has been dealt with by the religious institutions of the relevant denomination; in other words, the individual has been regarded as a member of a specific (ethno-)religious collective. Even in Muslim countries where Western criminal and administrative law have been implemented, civil law can fall under religious jurisdiction. The autonomy for non-Muslims in Muslim environments and the injunction in order to protect them from imposed regulations (dress code or alcohol consumption) is formally guaranteed by sharia. In many other contexts such issues would have been regarded as private matters, but not according to (conservative interpretations of) sharia. The ideals of autonomy are far from always a political reality though, and are always dependent upon local political circumstances.

Schooling and education have therefore always been important tools for keeping Islamic communities together as well as for theological cohesion. The term *madrasa* refers to schools for Islamic training, which provide both basic and higher education. Some *madrasas* have developed from large-scale schools into modern Islamic universities, some of them with branches worldwide, that are especially connected with the study of jurisprudence and the principles of how to implement sharia.

By far the best-known *madrasa* in the Muslim world is al-Azhar in Cairo. Its long history, renowned scholars and the sheer volume of its activities put al-Azhar in a special position of authority in the Muslim world. Al-Azhar has provided the educational background for a number of influential Muslim scholars over the centuries. In the absence of a formal institution for the provision of general guidance on moral and theological matters, al-Azhar has for centuries offered higher education and the services of a cadre of men of learning within all Islamic disciplines. The normative influence of al-Azhar, both in the past and today, cannot be overestimated.

Modern media have opened new paths for both raising questions and spreading responses and advice. These can take the form of talk

Al-Azhar: the leading educational institution in the Muslim world

Inaugurated in 970 during the Fatimid reign, al-Azhar developed into the most influential institution of learning in the Sunni world. Its principal is given the title *shaykh al-Azhar* (since 2010, this has been Ahmed al-Tayeb), whose opinions draw world attention. Even if there is no central religious authority in the Muslim world, the *fatwas* formulated by the *ulama* of al-Azhar have a considerable impact in the Sunni world due to the position this institution has in the Islamic realm of learning. The positions it takes on controversial issues and its verdicts have a global media spread and a normative impact. Statements from the head of al-Azhar are noted in the media as opinions held by the Muslim mainstream

Al-Azhar's core activities are structured around three faculties: theology, sharia and the Arabic language. After reforms in 1961, al-Azhar nowadays offers a curriculum in the liberal arts and sciences, as well as faculties for women, and it has had an increasing focus on international students. Considerable expansion has taken place during the last decades and there are several branches of al-Azhar's faculties and colleges outside Cairo, teaching well over 1 million students in Egypt and elsewhere.

shows on TV, blogs, Facebook, Twitter messaging, websites and official statements posted by influential institutions like al-Azhar in Cairo and the Turkish Directorate for Religious Affairs, Diyanet. The site islamopediaonline.org posts current debates in English and gives an overview of positions taken on, not least, politically hot topics.

The following example of how a question may be posed and how the answer can be formulated comes from the website Fatwa Online, which has close links to the radical reformists:

> Question: I married a Hindu woman a year ago, after she had embraced Islam – as far as I could tell. However, after the marriage it became apparent to me that she had not embraced Islam with her heart, and because of this, she continues to practise her religion. It is difficult for me to divorce her, because we have such a good understanding, and I try to encourage her to the best of my ability [to embrace Islam], and believe she will respond. So what is now legally required of me?

Response: It is quite possible she believes that what she is doing [in practising] some of the rituals of her religion does not nullify her belief in Islam. So you should call her to leave these practices, and if she acquiesces, then this is what is required. If she does not acquiesce, then tell her that you have not left these religious practices of yours, so there is no [legal] marriage between you. As it is known, if she is keen on [maintaining] this marriage, that will draw her to Islam, and if she refuses, even after such a threat, then there is no [legally binding] marriage between the two of you, [in which case] you are required to separate from her. Allah has complete knowledge [of all affairs].

The above has been translated and edited to an unknown extent by the managers of the website, but it illustrates how questions can be answered (rather than how questions are formulated), ranging from private concerns to issues with consequences for international politics. Several of the larger *fatwa* sites take obviously conservative or even radical Islamist positions, among them Yusuf al-Qaradawi's highly controversial IslamOnline or the Ministry of Religious Affairs in Saudi Arabia, and they are therefore rejected by many Muslims.

Marriage and divorce

Muslim family law functions in many countries over a wide spectrum from moral guidance to settling legal matters, and clearly illustrates the consequences of not separating civil and criminal law in sharia in modern societies. Marriage and divorce are issues of relevance in both Muslim majority and minority contexts. These issues also highlight how religious and social life are interwoven.

The framework for marriage (*nikah*) is a regulating agreement and a wedding as the social and religious celebration of this contract are situated at a crossroads between sharia, national civil code and local traditions, with individual emotions and family alliances. The scriptural tradition of the Qur'an is perhaps not always taken as an argument per se (in relation to local customs), but might be used as a tool of authority and legitimacy in order to preserve established custom. In Muslim contexts, men and women are both expected to marry and raise families. There is no tradition of celibacy or monastic life; asceticism was rarely practised even in medieval times, except rarely late in life after marital commitments had been fulfilled. The following words from the Qur'an are often used as a directive when celibacy is discussed: 'And monasticism they [the Christians] invented – We did not prescribe it for them, only seeking the good pleasure of God; but they observed it not as it should be observed' (Qur'an 57:27). Marriage is promoted from the perspective of personal security and community stability. Marriage and marital procedures constitute a link between local custom and scriptural tradition.

On the one hand, a wedding is from a strictly normative perspective a celebration of the chaste bride, who has hidden her beauty and attractiveness from public view, while from a social perspective it is a public exposure of her readiness to enter matrimonial life. There are considerable legal, social and personal implications to every individual marriage, and other agents are always involved in the surrounding ritual proceedings. More than in any other group of Muslim rituals, the agency of women is apparent in the customarily long preparations for a wedding. The Qur'anic view of marriage as a social institution is to a great extent focused around the links within a family in its declaration of rights and obligations.[12] But the wedding ritual is not a sacrament in Islamic tradition, although local life has its norms, standards and expectations regarding the proceedings. Formally, the signing of the marriage contract is preceded by a proposal that includes an offer (ijab) followed by an acceptance (qabul).

Islamic tradition does not require any specific wedding ritual to make a marriage legal. The performative act of announcing: 'I herby declare you man and wife' has instead its equivalent in the act of the signing of the marriage contract, which according to traditional fiqh makes a marriage valid (sahih).[13] In short, the concept of nikah can have several meanings. It can refer to marriage as a social institution, to the contract itself or to the wedding and its ritual proceedings. From the point of view of sharia, marriage is an agreement between two individuals (though often represented by their families) sealed with this written document and, from a local perspective, the exchange of gifts between the families plays an equally confirming role. Many Muslims, however, regard the actual signing as a public pronouncement to the local community of the definitive uniting of two families after a period of negotiation. In many Muslim communities there is a period equivalent to engagement (khitba, 'mutual acceptance') or betrothal, indicating that an offer of marriage has been made but not constituting a legal act. Even where no such formalities are made, if

Fig. 6   A woman signing a marriage contract (*nikah*). The text of the contract gives
the names of the couple, indicates their respective lineage and specifies the bridal gift
(*mahr*). A marriage contract can also stipulate the economic conditions in the event of
divorce and for inheritance. (*Getty Images*)

signs of marital interest are expressed by either family, word spreads
and becomes local knowledge.

The consent of both parties is formally required for an agreement,
although a male representative or matrimonial guardian (*wali*) of the
bride (from the paternal side of her family) can sign the marriage
contract with her or, as is often the case according to local customs,
instead of her. Two male adult witnesses (pl. *shuhud*) also have to be
present at the moment of the signing in order to make the marriage
valid. The text of the contract gives the names of the couple, indicates
their respective lineage (in order to avoid the marital impediment of a
couple being blood relatives) and specifies the bridal gift (*mahr*) in
terms of money, gold, property, consumer goods or labour. A
marriage contract can also stipulate the economic conditions in the
event of divorce and for inheritance.

A bridal gift should, according to sharia, be indicated in the
marriage contract.[14] It should specify what the woman is guaranteed if

divorced or widowed. *Mahr* could be translated as 'dowry', but the term has wider implications, as it is, in principle, a form of insurance for the woman. It is supposed to remain her own property, but can be spent to meet her family's needs at any time in the marriage. Customary practice around *nikah* and *mahr* shift not only between regions, but often between social groups living in the same place. The *mahr* is in most cases to be paid before the marriage and is regarded as an assurance that the marriage will soon follow. In some Muslim contexts, a 'bride payment' is also customary. This payment consists of money or commodities passed from the groom (or his family) to the bride's family when the marriage is sealed or in order to finalize the marriage negotiations.

A third major economic transfer is the trousseau the bride brings to her new home, which is sometimes prepared for years beforehand by herself and her female relatives. Where this tradition is observed, the trousseau normally consists of textiles for the household, kitchen utensils and commodities. A popular interpretation of the custom is that, by her handicraft, the bride proves herself to be a capable worker. All these economic transactions, as well as regulations about who to marry, were of utmost importance in pre-modern societies in order to bind local communities together. In a contemporary context, the trousseau can consist of an apartment bought for the young couple by the bride's father, which indicates not only a change in the character of the gift (it still ties the younger to the older generation), but also a more radical social shift: young couples setting up households of their own from the beginning.

Muslim marriage rituals do not usually take place in a mosque, but in private homes or at the office of a judge (*qadi*) or an imam. In many countries, a visit to the registrar's office − or, rather, the legal document produced by the registrar − constitutes the definitive marriage certificate and is regarded as the public announcement of the union, whereas the wedding ceremony has private and religious meanings. Hence, a distinction must be made, as in all religions, between the wedding as a social and religious event and marriage as a regulating institution. There is a far more elaborate theological discourse regarding the latter. The signing still takes place in separate rooms for men and women and the ceremony can to some extent be regarded as a kind of parallel ritual. When the imam or *qadi* officiating at the wedding ritual announces its conclusion, those present offer a prayer, reciting the first *sura* of the Qur'an, al-Fatiha, in unison. This can be followed by a short sermon or a speech to the couple, but this is far from always being the case.

The wedding celebrations start after the signing of the marriage contract and follow local custom; in other words, they can take many – more or less elaborate – forms. Recent years have seen a tendency towards very costly weddings among the urban middle classes. This has definitively affected the marriage pattern in many Muslim countries, above all raising the marriage age (as young people save up for a long time) and marriage across social borders. To give couples of less means a chance to marry, mass weddings have consequently been introduced, supported by welfare endowments.

A most important part of Muslim marital jurisprudence is the legal impediments to marriage as stipulated in the Qur'an and specified in detail in traditional *fiqh*. One verse in the fourth *sura* of the Qur'an, 'The Women', has had a wide impact on family structure and the conceptions of family and family relations in most Muslim cultures, as it states:

> Forbidden to you are your mothers and daughters, your sisters,
> your aunts paternal and maternal,
> your brother's daughters, your sister's daughters,
> your mothers who have given suck to you,
> your suckling sisters, your wives' mothers
> your stepdaughters who are in your care,
> being born of your wives you have been in to –
> but if you have not yet been in to them
> it is no fault in you – and the spouses
> of your sons who are of your loins. (4:23)

This restricting of marriage to within a specific group and thus limiting the number of possible spouses is done in many cultures. The cultural norms regarding the social borders within which marriages can be made vary throughout the Muslim world. In short, it is forbidden (*haram*) to marry:

- a person of close blood relationship (4:22–23);
- a person brought up by the same wet-nurse.
- a person of another faith, i.e. a Muslim woman is not allowed to marry a non-Muslim, but a Muslim man can marry a woman from 'the people of the Book', i.e. Christian or Jewish, though it is generally understood that acceptance of marriage implies that she

will convert (the acceptance of a Muslim woman's marriage to a non-Muslim would, according to the traditional line of reasoning, be the same as accepting that she leaves Islam, i.e. becoming an apostate) and that the offspring will be brought up in the Muslim faith.

In addition:

• a woman cannot remarry before the stipulated 'waiting period' (*idda*) after a divorce (most often three months, in order to identify pregnancy).

Radical changes have followed urbanization and international migration, and have implications on ritual performances, as customs merge in new contexts. This development has also been greatly affected by global poplar culture regarding romance as well as the influence of modernist reforms stressing civil liberties and the individual as a legal and social subject. The preference for marriage based on personal choice has also increased, as have young people's expectations regarding married life. Many experience conflicts between, on the one hand, adherence to religious and traditional norms emphasizing family values and chastity and, on the other, influences from popular culture that presupposes other possible relationships between the sexes. The shifting traditions when arguing for sharia-based verdicts is not only a question of ethnographic data, it is a core issue when legal pluralism is accepted, such as in the UK. Whose interpretation of sharia is valid? In Canada groups of Muslim women have strongly opposed parallel legal systems.

Divorce (*talaq*) is usually phrased in traditional *fiqh* as permitted but not encouraged. It falls conventionally under the category *makruh* – disliked; neither forbidden nor encouraged. As divorce is mentioned in the Qur'an as a social fact, the status of the divorcee has not been stigmatized in Muslim cultures as it has in most traditional Christian contexts, where divorce has often not been an option at all.

The agreement in the marriage contract establishes the economic conditions of the marriage, but local custom does not always allow the woman what she is formally entitled to as stipulated in the individual marriage contract. According to the rules of *fiqh*, the father is always the *wali* of his children and therefore has custody (*hadana*) of the children and the duty to pay maintenance when younger children stay with their mother. Traditionally, a divorced woman moved back to her father's household. However, in modern times and urbanized contexts, other options are open to divorced women. Nevertheless, as stated above, local custom is as important as, if not more than, sharia when it comes to the regulation of divorce.

Economic transactions

An important aspect of sharia is the regulation of economic transactions. As discussed in previous chapters, the normative sources from the formative period of Islam bear witness to its background in the trading community, and the Qur'an displays both concrete regulations and uses economic relations as metaphors. Whole sections in the *hadith* collections are devoted to economic transactions: sales, loans, partnerships and conditions for business. Others are closely related to family law, such as bride wealth, inheritance and marriage contracts.

In relation to sharia the concrete possibilities to perform welfare there are some economic constructions of special interest. The inauguration of an endowment (*waqf*) has a long history in Islamic tradition. The term is often translated as 'pious endowment or foundation', as a charter explaining the foundation's aims and the regulation of its activities is required by Islamic law. Throughout history, the mosque has been far more than a place for prayer and sermons; it has also been one of the prime arenas for social work. Many important welfare activities, such as education and healthcare, have their economic base in such a *waqf*. These activities can carried out in the vicinity of mosque compounds, be performed by appointed executors or Sufi orders in commemoration of an individual, a family or an event. Schools, libraries, soup kitchens and hospitals in the Muslim world have often been organized as endowments, as the *waqf* structure ensures stability in terms of access to funding and loyalty to its cause, as stipulated in the charter. Throughout history, women have taken the initiative in establishing foundations for a worthy cause or in commemoration of an individual, and have been able to use them as platforms for engagement in welfare and education.

Islam, human rights and democracy

Human rights is an area where Islamic tradition has clashed with the concept of individual civil liberties, and discussions have focused on whether Islam and democracy are compatible and whether traditional Muslim societies can change to a democratic course under Islamic governance. Some Muslims thinkers have embraced the unity of Muslim values and democratic variety, while others have rejected the thought of representative decision-making replacing sharia, making reference to the concept of *tawhid*: Allah's unity cannot be replaced by differing human opinions.

These debates have to a large extent focused on whether universal human rights (*huquq al-insan*) are compatible with sharia or are a Western construction and part of colonial attitudes. The concepts political rights and civil liberties are undoubtedly part of the Enlightenment legacy, with their historical roots in Western Europe and the USA, where individual prerogatives and emphasis on the legal subject and citizenship are expressed in the Declaration of Independence: 'All men are created equal'. The United Nations' Universal Declaration of Human Rights of 1948 follows that tradition when it underlines unconditional equality before the law as its fundamental principle and point of departure.

Legal egalitarianism is often rejected in principle from an Islamic position, as one of the fundaments in sharia is the division between legal subjects: men and women, Muslims and non-believers, pure and impure. Instead, collective identities, with rights and obligations, are placed above individual civil liberties. The meeting point between claims for universal human rights and defence of sharia bring sensitive topics to light: gender equality, inter-religious marriage and custody over children, to which there are no unanimous Islamic answers.

There are several Islamic responses to the UN Declaration, which can be read from different angles. Some of them are complete rejections of universal rights. Other modes of reasoning formulate parallel sets of rules that promote (more or less) the same rights without accepting legal egalitarianism as a point of departure. One example of the latter is the Cairo Declaration on Human Rights in Islam (1990), formulated by the Organization of the Islamic Conference (OIC). Although not ratified, this document is stated to be a guide for the 25 nations whose foreign ministers agreed to sign the text. To a large extent, the issues are the same as those brought up in the UN Declaration. It is above all the last two articles, which clearly state that sharia is the sole basis of jurisdiction, that have caused controversy over whether the declaration is universally applicable and whose interpretation of sharia would be the valid one. Article 24 states that 'All the rights and freedoms stipulated in this Declaration are subject to the Islamic Shari'ah' and article 25 that 'The Islamic Shari'ah is the only source of reference for the explanation or clarification of any of the articles of this Declaration'. Defenders of the Cairo Declaration point to democratic values within Islam, while its critics regard the document as proof of either the unwillingness among the many autocrats in the Muslim world to implement democracy or a position generally critical of any political place for religion in a democracy.

The issue of punishment is one area of debate around human rights and sharia. The punishments explicitly stipulated in the Qur'an (*hudud*; sing. *hadd*, literally 'limit') for crimes such as theft, adultery and apostasy are sometimes named 'sharia punishments', which might give the impression that sharia always stipulates particularly harsh penalties and that it connotes a given set of rules instead of differing schools of interpretation. The definitions of these 'limits' could therefore be contrasted with Muslim arguments against the death penalty and the inviolability of individual lives.

Not only has sharia as the point of reference been a problematic position, but also the very definition of human existence in relation to Allah as creator and ruler.

Theological and philosophical reasoning that seeks to combine Islam and democracy points to two classical Islamic concepts: the general good (*maslaha*) or public interest as a basis of legal decisions, and consultation (*shura*). The concept of *shura* has been institutionalized to a consultative and advisory body (also named *shura*) in public affairs. There has been a long discussion in the field of Islamic sciences over the nature of good (i.e. Islamic) governance. The Qur'an praises those who avoid conflict – 'those who answer their Lord, and perform the prayer, their affair being counsel between them, and they expend of that We have provided them' (42:38) – and recommends consultation. Some thinkers therefore put forward *shura* as the Islamic alternative to democracy.

There are proposals from other perspectives as to how to cope with shared issues among Muslims and non-Muslims and how to identify shared platforms for solutions irrespective of religious inclination. Abdullahi Ahmad an-Naim (b. 1946), the Sudan-born American legal scholar, has in his academic studies *Towards an Islamic Reformation* (1990) and *Muslims and Global Justice* (2010) attempted to combine

The Cairo Declaration on Human Rights in Islam

The Cairo Declaration on Human Rights in Islam was agreed upon by the Organization of the Islamic Conference (OIC) in August 1990 to serve as general guidance for the member states in the field of human rights. It states:

> Article 1:
> (a) All human beings form one family whose members are united by their subordination to Allah and descent from Adam. All men are equal in terms of basic human dignity and basic obligations and responsibilities, without any discrimination on the basis of race, colour, language, belief, sex, religion, political affiliation, social status or other considerations. The true religion is the guarantee for enhancing such dignity along the path to human integrity.
> (b) All human beings are Allah's subjects, and the most loved by Him are those who are most beneficial to His subjects, and no one has superiority over another except on the basis of piety and good deeds.

It ends with two paragraphs that have caused problems in terms of reconciling the Cairo Declaration with the universalism of the UN Declaration of Human Rights:

> Article 24:
> All the rights and freedoms stipulated in this Declaration are subject to the Islamic Shari'ah.
> Article 25:
> The Islamic Shari'ah is the only source of reference for the explanation or clarification of any of the articles of this Declaration.

philosophical reasoning with the proclamation of a global morality. From his point of view, sharia is to be understood as interpretation and therefore is always a subject to change and contextualization.

Divine law and human shortcomings

No human activity falls outside sharia and all deeds and opinions can be classified according to a scale from the mandatory to the forbidden. All activities can also be categorized according to their ritual (or, more strictly, legal) purity. The uses of the concept of *halal* have broadened with the establishment of new lifestyles in Muslim majority contexts and in the diaspora. It tends to include not only what is permissible to eat and do, but also a conviction that things are sound and healthy from a Muslim perspective.

The implementation of sharia has always been a source of conflicting arguments as to what path to take when evaluating statements in the canonical literature. Regardless of the strict hierarchy accepted by all Muslims between the Qur'an, the *hadith* and the *sira* texts accounting for the life of Muhammad, four law schools have developed in the Sunni world since the eighth century that have had an impact in different regions of the Muslim world. Whether to accept the consensus (*ijma*) that follows the established custom in a specific environment or whether 'imitation' (*taqlid*) is the path to follow in order to ensure that the intentions of *sunna* and sharia are respected has been an ongoing theological dispute. Sharia as the framework for public and civil relations therefore looks very different in various Muslim environments. Changing living conditions since the late nineteenth century (increasing urbanization, migration and education) have also altered the conceptions of what a righteous Muslim life is. Actors other than the *ulama* take it upon themselves to pronounce their interpretations of Islam. Issues of women's rights, civil liberties, democracy and environmental protection have become themes in some contemporary Islamic theology, while an increasing conservative trend is also noticeable.

Further reading

Cook, Michael, *Commanding Right and Forbidding Wrong in Islamic Thought* (Cambridge: Cambridge University Press, 2000).

Hallaq, Wael, *A History of Islamic Law* (Cambridge: Cambridge University Press, 1997).

——, *An Introduction to Islamic Law* (Cambridge: Cambridge University Press, 2009).

Hefner, Robert, *Sharia Politics: Islamic Law and Society in the Modern World* (Bloomington, IN: Indiana University Press, 2011).

Mayer, Ann Elizabeth, *Islam and Human Rights: Traditions and Politics*, 5th edn (Boulder, CO: Westview Press, 2012).

Otto, Jan Michiel (ed.), *Sharia Incorporated: A Comparative Overview of the Legal System in Twelve Muslim Countries in Past and Present* (Leiden: Brill, 2010).

Vikør, Knut, *Between God and the Sultan: An Historical Introduction to Islamic Law* (London: Hurst, 2005).

Weiss, Bernard (ed.), *Studies in Islamic Legal Theory* (Leiden: Brill, 2002).

Zaman, Muhammad Qasim, *The Ulama in Contemporary Islam: Custodians of Change* (Princeton, NJ: Princeton University Press, 2002).

Zubaida, Sami, *Law and Power in the Islamic World* (London: I.B.Tauris, 2003).

Chapter V

The Festivals of the Muslim Year and Lifecycle Rituals: Community and Celebration

The Friday midday prayer with its sermon (*khutba*) is the backbone of Muslim communal ritual gatherings. Although this is in most cases a mono-gendered ritual, it must be regarded as the most central of the Muslim rituals, as it constitutes the nexus of the regular daily *salat* prayers. The stipulated prayers of the day and the week are, however, part of a web of other rituals. This chapter will deal with significant celebrations of both religious and social importance, and it is divided into two sections: the festivals in the Muslim calendar and Muslim lifecycle rituals.

The varying rituals of the lifecycle and the different ritual spaces for men and women as well as the rapidly changing forms of celebration in diaspora communities, are the inevitable lens of variety through which any generalization must be viewed.

The rituals discussed in this chapter can, more or less, be characterized as family events with both religious and social references. A recurring theme for both the lifecycle rituals and the yearly celebrations will therefore be the relation between local custom and learned legal discussions related to theology (*kalam*) and jurisprudence (*fiqh*). What is regarded as a traditional festival custom in one context is considered repellent in another. These rituals relate to the theological distinctions between the categories of *ibadat* (stipulated ritual observance or worship) and *muamalat* (interpersonal interaction or social obligations). The *ibadat* (sing. *ibada*) are conventionally defined as the absolute (religious) duties in relation to God, and are sometimes referred to as canonical, emphasizing the strong support for these customs in Islamic legal texts. Usually, the following obligations and their accompanying rituals are regarded as *ibadat* and it is not uncommon to see the term translated simply as 'worship': ritual purification (*tahara*), the five daily *salat* prayers, funeral obligations, alms (*zakat*), fasting (*siyam*) and pilgrimage to Mecca at least once in a lifetime (*hajj*). *Muamalat* (sing. *muamala*) on the other hand imply social obligations in relation to other humans (especially family) of a legal, moral and economic character – in practice often connected with ritual activities. Among what is conventionally defined as *muamalat*, with its strong emphasis on social agency, ritual or other forms of pious obligation we find: naming ceremonies, marriage and divorce. The rituals accounted for in this chapter fall into both *ibadat* and *muamalat* and the distinction between them might appear unimportant from an individual's perspective, though, throughout history as well as in contemporary times, they have been at the heart of many theological debates on ritual performance and on gendered issues because the performance of them touches the basic classifications that determine the definitions of authority, possible agency and spaces of activities. Traditional *fiqh* classifies human acts and activities into five categories (*al-ahkam al-khamsa*) as discussed in Chapter 4: from obligatory religious duties to the forbidden. The concept *halal*, permitted and lawful, has its absolute contrast in the concept *haram*.

The division of this chapter can, like every typology, be contested, but it enables us to emphasize everyday practices rather than theological categories. The rituals presented here are celebrated in most, but not all, Muslim communities (in some, certain celebrations are even rejected as un-Islamic or as innovations). However, they vary in the manner in which they are performed or celebrated in their wider social context – and differ perhaps even more in terms of the meanings that the performers invest in them, especially in relation to social stratification, age and generation. Some of the ceremonies mentioned in this chapter (like *mawlid* and *dhikr*) are important parts of both yearly celebrations and regular prayer activities.

Few things vary more than the social contexts in which lifecycle rituals and yearly celebrations are set; this is as true for Muslim environments as for any other cultural milieu. Ritual participation is from such a perspective connected with identity and belonging, especially in societies where alternative modes are competing or cultural transformations are at stake. The objectives for individual participation involve the modes of everyday life as well as conscious individual choices. The impact of processes such as urbanization, migration and encounters with other ways of living as a Muslim or with other religious or secular lifestyles – in short, the conditions of modernity and the options for individual choices and access to new pious meeting grounds – have had a considerable impact on Muslim rituals ever since the late nineteenth century. A traditional Muslim funeral service, for example, is conventionally attended only by men, while women's mourning gatherings are usually defined as social rather than religious events. In new social contexts controversies around women who demand to attend emerge, and hereby new funeral traditions start to develop, as well as the formulation of conservative criticism. It is in this zone between convention and change that we find many contemporary Muslim rituals. Lifecycle rituals differ significantly from one another when regarded from a gendered perspective. Not only do males' and females' rituals take different expressive forms, but the social impact of the rituals on the individual lives of the agents can also be worlds apart. In most cultures, certainly not only Muslim, lifecycle rituals continue to constitute a social manifestation of the legitimacy of stable gender roles.

Holidays of the Muslim year

Muslim ritual life follows both the lunar and the solar cycles. The lunar calendar provides the structure for the Muslim yearly ritual cycle and its festival calendar, while the daily *salat* prayers are performed according to the movement of the sun (from dawn to dusk) and some local celebrations also follow the solar calendar. The sunset marks the beginning of the new day; consequently many celebrations commence in the evening. The calendar regards the appearance of the new moon as the start of a month and has 12 months with 29 or 30 days. The Islamic calendar is completed in a 33-year cycle. It makes the Muslim festivals movable backwards in relation to the solar calendar. The Qur'an states: 'They will question thee concerning the new moons. Say "They are appointed times for the people, and the Pilgrimage"' (2:189). Therefore the public announcement of the beginning of a festival is part of its ritual framework.

Two of the Muslim months are especially associated with major holidays, but of a very different character: Ramadan and Muharram. The month of Shawwal is also thought of as especially blessed and favourable for decisions and important events such as signing marriage contracts or moving house. The following presentation of Muslim festivals will follow the lunar cycle, starting with the first month of the Islamic calendar.

The structure of the Muslim lunar calendar and its ritual cycle

'Id Mubarak!' ('Blessed festival!'), the frequent salutation during the two major festivals, implies the wishing of the general blessings of the period upon the addressee.

Two festivals are traditionally called *id* or *eid*, though the term is not used in the Qur'an, nor are any performances of festivals mentioned: Id al-Fitr, the breaking of the fast observed during Ramadan, and Id al-Adha, the sacrifice in remembrance of Abraham's loyalty to Allah and performed all over the Muslim world while the pilgrims to Mecca are completing their rites. Both festivals are embedded in a larger web of celebrations. Other celebrations are referred to as *laylat*, meaning 'night', as they start after sunset.

The following are the names of the months in the Muslim calendar with an indication of the most important festivals (some of these celebrations are generally accepted, while some are contested as either folk custom or *bida*):

Muharram
1 Al-Hijra (Muslim New Year's Day)
10 Ashura
Safar
Rabi al-Awwal
12 Mawlid al-Nabi (celebration of the birth of Muhammad)
Rabi al-Thani
Jumada al-Ula
Jumada al-Akhirah
Rajab
The first night to Friday (*raghaib*) is commemorated as the time when Amina conceived Muhammad
13 Birthday of imam Ali (Shi'i)
27 Laylat al-isra wa-l-miraj
Shaban
Laylat al-Baraat (the night of forgiveness). On this night of the full moon Muhammad's entry into Mecca is remembered; it is thought of as the night when the fate of the coming year is established.

Ramadan
The month of fasting, which includes the following special festivals:
19 Commemoration of the battle of Badr
27 (or one of the last odd-numbered days) Laylat al-Qadr, celebrated
   in commemoration of the revelation of the Qur'an
Shawwal
1–3 Id al-Fitr, the breaking the long fast during Ramadan
Dhu al-Qada
Dhu al-Hijja
10 Id al-Adha, the festival of sacrifice in commemoration of Abraham
   and Isaac
18 Id al-Ghadir (Shi'i festival in remembrance of Muhammad's last
   sermon)

The ritual year with its stable scheme of festivals observed by most Muslims nevertheless has many local variants, as have the lifecycle rituals discussed in the second part of the chapter.

Muharram

Muharram, the first month in the Muslim lunar calendar, has a solemn character among the various groups of Shi'is, whereas the commemoration is observed in other modes among Sunni Muslims as a month of special blessing, if at all. The first ten days of Muharram are a period of grief and mourning over the major martyrs in Shi'ism. The month starts with an optional fast, leading to the tenth day of the month, Ashura. This is the commemoration of the martyrdom of the grandson of Muhammad, Husayn, who died in the battle of Karbala in CE 680.

The rituals and narratives of Muharram have a special significance in Shi'i communities worldwide, but also in old, formerly Sunni, Ottoman areas, such as Turkey and the Balkans, where the legendary history of martyrdom is remembered at prayer meetings and during *mevlud* recitations. In Sunni parts of the Muslim world, Muharram is considered to be a month of special blessing. The elaborate Shi'i rituals during Muharram are presented in Chapter 7. In large parts of the Muslim world, there is no special celebration of Ashura day like the performances among Shi'i Muslims. Rather, other significant historical moments are connected to this day. It is regarded as the day of creation, Abraham's birthday or the day when the Kaaba was constructed. Fasting is generally recommended for the tenth day of Muharram to mark it as a day of importance.

The first day of the month, Al-Hijra, is the Muslim New Year's Day and is named in commemoration of Muhammad's migration (*hijra*) from Mecca to Medina in CE 622 and the establishment of a new community of believers. This important event constitutes the symbolic start of the year. New Year's celebrations are not uncommon on this day, and not necessarily only with religious connotations.

Rabi al-Awwal

The tradition of celebrating the birthday of Muhammad (Mawlid al-Nabi; Arabic *mawlid* or *mawlud* – meaning 'birth'; Turkish *mevlud*; Persian *mowlud*) on the twelfth day of Rabi-Al-Awwal developed in the thirteenth century and spread to large parts of the Muslim world. The poetic and ritual traditions surrounding the celebration of the prophet's birth are not only deeply embedded in local custom; they have also been the source of sophisticated aesthetic expression.

Süleyman Çelebi's widely known early fifteenth-century collection of poems in praise of the prophet takes the narratives of the birth of Muhammad as a point of departure. The poems are also sung during other commemorative events of a joyous or poignant character, when sending a group on the *hajj* or receiving them back. The most cherished part is from the fifth section, welcoming the newborn prophet, at which the worshippers rise with their right hand on their chest. It reads in MacCallum's translation (1943: 23f.):

> Welcome, O matchless Sultan, thou art welcome,
> Welcome, O Source of Knowledge, thou art welcome.
> Welcome, thou Secret of the Koran, welcome,
> Welcome, Affliction's Cure, thou art most welcome.
> Welcome, thou Nightingale of Beauty's garden,
> Welcome, to him who knows the Lord of Pardon.

The *mawlid* celebration is far from only a ritual in the yearly cycle. Narrative poems are widely appreciated when celebrating joyous events and commemorating the dead, and is by some considered contested ritual practice. The rituals can be performed in mosques, by Sufi circles or in private homes, and are often highly emotional.

Women are frequently active as organizers of events, ritual leaders and reciters, and as participants in the circles around the reciter, they follow the recitation intensely and join in the choruses between the narrative stanzas.

Another cherished collection often recited from is the thirteenth-century *Poem about the Mantle*, in praise of Muhammad, by Qasidat al-Burda (the poem is therefore often referred to as simply 'Burda'). The tone is affectionate and the mantle represents the sense of being protected by Muhammad. The tone is even more devotional in this poem – an example of how emotional closeness to Muhammad is expressed:

> If I have committed sins, yet my pact with the Prophet is not broken,
> Nor is my bond with him severed.
> Surely by my name Muhammad I fall under his protection.
> And he is the most faithful of all creation to his convenants.
> (145–6; trans. Stetkevych, 2010:142)

Rajab

Together with the two following months, Shaban and Ramadan, this month is considered to have a holy character, and periodic fasting is recommended. The first night to Friday of Rajab is celebrated as the time when Amina conceived Muhammad and when Allah's grace is supposed to be especially great for those who repent. The night is therefore also known as 'the night of wishes'.

On the thirteenth day of Rajab, the birth of the imam Ali is celebrated by Shi'is.

On the twenty-seventh is Laylat al-Miraj (or *laylat al-isra wa-l-miraj*), celebrated in commemoration of Muhammad's Night Journey (*isra*) from Mecca to Jerusalem and his ascension (*miraj*) to the Seven Heavens (as discussed in Chapter 2).

Shaban

Shaban is the second of the holy months and, among pious Muslims, is a period for preparations for the long fast during Ramadan. On the fifteenth is Laylat al-Baraat, the night of forgiveness, celebrated on the night of the full moon (in the middle of the month); this is the night when all sins can be forgiven of those who turn to God and when the destinies for the following year are thought to be settled. This day is also thought among Shi'i Muslims to be the birthday of the Mahdi, the coming redeemer.

Ramadan

Ramadan is the ninth month and was probably already a special period in the pre-Islamic yearly cycle. It is perhaps the most renowned Muslim month and is referred to as 'the holy month' (al-shahr al-haram).

Fasting (sawm) for the whole month is mandatory, as it is one of the five pillars of the faith (arkan). Adults should refrain from food, drink, smoking and sexual activities during the hours of daylight. Children, the sick, women who are menstruating, pregnant or nursing and people travelling are excepted. Besides the stipulated prohibitions, pious Muslims are required to stay away from pleasures and concentrate on spiritual matters. The second sura states: 'eat and drink, until the white thread shows clearly to you from the black thread at dawn; then complete the Fast unto the night' (2:187). In certain phases of the 33-year cycle, when Ramadan falls during the summer, the heat can be a real challenge; drinking is forbidden, as is even to swallow saliva. An illegitimate break of the decree means failing to respect the demands of Allah and requires compensation. Such repentance is most often done by feeding the poor.

A word like fasting might sound gloomy, as does abstinence, but Ramadan is perceived as a joyous period, with a strong emphasis on breaking the fast, and the accompanying social events which take place after sunset. Ramadan is regarded as a blessed month, when people feel especially close to the grace of Allah. The fasting period is an exercise in controlling physical needs as well as cultivating spiritual endeavour. Ramadan is both a period of intense piety and a time of frequent public events. It is very much a family-oriented period, as the evening meals play a major role in local interaction. The meal when breaking the fast (iftar) at the end of the day when the sun sets is a time for the gathering of families and friends. In order to mark the break, the first thing to eat is often a date, and ideally one from a gift brought back from a pilgrimage to Mecca. The meal before dawn (suhur) is, if it can be afforded, sturdy enough to prepare for a new day of fasting.

Activity in the mosques is vigorous during Ramadan, with colourful decorations on the outside and invitations to participate, even to those who are not regular mosque-goers. Readings of sections of the Qur'an are organized, culminating with celebrations of the revelation of the Qur'an. Traditionally, a systematic division of the Qur'anic text into 30 or 60 equal parts (ajza) is made, to be read one each night in order to complete the reading of the whole Qur'an during Ramadan. A number of additional prayers and special forms of prayer are connected to the fasting period and take their character from local cultural expressions. During Ramadan, women are more visible in the mosques and in the courtyards, and engage in recitations and prayers.

Voluntary additional nocturnal prayers (tarawih), with up to 40 additional prostrations and movements (rakat) during the last prayer of the day, are performed. The gatherings during the nights of Ramadan can develop in an intensive mode. Sufi orders are particularly active during Ramadan, with night-long vigils and repetitive emotive performances in mosques.

On the nineteenth of Ramadan, the decisive battle of Badr (in CE 634), when early believers fought Meccans, is remembered during a nocturnal vigil, when the names of the 305 Muslim fighters who died in the battle are uttered and blessings are pronounced over their names.

The last ten nights of Ramadan are regarded as especially holy and people try to find time for more intense prayers and readings from the Qur'an. The very pious can spend the last ten days in a kind of retreat (itikaf) in a mosque – within a marked space, but joining the collective five daily prayers – to focus on prayer and Qur'an reading.

The first revelation of the Qur'an is thought to have come to Muhammad during Ramadan. On the twenty-seventh of Ramadan (or one of the last odd-numbered days; in Shi'i communities on the twenty-third), Laylat al-Qadr (kadir gecesi in Turkish) – 'the Night of Power' – is celebrated in commemoration of the night when the Qur'an was revealed to Muhammad by the angel Jibril, fixed in pious history to year CE 610. By some it is believed to be the holiest night of the month. The Qur'an states: 'The Night of Power is better than a thousand months' (97:3). According to tradition, Muhammad's wife Aisha said that 'this night is in the soul of the prophet'. This is also the night when the fates of the coming year are supposed to be established, and all – not only the very pious – perform a vigil with intense prayers to make the New Year a good one.

Shawwal

The breaking of the last fast of Ramadan marks the beginning of the following month. When the new moon appears it signals the end of Ramadan and the fast; and a special *id* prayer is said in mosques. From the first to the third of Shawwal, Id al-Fitr (*Şeker Bayramı* in Turkish) is celebrated. Id al-Fitr is very much a family holiday and is preceded by much travelling to join relatives and friends. The feast continues for three days, with gifts, special foods and visits and a special festive charity (*zakat al-fitr*) is stipulated for the holidays.

Even though Ramadan is over, a six-day fast during the month is recommended, and is followed by the very pious.

Dhu al-Hijja

This is the month of the pilgrimage to Mecca and it ends the Muslim calendar. Fasting is recommended for the ninth of the month, as a preparation for the feast on the following days. The Festival of Sacrifice Id al-Adha (or Id al-Qurban) (*kurban bayramı* in Turkish) is celebrated for several days, starting on the tenth. Along with Id al-Fitr at the end of Ramadan, Id al-Adha is one of the two major festivals for many Muslims and it is therefore sometimes referred to as the Great Feast (Id al-Kabir).

The celebrations follow the pattern inaugurated by Muhammad in Medina, as recorded in the *hadith* literature and the *sira* narratives. The background is the shared narrative of how Abraham almost carried out the sacrifice of his only son, proving his utmost obedience to God, but the angel Jibril replaced him with a ram. The Qur'an does not provide a full-length narrative, in contrast, for example, to the story in Ibn Ishaq's account of the life of Muhammad. It only briefly indicates Abraham's loyalty to Allah (37:102–103).

Traditionally, the sacrifice takes place at home. In urban areas, however, the animals are taken to a large mosque, where they are slaughtered in the courtyard by the local imam or an assistant. The sacrificial animal is brought back home and is cooked and consumed over several days of family gatherings; parts of it are generally distributed to the poor. As with *salat* and other ritual activities, the sacrifice requires the proper intention (*niyya*) to be pronounced and must be followed by prayers and blessings. This is perhaps the most important festival in the Muslim calendar. The ritual activities to some extent run parallel with the ceremonies closing the pilgrimage to Mecca, where sacrifices also take place to commemorate Abraham's willingness to follow the commands of Allah. Hereby, the local ceremonies are linked to the rituals performed at the epicentre of the Islamic world.

The two major festivals, Id al-Fitr and Id al-Adha, both celebrate a fundamental principle in Islam, obedience to God, and are connected to two of the five pillars of Islam. In the first case, the fasting period of Ramadan and in the second the pilgrimage to Mecca – also for those who don't travel, but perform the sacrifice at home.

Lifecycle rituals

The ceremonies celebrating changes in the lifecycle of an individual appear closely embedded in local customary practice, family law according to sharia and under the impact of modernization processes, social reforms and educational programmes. Interpretations of Muslim family law, especially when it comes to practices surrounding marriage and divorce, are directly linked to the status of women and gender relations. Since the late nineteenth century, the various modernist movements in the Muslim world have, with their more or less secular and national agendas, had a substantial impact on how traditional rituals are performed and reformed, and how they have been challenged by growing religious intolerance. The issue of interpretation (*ijtihad*) and how to draw conclusions from the normative corpus in relation to contemporary circumstances has been greatly debated – especially the legal methodology of how to determine sharia verdicts.

This section will discuss four groups of ceremonies during a person's lifespan: birth and naming, coming of age rituals, marriage and wedding, death and funerals. These are the rituals that are performed in most cultures to mark the key transitions in life. Changes in social status and acceptance into a collective are not always, but commonly in most cultures, marked with an outer sign in dress or otherwise. In Muslim contexts, they are of course inscribed in the local understanding of Islamic concepts and categories.

Birth and naming

Most cultures mark, in one way or the other, the arrival of a baby as a new member of the community. In the Muslim world, there are few examples of elaborate rituals of this kind. None of these ceremonies are regarded as compulsory; instead, they are to a great extent reflections of local family structures and other social conditions. In general, there are ceremonies for the baby shortly after the birth and seven days later, as well as purification rituals for the mother 40 days after she has given birth. Many rituals surrounding birth and giving birth follow the pattern below, where post-natal dangers, medical as well as magical, are confronted.

Shortly after birth, the newborn is washed and covered in a clean (white) cloth. It is a transitional ritual, marking the separation from the mother. This very first act has a double meaning of covering the infant's human nakedness as well as protecting it from attacking spirits and the evil eye. The foetus is naked (and innocent) in the womb, but the baby arrives in the world as a human and must therefore be covered.

The testimony of the one God in *shahada* – or the *shahada* phrase of Allah's oneness included in the full call to prayer (*adhan*) – is then read into the right ear of the newborn (and sometimes the second call to prayer (*ikama*) into the left.[15] The infant should be made aware from the beginning of the essentials of Muslim dogma: absolute monotheism and that Allah's message was brought to mankind through Muhammad. Of equal significance to the first sound is the first taste on the tongue. According to a *hadith* Muhammad showed through a symbolic act how a newborn should be greeted with sweetness:

> The Prophet took a date, chewed it, took some of it out of his mouth, put it into the child's mouth and did Tahnik [chewed fruit juice] for him with that, and named him 'Abdullah' [= a servant of Allah]. (Sahih Bukhari 7:66:379)

The first nourishment before the mother starts breast-feeding should be something sweet: chewed dates, honey or some fruit juice (*tahnik*). It is a symbolic 'meal' and implies wishes for a sweet life. Both these rituals could be summarized as symbolic acts, as manifestations of the baby being included in the parents' religious identity and framed by good wishes.

There is a fourth ritual act at the moment of birth, which is far from being as common as the former three. In some Muslim communities, a piece of paper with an inscription from the Qur'an (*sura* 113 or 114 are not unusual choices) is embedded as protection in the swaddling or in the cradle. Amulets, beads or ribbons could also be attached to the baby's clothes: the little eye protecting it from the evil gaze or Fatima's hand.

> ***Sura* 113, the second last in the Qur'an, is, like some of the other very last chapters, formulated as a prayer:**
>
> > Say, 'I take refuge with the Lord of the Daybreak
> > from the evil of what He has created,
> > from the evil of darkness when it gathers,
> > from the evil of the women who blow on knots,
> > from the evil of an envier when he envies.'
>
> The *sura* is formulated as an imperative to use as a specific prayer when seeking the protection of Allah. The phrasing is a petition in a world of danger. 'The women who blow on knots' is a reference to sorcery. In many folk traditions, infants are thought to be a target for cunning people, especially of their evil gaze that could harm the infant.

The seclusion of the mother for seven days after giving birth has traditionally not been uncommon, but not necessarily complete seclusion, and the custom is quickly fading away in urban environments. The mother and child would then in some Muslim environments rest in a special bed decorated with charms, as the focus of visitors bringing good wishes and gifts.

After seven days, the critical post-natal period having passed, a new set of rituals takes place. The naming of the child (*tasmiya*) is a significant act, as the name implies both personal identity and protection as well as religious and familial belonging in a community.[16] The name is thought by many to have an impact on the character of the child and on its development. As indicated in the previously quoted *hadith*, names from legendary history (such as Aisha or Ali), names with positive significance (such as Noor [light] or Gül

[rose] in Turkish) or names from earlier generations of the family are not uncommon. The name-giving indicates inclusions, but not an initiation like the Christian baptism, according to the principle 'all humans are born Muslim'.

The ritual viewed foremost as a specifically Muslim birth ritual is the hair-cutting ceremony (*aqiqa*, meaning offering) – with or without an accompanying animal sacrifice. The head of the newborn baby is shaved as a sign of its being a humble servant of Allah, and the hair is collected. Ideally, the weight of the hair in silver is distributed to charity. In some wealthier Muslim communities, the hair-cutting ceremony is accompanied by the slaughter of an animal (often a sheep), as the offering (*aqiqa*) proper. The meat is afterwards partly consumed at a family feast as well as partly distributed to the poor. In areas where *mawlid* gatherings are customary, a reciter may be invited to the seventh-day celebrations to perform a recitation from Süleyman Çelebi's poem in praise of the birth of the prophet or other widely spread poems and songs on the same theme.

As previously mentioned, post-natal seclusion is not a widespread custom. Nevertheless, in some Muslim communities, the mother undergoes a purification ritual 40 days after the delivery whereafter she is reintegrated. The atmosphere is mostly joyous and includes festivities, since she, after her liminal period, returns not only to family life (and life goes back to its normal structures), but also to her full ritual obligations.

The age for boys' circumcision varies; in some environments, the operation is carried out on infants (as in the Jewish tradition), in others when the boy is old enough to recite from the Qur'an. Circumcision can even function as a coming-of-age ritual, which implies that the male, from now on, has the religious obligations of an adult. The custom is not mentioned in the Qur'an, and there have therefore been legal disputes as to whether it is to be regarded as mandatory. However, in local contexts, strong cultural norms surround the ritual and it is an occasion for family festivities. Arguments in favour of the custom call upon loyalty to tradition, or conceptions of purity.

Coming-of-age rituals

Islamic tradition in general has no stipulations for any coming-of-age rituals equivalent to Christian confirmation. In many contexts, however, an early agreement of marriage between families (if not always the wedding) serves a similar purpose. The step between childhood and married life can therefore sometimes be very short. There are few examples of formalized ceremonies, and most of them relate to local custom rather than being rituals claiming an Islamic background. In some cultures, the start of menstruation or other signs of physical maturity require a rite of passage to mark the shift to adult status. A number of African rituals of this kind, where Islamic links are more or less pronounced, have been documented.

Starting to wear the *hijab* as a sign of female modesty and obedience can, especially in urban environments and in the diaspora, constitute a less ceremonial but nevertheless ritualized way of indicating that the young woman from now on intends to fulfil her Muslim duties and behave in accordance with moral expectations. In some Muslim communities, a youngster takes an oath after puberty to thereafter take individual responsibility for following the demands of Islam. Young women usually do so somewhat earlier than young men, and the oath ceremony is followed by family celebrations.

Marriage and weddings are obviously important lifecycle rituals, but these are discussed in Chapter 4 in relation to sharia.

Death and funerals

Attendance at rituals related to death, such as funerals, is an obligatory collective duty (*fard kifaya*) according to sunna and sharia for men, but not for women. The rituals men are supposed to take part in are to a great extent public – they take place in the vicinity of a mosque and at the cemetery – whereas women's rituals are mostly performed in domestic spaces, where many of the responsibilities for the social interaction, such as visits to convey condolences during the period of grief are fulfilled. Dead women are usually not followed to the grave by other women.

Death (*mawt*) and the afterlife are frequent themes in the Qur'an. The focus is often on eschatological matters such as resurrection and Judgement Day, fate and measured time, repentance and forgiveness. One stanza of the third *sura* that is often referred to in popular pious literature and in sermons reads:

Every soul shall taste of death; you shall surely
be paid in full on the Day of Resurrection.
Whosoever is removed
from the Fire and admitted to Paradise,
shall win the triumph.
The present life is but the joy of delusion. (Qur'an 3:185)

The sequence of rituals that eventually leads to the interment can be
said to start with the activities around the dying individual to prepare
him or her for the judgement on the day of resurrection. The
customs vary, but certain features are common to many places in the
Muslim world.

Ideally, the face of a dying person should be turned on its right side
and face the Kaaba in order for the person to be prepared for
Judgement Day, and the *shahada* should be read into his/her ear. In
pious teaching, it is often stressed that the moment of death is the
transition from life on earth to eternity and is sometimes believed to
carry symbolic messages. Attention should therefore be paid to the
person's last words and, in some contexts, signs at the moment of
death such as sudden changes in the weather, cries from birds and
animals are interpreted, in most cases in relation to conceptions of fate
and the destiny of the dead or narratives about angels and demons
fighting over the soul.

Good manners in relation to the dying is intimately connected with
the honour of the house. Disrespectful behaviour brings shame on the
family. The extended family should be notified about the situation and
visitors will gather by the deathbed at home or at the hospital. They
should not only bid farewell and offer comfort to the dying but also
remind her/him to ask for forgiveness and Allah's blessing.

The strong cultural code not to leave the dying alone has received
more attention in an age of international migration, with family
members spread over long distances. There is a rich corpus of folk
narratives about angels and demons fighting over the soul that is about
to transit and the importance of supporting prayers and care. If
possible, when death approaches, *sura* 36, commonly referred to under
its Arabic heading Ya Sin (the two first letters in the text of the *sura*)
and known as 'the heart of the Qur'an' is recited. This sura, often read
integrated in rituals as a prayer, is to be recited to the dying by the
family members gathered around the deathbed.

The beginning of *sura* Ya Sin reads:

By the Wise Koran,
thou art truly among the Envoys
on the straight path;
the sending down of the All-mighty, the All-wise,
that thou mayest warn a people whose fathers were
never warned, so they are heedless.
The word has been realized against most of them,
yet they do not believe.

The text is not a prayer, but rather a lengthy summary of the core issues of Islamic belief, and the 83 stanzas of the *sura* are focused on the responsibilities every human has when contemplating the final judgement (36:2–7).

However, the normative views of death and dying in the canonical literature are very different from the conditions of death that often prevail at modern hospitals, morgues or funeral homes today. The conflict between what is considered proper according to tradition and according to life as it is lived today can be very painful from an individual point of view. In diaspora milieus as well as in Muslim majority urban settings, the professionalization and institutionalization of death and funerals are apparent, and new agents, who are neither domestic nor public, take over in novel spaces what used to be a very tactile last contact with a close relative.

Whatever variations there may be in Muslim funeral traditions in terms of belief and rituals, one shared feature is the absolute demand to complete the proceedings of the funeral and burial without delay (within 24 hours). This imperative is not always possible to obey in urban and transnational milieus. The norms and ideals for the funeral ceremony presupposes a tight local community with close communication and immediate access to spaces like a mosque and that the mourners lives relatively close by. Modern living conditions and migration have changed this. In principle, however, most Muslim funeral rituals follow the pattern outlined below.

The deceased (*janaza*) is placed on a stretcher covered by a clean cloth. The people around the body take the first steps in preparing the deceased person for the grave by closing the eyes and the mouth, turning the head to the right and directing the body towards Mecca as if in prayer. The announcement of the death of a community member is an important social task that increases the number of visitors to the house in grief. Traditions vary as to when condolences are paid and what formulas, symbols and customary behaviour are in use. In some places, the custom is that absolutely no such visits should take place until after the purification and interment.

Death in itself is indeed very physical, and the treatment of the body follows a strict pattern of decorum and purification. The washing of the corpse (*ghusl al-mayyit*) differs according to the sex of the deceased. Female bodies can only be washed by women, and men's by men. Three or four members of the immediate family perform this task, or paid corpse-washers with insights into the proper rituals. The location of the *ghusl* is an isolated room (it may well be in the home of the deceased) – it is secluded, but still at the social nexus of the funeral activities – and the private parts of the body (from the waist to the knees) should always remain covered during the purification ritual.

The washing of the corpse is regarded as the final major ablution (*ghusl*), preparing the dead for resurrection. It combines the tactile with the spiritual, the functional with the eschatological, and begins with a *basmala*, 'In the name of God, the Compassionate, the Merciful'. As indicated in the *hadith* literature, the body is always washed an odd number of times. The purification is to be started on the right side of the body, which must never be completely bare, but should remain partly covered. All impurities and excrements should be removed from the body. The use of camphor is therefore argued for, as it is regarded to be in accordance with halal rules, takes away the odour and is claimed to be hygienic. Scented water is used not only for its fragrance; the scent is also associated with prayers as both reach Allah in a pleasurable way.

The next step is the ritual shrouding (*takfin*). A male body should be swathed in five unsewn sheets of clean white shroud (*kafan*) to symbolize an easy resurrection. The first is to extend from the head to the waist; the second extends from the chest to the knee; the third is a seamless shirt, folded and cut open in the middle so that it can be passed over the head and cover the whole upper part of the body (back and front) down to the knees; the fourth should cover the whole body; and the fifth should also be swept over the whole body and tied at the head and under the feet. Two additional sheets for a woman include a head covering and a cloth covering the breasts. After the washing and shrouding, the deceased is considered ready to utter the same phrase as the believer on *hajj*, 'Here I am, Allah' (*talbiya*), on Judgement Day. The corpse should now be carried to the cemetery on a bier or in a wooden coffin as soon as possible. The coffin is usually covered in a green cloth during the procession and passers-by should stand still to pay their respects.

The funeral procession (from the mosque to the cemetery) plays an important part in *hadith* literature dealing with burials. According to the *hadiths*, is it obligatory for local men related to the dead to join a funeral procession and thereby show respect for a deceased member of their community. In most Muslim contexts, women do not participate in the public aspects of the funeral ceremony. It is a ritual in the local community when the family's respect for the dead is demonstrated.

The second public ritual in the sequence is the funeral prayer (*salat al-janaza*), which should take place as soon as possible after the shrouding. Not necessarily, but conventionally, it is performed at the local mosque immediately after the noon prayer (*zuhr*). Often, the prayer for the dead is held in the courtyard or an adjoining room of the mosque. Death and the dead have a certain contaminating quality that contradicts the ritual purity of the prayer room. The funeral prayer at the mosque is both a public ceremony and a private one for those in grief: on the one hand, all measures are taken to clean the body in every sense and prepare the deceased for eternity; on the other, a mosque is at all times regarded as an area ready to receive people who want to pray.

Except for pronouncing the *takbir* four times and the closing blessing on Muhammad (*taslim*), this prayer is a silent one and is made standing. Otherwise, the participants must observe the usual imperatives (accurate intention (*niyya*) and at least the minor ablution (*wudu*) required for prayer), and the ritual is led by an imam, who stands between the congregation and the coffin. In many places, women do not participate in this prayer, but if they do, they stand behind the men and children irrespective of whether the deceased is a man or a woman.

Women do not attend the final part of the funeral ceremony, the interment. The body is placed with the face turned towards the Kaaba, symbolically ready for the Day of Judgement. The burial ends with prayers at the grave. The body should be in contact with the earth and the shrouded body is therefore placed directly in the grave; if a coffin is used, a small hole is made in the bottom to ensure the connection. The seamless shroud and the body on the ground are symbols of an easy resurrection for the faithful. *Sura* 3:185, quoted above, which states that all souls shall taste death and will be rewarded or punished according to their deeds, is generally recited.

The cultural codes for emotional expressions at deaths and funerals vary by necessity, many post-burial ceremonies have little or no direct Islamic connection, this is, they are not prescribed in canonical literature or in didactic funeral manuals. Nevertheless, the participants recognize grieving ceremonies as proper Muslim behaviour as they are deeply embedded in local culture, although lamentations or wailing after a burial are condemned by more conservative Sunni Muslims. The period of grieving follows a certain rhythm. After seven and/or forty days, as well as after one year and sometimes on every anniversary of the death, commemoration ceremonies are performed. Prayers are said at home or in the local mosque, and a visit to grave is sometimes made.

Losing a spouse opens up the question of remarrying. A widow, like a divorced woman, has to respect the waiting time (*idda*).[17] The reasons given in local contexts are often dual: the widow has to fulfil her obligations to her deceased husband in terms of all the social activities surrounding a death, such as receiving visits and condolences, and it must be established whether she is pregnant or not (determining fatherhood).

The *hajj*

The pilgrimage to Mecca (*hajj*) is the fifth pillar of Islam, and it is formulated as a command in the Qur'an (2:196–197; 3:97; 5:95–97). Therefore, every adult Muslim of sound physical and mental health must go to Mecca and perform the stipulated rituals at least once in his/her lifetime. Even though the annual number of pilgrims is restricted, more than 2.5 million visit the holy sites in what today is Saudi Arabia during the pilgrimage month. Lack of economic means and illness are legitimate reasons for not going on the *hajj*, and to a majority of the Muslims of the world the *hajj* remains an unreachable dream. Only Muslims are allowed; non-Muslims are not even permitted to visit Mecca. Women can in principle not go on the *hajj* without accompanying men responsible for them, modern package travel puts the issue of custodians in another light and some groups of women go together. Travelling with relatives though remains the norm. The numbers of pilgrims have been steadily increasing since the 1970s, as globalization, modern transportation and package deals (specialized travel agents offer organized tours, complete with tickets and visas) have made the *hajj* more accessible. Those who have the means sometimes go more than once. There is a rich literature of manuals on preparation for the *hajj* and guidance to the sites, which contributes to the sense of unity in the encounter between Muslims from all over the world.

The pilgrimage is to be performed during the last month in the Muslim calendar, Dhu al-Hijja, in order to be recognized as a complete *hajj*. The pilgrimage period is therefore between the end of Ramadan and *Id al-Adha* (the Feast of Sacrifice). The sending-away and receiving-back of family members is also a major community event. A pilgrimage to Mecca at another time of the year is known as *umra*.

The Kingdom of Saudi Arabia is the current custodian of the holy places in Mecca and Medina, a position fought over throughout history. Since the 1960s, the *hajj* has been organized by the Organization of the Islamic Conference (OIC) and Muslim countries have certain quotas of pilgrims per year. All Muslims, of any faction, are in principle welcome, although conflicts occur, not least between Sunni and Shi'i Muslims. The sheer number of pilgrims demands large-scale logistics for hygiene to prevent the spread of epidemics, for safety to protect pilgrims from being trampled when vast crowds move during the rituals and to prevent fires in the enormous tented camps.

The movements and rituals follow a strict pattern. Like all *ibadat* activities, the *hajj* should start with the pronouncement of the proper intention (*niyya*) – and this in a state of ritual purity and an absolute requirement for pilgrimage and fast in order to make it valid. Men are required to wear a special white outfit (*ihram*) consisting of pieces of cloth draped around the body, which must be put on before entering Mecca, and women commonly wear a simple white outfit. During the *hajj*, no signs of wealth or status should be shown; shaving or cutting nails and hair during the *hajj* is not permitted. The garment can be put on at six stations (*miqat*) before entering Mecca. *Ihram* is also the term for the state of purity required before the visit to the holy places.

On the way to Mecca, the pilgrim should chant the prayer phrase 'Here I am, Allah, at your service, here I am' (*talbiya*, sometimes called *labbayka*, i.e. the first words of this prayer 'Here I am'). Before the eighth day of the month, the first circumambulation (*tawaf*) – seven times around the Kaaba – should be made, along with the run (about 400 metres, but it is hard to move fast among all the pilgrims in the heat) between the hills Safa and Marwa – also seven times – in remembrance of Hagar's desperate search for water for her son, Ismael. Today, the route is within the complex of the Grand Mosque in Mecca. The rituals connect the participants to a historical chain and the narratives that form the basis of the rituals. The Kaaba is referred to as 'the House of Allah' or simply 'the House'; the structure is supposed to have been built by Abraham and even to be the place where Adam worshipped. Abraham plays a substantial part in the narratives surrounding the *hajj*, which emphasize the genealogy of piety. The black stone on one of the doors is believed to have been there from the beginning and every pilgrim tries to touch it during the circumambulation. The Kaaba is the pre-Islamic cult site that Muhammad cleared of idols and through his example the standards for a proper *hajj* are set, as depicted in the *hadith* literature and in the *sira* narratives, especially the narratives of Muhammad's *hajj* in 632. The black cloth (*kiswa*) covering the Kaaba is decorated with Qur'anic verses embroidered in silk and gold weighing 450 kilogramme. The *kiswa* is renewed every year and pieces of the *kiswa* are cherished gifts to bring back home; these are purchased through donations to charities. The Kaaba and the Grand Mosque in Mecca are today linked in one enormous complex of buildings. Since the restoration and expansion in 1988, it can accommodate 1 million visitors.

On the eighth day of the month, when the visits and rituals at the holy sites start, another *tawaf* takes place and pilgrims leave for Mina and stay there overnight. The next day, pilgrims go to Mount Arafat, 'the Mountain of Mercy', and spend time in contemplation on the summit, where a sermon is given. This is considered by many to be the most significant moment of the *hajj*. On the tenth day, seven stones are thrown against three pillars in Mina, representing the stoning of Satan by Abraham when Satan tried to tempt him to disobedience. Thereafter a sheep or a goat is slaughtered. This is the day on which Id al-Adha is celebrated all over the Muslim world. Not everyone can afford to have an animal slaughtered, but it is possible to buy a share in a slaughter (*qurban*) and have the meat distributed to the poor. Nowadays, the meat is stored in enormous freezers and warehouses for effective and hygienic handling.

During the following days, the circumambulation is performed once again, as is the stoning of Satan, this time three stones against each of the three pillars. The *hajj* reaches its end as the pilgrims return to Mecca and blessed water from the *zamzam* well is drunk and collected in bottles and cans to be taken back home as precious gift or to be consumed when grace is said for a safe return. Most pilgrims take the opportunity to visit Muhammad's mosque and grave in Medina before leaving for a third *tawaf*.

Modern media and communications make it easier to follow the *hajj*, to take part at a distance through TV, film clips on the internet, Facebook or Twitter. Memorabilia brought back is not just for souvenirs, but is regarded as carrying blessings (*baraka*) that confirm a bond between giver and receiver.

Muslim festivals and celebrations

Muslim identity is not expressed only through daily pious practices – even if *salat* prayers are mandatory. The celebrations in the lunar calendar also play a major role in manifesting religious and social belonging to family and community.

Two of the Muslim festivals are of special importance as a time when families gather, if possible: Id al-Fitr, celebrated when the final fast of Ramadan is broken, and the commemorative Festival of Sacrifice, Id al-Adha, celebrated during the pilgrimage month by both pilgrims in Mecca and those at home. Both festivals connect to central narratives in the Islamic faith: the successful completion of the fast and Abraham's loyalty to Allah when commanded to sacrifice his son.

Rituals are inscribed in larger family celebrations such as lifecycle rituals, which mark the shifts in life that are important to most people: name giving, coming of age, marriage and death. Most of these rituals also have a profound local colour. The performance of a ritual connects a participant to a collective and its history as well as being a means to express personal religiosity. The piety practices discussed above follow the instructions in the canonical texts of Islam, but find many expressions depending on social and cultural context.

Celebrating the birth (*mawlid*) of the prophet is part of the yearly calendar of events, but the prayers and song traditions connected with this festival are also used for the commemoration of deceased family members and saints or to mark special events in the family or community (such as homecoming from *hajj* and young people leaving home for education or military service). Even if contested, as accretions, by some conservatives, to participants the *mawlid* is a confirmation of closeness to Muhammad and to the local community. These gatherings mostly take place in premises other than a mosque and are an indication of the general importance of private spaces as sites for Muslim religious practice.

The *hajj* is an obligation that not all Muslims can fulfil, but some of its rituals are mirrored in the celebration of Id al-Adha. Today, events at Mecca are followed daily on television and via other media throughout the pilgrimage period. Still, sending away and receiving back pilgrims are important events, as is the circulation of *hajj* gifts by the returners.

Most local performances of a festival or ritual balance what is prescribed by local convention with more general religious norms; ritual leaders interact with the participants and connect to current circumstances (in themes for prayers and sermons, as well as in the length and emphasis of the rituals). Many theological debates over the centuries have rarely affected broader groups until the moment the way a festival or ritual is perfomed becomes a marker of identity and belonging in a conflict of sorts. But those who deem some ritual practices to be un-Islamic because of their local flavour have caused both social distress and emotional discontent.

Further reading

Bowen, Donna Lee and Evelyn A. Early (eds), *Everyday Life in the Muslim Middle East*, 2nd edn (Bloomington, IN: Indiana University Press, 2002).
Buitelaar, Marjo, *Fasting and Feasting in Morocco: Women's Participation in Ramadan* (Oxford: Berg, 1993).
Grunebaum, Gustave, *Muhammadan Festivals* (New York: Henry Schuman, 1951).
Hawting, Gerald (ed.), *The Development of Islamic Ritual* (The Formation of the Classical Islamic World) (Aldershot: Ashgate, 2006).

Hillenbrand, Robert, *Islamic Architechture: Form, Function and Meaning* (Edinburgh: Edinburgh University Press, 1994).

Özdemir, Adil and Kenneth Frank, *Visible Islam in Modern Turkey* (Basingstoke: Palgrave Macmillan, 2000).

Porter, Venetia and Saif Liana (eds), *The Hajj: Collected Essays* (London: The British Museum, 2014).

Schielke, Samuli, *The Perils of Joy: Contesting Mulid Festivals in Contemporary Egypt* (Syracuse, NY: Syracuse University Press, 2012).

Chapter VI

Between Canonical Obligations and Devotional Practices: Everyday Religiosity

This chapter is divided into two sections based on a distinction between the prescribed canonical prayers and the wide range of emotive forms of prayer that are popular all over the Muslim world. Such a distinction could, of course, be disputed, as, to many Muslims, the five daily *salat* prayers definitively have the character of a possibility to express personal piety. The regular prayers constitute a distinct rhythm for individuals and communities, and the framework of the daily prayers also allows space for personal prayers and contemplation. But while the latter are optional (depending on local tradition, personal choice and inclination), the *salat* prayers are mandatory and non-negotiable.

There are also ritual activities that fall between the two categories. Qur'an recitation, for example, is a vital element in both these domains of piety, as well as playing an important role at domestic prayer gatherings and in individual expressions of faith. The way in which ritual activities are embedded in daily life indicates how difficult it is to separate religious and social activities. The intensified readings from the Qur'an during Ramadan form the basis of major ritual gatherings in many mosques, which include prayers of a sometimes intense character. These are also occasions when women frequent the local mosques to a greater extent than usual. Both the stipulated categories relate to rituals of a collective character, although most of the prayer schemes can be performed in solitude.

The Friday midday sermon, with its accompanying elements of prayer and recitation, which used to be a strictly communal gathering, can now be listened to on CD, watched on TV or accessed via the internet. This developing media situation points at two important aspects of contemporary religiosity in general, not only in Islam. First, religion is increasingly performed individually and on the basis of personal preference and living conditions, and is less dependent on the local community and on specific times for rituals – as people lead professional lives that cannot always match the old community rhythm. Second, due to the rapid development of virtual modes of expression, religious performance is less dependent on traditional spaces; alternatives are available that are independent of time and place.

The last of the pillars (*arkan*) of Islam are all of a ritual kind. The *salat* prayers, by tradition placed second after the monotheistic capstone, serve as a daily reminder of the fundamental concepts of Islam. These are public ritual practices, with an obvious social impact that indicate and confirm identity, which could be of religious, ethnic or cultural character depending on the context. Collective rituals always have disciplining elements, as they regulate community life. The Islamic reform movements that have sprung up in various directions since the late eighteenth century have had a tendency to emphasize collective prayer, the daily *salat* prayers and the Friday sermon as the authentic nexus of Islamic rituals, whereas other forms of collective prayer are disapproved of, if not condemned. The public performance of Islam has traditionally been a strictly male affair, although the alternative spaces women have had access to throughout history are now generating more interest. Recent developments, however, indicate that women are to an increasing extent also part of public ritual life. They are taking up leading positions – not necessarily as imams but in functions with the same influence.

To many Muslims, the more emotionally oriented performances, in private or public, constitute the very nexus of the religion, and in many ways the veneration of saints, 'friends of Allah' (sing. *wali*, pl. *awliya*; *dust* in Persian and *dost* in Turkish) and other holy persons can be put in contrast to the canonical rituals of the mosque, especially in terms of authority, leadership and the strictly kept ritual format. Pious narratives tell of the saints' ability to guide, heal and warn. Even after their death, they serve as mediators, as they are thought to be able to bring the visitors' prayers forward to Allah. Hence the accusations of polytheism (*shirk*). These devotional practices indicate personal commitment, not that they have to be less collective from a performance perspective. They are individual, have a more emotional character and are more varied in forms of expression than the obligatory prayers; they are not canonical and therefore also a target of orthodox criticism. The performance of these rituals is closely related to social consistency, rather than to the organization of a local mosque, and they often bestow a sense of cohesion beyond the given networks. Furthermore, many of the devotional rituals are connected with Sufi traditions; these will be dealt with in the second part of this chapter.

General discussions about religion and the public sphere are closely linked to issues of understanding modernization and secularization. Even if many devotional practices have a long history in local environments, they must by no means be understood as pre-modern, as they have always changed over time and adapted to new conditions. Neither is the following an attempt to emphasize any dichotomy between the obligatory and the supplementary in Muslim piety. Nevertheless, in the early normative literature there is an emphasis on individual conduct in public domains as a mode of confirming religious belonging.

Housing in Muslim cultures has been organized in a number of ways and the distinction between private and public has always been complicated. A separation between the sexes has guided how social and religious life is organized. The women's quarters (*harim* – from *haram*, forbidden or restricted to visitors, or *purdah* in Urdu) have traditionally been separated from areas where guests are received and which constitute a contact zone with outside space.

In some rooms, the direction of Mecca may be indicated by a framed picture of the Kaaba or a *hajj* souvenir. The presence of prayer rugs is used to indicate ritual spaces, while other objects like rosaries, copies of the Qur'an or calligraphy are used to establish the necessary symbolic boundaries. Even if several individuals pray (gender separated) in the same private room, these are regarded as individual prayers and are not collectively conducted by a prayer leader.

Traditionally, meetings in mosques outside prayer times and local pilgrimages, such as visiting shrines (sing. *ziyara*, pl. *ziyarat*; the term can refer to both the ritual and the site for the pilgrimage), have been platforms for women taking up ritual responsibilities. Modern life and women's greater participation in the labour market have changed the patterns of women's prayer meetings. Strictly domestic premises are to a great extent replaced by semi-public or public spaces.

From early times, Muslim doctrine and practice have emphasized the public aspects of religious life. This visibility, where ritual performance confirms affiliation and commitment, still marks Islam as a distinct path to follow. The witnessing of faith (*shahada*) is a public declaration; the obligation (for men) to attend the communal Friday prayer and the descriptions of the ideal society in the Qur'an and the *hadiths* deal to a great extent with the ideal public conduct of Muslim individuals and collectives.

Islamic theology makes a distinction between the ritual categories of *ibadat* and *muamalat*. The *ibadat* are conventionally defined as the absolute (religious) duties in relation to God. They are sometimes referred to as canonical, hereby emphasizing the strong support they have in Islamic legal texts in contrast to local piety practices. Usually, the following obligations and their accompanying rituals are regarded as *ibadat* and it is not uncommon to see the term translated simply as 'worship': ritual purity (*tahara*), the five daily *salat* prayers, the funeral obligations, alms (*zakat*), fasting (*siyam*) and pilgrimage to Mecca once at least in a lifetime (*hajj*). Muamalat (sing. *muamala*), on the other hand, imply social obligations in relation to other humans, especially family, of a legal, moral and economic character – in practice often connected with ritual activities. What are conventionally defined as *muamalat* include naming ceremonies, marriage and divorce. The rituals described in this chapter fall into both categories, and the distinction between them might appear obsolete from a local perspective. However, throughout history, as well as in contemporary times, this distinction has been at the centre of many theological debates on correct ritual performance and on gendered issues that determine the definitions of authority, possible agency and spaces of prayer activities.

Daily canonical prayers

The five daily *salat* prayers sometimes transliterated *salah; namaz* in Persian, Turkish and Urdu) constitute the rhythm of Muslim ritual life. Daily prayers at specified times go back to the Jewish and Christian traditions, where such communal gatherings constituted the backbone of public religious performance. Jewish tradition calls for three prayers a day and the Christian tradition five. Islamic practice took form in relation to these practices and indicates both a direct continuation and a distinction in form. The direction of prayer towards Mecca was perhaps the most manifest indication of the attempts in early Islam to establish an Arabic focal point rather than the initial one, towards Jerusalem.

The technical performance of the five daily *salat* prayers is comparatively uniform among the Muslims of the world, whereas the social organization around worship (community life) and the architectonical constructions for worship (the mosque) display a rich variety. Muslim tradition emphasizes the prayers as such and the purification rituals that precede them as linked to the origin of Islam. The hagiographical story in the text box below indicates Muhammad's pious wife Aisha as the source for the chain going back to Muhammad being instructed to pray by the angel Jibril himself and passing on the tradition to his first wife Khadija. It should be noted that according to this normative text the ablution and the prayer play an equal part of the ritual as a whole.

> **The beginning of the revelations when Muhammad is approached by the angel Jibril, as described in Ibn Ishaq's biography (sira) of Muhammad**
>
> A learned person told me [Aisha] that when prayer was laid on the apostle [the prophet] Gabriel came to him while he was on the heights of Mecca and dug a hole for him with his heel in the side of the valley from which a fountain gushed forth, and Gabriel performed the ritual ablution as the apostle watched him. This was in order to show him how to purify himself before prayer. Then the apostle performed the ritual ablution as he had seen Gabriel do it. Then Gabriel said a prayer with him while the apostle prayed his prayer. Then Gabriel left him. The apostle came to Khadija and performed the ritual for her as Gabriel had done for him, and she copied him. Then he prayed with her as Gabriel had prayed with him, and she prayed his prayer. (Ibn Ishaq 158, trans. Guillaume, 1955: 112)

The canonical prayers are ascribed in the normative literature at several places and the *hadiths* instruct in detail. The Qur'an states: 'Thou seest them [the believers] bowing, prostrating, seeking bounty from God and good pleasure. Their mark is on their faces, the trace of prostration' (48:29) and the *hadith* literature, with its longer narrations, depicts the following scene:

Narrated Abu Huraira:
Allah's Apostle entered the mosque and a person followed him.
The man prayed and went to the Prophet and greeted him. The
Prophet returned the greeting and said to him, 'Go back and
pray, for you have not prayed.' The man went back prayed in the
same way as before, returned and greeted the Prophet who said,
'Go back and pray, for you have not prayed.' This happened
thrice. The man said, 'By Him Who sent you with the Truth, I
cannot offer the prayer in a better way than this. Please, teach me
how to pray.' The Prophet said, 'When you stand for Prayer say
Takbir and then recite from the Holy Qur'an (of what you know
by heart) and then bow till you feel at ease. Then raise your head
and stand up straight, then prostrate till you feel at ease during
your prostration, then sit with calmness till you feel at ease (do
not hurry) and do the same in all your prayers.' (Sahih Bukhari
1:12:724)

Both the Qur'an and the *hadith* literature stipulate regular prayers,
although the detailed rules are formulated in the former. The Qur'an
states: 'perform the prayer at the two ends of the day and nigh of the
night [in the hours of the night]; surely the good deeds will drive away
the evil deeds. That is a remembrance unto the mindful' (11:116f.).

The custom of five daily prayers is connected with the narratives of
Muhammad's Night Journey, when the encounter with Moses and
Jesus established the genealogy between the religions as well as
showing the particularities that define Islam as the final revelation.

The names of the five daily *salat* prayers are:

- Salat al-Subh or Salar al-Fajr (morning prayer) – to be performed
  just before dawn;
- Salat al-Zuhr (midday prayer) – to be performed at midday;
- Salat al-Asr (afternoon prayer) – to be performed before the sun
  sets;
- Salat al-Maghrib (sunset prayer) – to be performed just after dusk;
- Salat al-Isha (night prayer) – to be performed at the beginning of
  the night, when it is completely dark.

In Muslim communities a call from the mosque's minaret alerts
believers that it is time to pray. Urbanization and professional life,
migration and frequent travel require other tools: handy calendars and

tables nowadays give the correct time for prayers at a particular place as well as mobile phones programmed to keep track of the correct time and may also come with a compass indicating the direction towards Mecca.

Instructions on how to perform *salat* can be found in booklets and brochures all over the world. They often include additional prayers and give simplified transliterations into the local alphabet of the most frequently read *suras* of the Qur'an in order to help the congregation follow the recitation. Basically, the requirement to perform *salat* is thought of as an issue between the individual and Allah. By tradition, however, collective performance is regarded as commendable. This brings a gender aspect to the topic, as women to a much lesser extent perform *salat* prayers, either collectively or in public spaces.

In principle, any male Muslim may take up the role of leader of collective prayers, that is, act as imam (although in practice the role associated is with authority). The concept imam should therefore not be translated as 'clergy' or 'priest', as it is not an ordained position. The term is often literally translated as 'model' or as 'the one who takes the lead [in front of the rows of praying individuals]'. The prayer leader was traditionally connected to the mosque as a particular ritual place and, of course, this respected person has always had authority related to learning and competence, even though serving as an imam is not necessarily the same as holding a formal office. Today, however, an imam to a great extent also serves as a community leader and the title implies the role of a representative as well as a position in an organized hierarchy. It must be underlined that in Shi'i Islam the concept imam has quite another meaning (see Chapter 7).

Muslim tradition prescribes certain unconditional requirements for the correct performance of the *salat* prayers. The Qur'an states: 'We will surely turn thee to a direction that shall satisfy thee. Turn towards the Holy Mosque [Mecca]; and wherever you are, turn your faces towards it' (2:144). The following have always been common features of proper *salat* conduct:

1. Every daily prayer requires the cleansing of any impurity on the body in order to achieve the stipulated state of symbolic, mental and physical purity before starting the *salat*. Ritual purity (*tahara*) is attained by the the lesser cleansing (*wudu*) before prayer.

2. Correct covering of the body at prayer time is stipulated.
    Men should cover their bodies between the navel and the
    knees and women are obliged to cover the whole body
    (except hands, feet and face). Spatial separation between the
    sexes is taken for granted.
3. A praying individual should face Mecca (*qibla*).
4. Worshippers should respect the regulated time for each *salat*
    even if not praying at a mosque.
5. The *salat* must be performed with the accurate intention
    (*niyya*). This concept is an indication that rituals are a
    question not only of external conduct, but also of the
    thoughts that determine bodily movements.

The rules of purity vary according to the acts the praying person has carried out prior to prayer.

Minor ablution (*wudu*; Pers. and Turk. *abdest*) is always required before *salat*:

> It starts 'In the name of Allah, the Compassionate, the
> Merciful' the *basmala* formula and is followed by the
> witnessing of faith (*shahada*) before the washing of the
> face, the arms and elbows begins. Parts of the head should
> be rubbed with wet hands as also hands and feet including
> ankles.' Sahih Bukhari 1:4:193

The classical mosque compound has a fountain for ritual ablution in the courtyard, while modern mosque premises may offer a washroom instead. Major ablution (*ghusl*), including regulated cleansing of the whole body, is required in order to transform a ritually impure (*najis*) state into a pure (*tahir*) one. One *hadith* tells:

> Narrated Muhammad Ibn Ziyad
> I heard Abu Huraira saying as he passed by us while the
> people were performing ablution from a utensil containing
> water, 'Perform ablution perfectly and thoroughly for
> Abul-Qasim (the Prophet) said, "Save your heels from the
> Hell-fire."' (Sahih Bukhari 1:4:166)

Women are required to perform major ablution after menstruation and childbirth.

The formula 'Allahu Akbar' is to be recited silently before every ritual act, without which it is not valid.

Each *salat* prayer must meet the following six criteria:

1. It must be pronounced in a standing position (*qiyam*);
2. It must open with praise for Allah (*takbir*): '*Allahu akbar*' – God is greater;
3. This must be followed by a recitation (*qiraa*) from the Qur'an;
4. The prayer must proceed with the act of deep bowing of the upper part of the body and the placing of the palms of the hands on the knees (*raka*); taking this position is combined with the recitation of the first *sura* of the Qur'an, al-Fatiha.
5. This is to be followed by prostration (*sujud*);

The *taslim* salutation, 'Blessings be upon Muhammad', is the concluding part of the *salat*.

6. The final sitting during the *salat* involves the pronouncing of the testimony of faith (*shahada*).

A *raka* (pl. *rakat*) forms one unit in the five *salat* prayers over the day, and the number of *rakat* differs between the five *salat* prayers, some being mandatory while others are optional for spiritual training or as a part of the celebration of festivals. '*Allahu akbar!*' (*takbir*) and the first *sura* of the Qur'an, al-Fatiha, commences each *raka* and is followed by a bow and two prostrations (face touching the floor) and the utterance of *shahada* sitting on the knees. The sequence is closed with *takbir* and al-Fatiha once more.

Additional (nocturnal) prayers of 20 or more *rakat* during Ramadan (*tarawih*) is a very popular practice and can generate large crowds in mosques for events that may also include more explicitly emotive prayers. During the rest of the year, other supplementary prayers (*nawafil*) can be performed after one of the *salat* prayers, usually after the night prayer. The motivation is often a special cause or wish and the prayer resembles votive prayers in general. One *hadith* states: 'Narrated Ibn 'Umar: The Prophet had said, "Offer some of your prayers (*nawafil*) at home, and do not take your houses as graves"' (Sahih Bukhari 1:8:424). The *suras* most frequently recited during *salat* include al-Fatiha and the Throne Verse (Ayat al-Kursi 2:255), both quoted in Chapter 1.

Muslim tradition does not specify a day of the week as particularly holy or as a day of rest, but Friday has always played the same role in communal religious activities and social family traditions as Saturday and Sunday do in Judaism and Christianity.

Friday midday prayer

Friday midday prayer (*juma*), with its preceding sermon (*khutba*), differs from the midday prayer on other days. The basic meaning of community (*umma*) is 'those who gather to pray together on Fridays', which throughout history has included the Muslim community worldwide. Traditional jurisprudence stipulates *juma* as an obligatory congregational prayer for men, to be performed in the mosque. Usually, *juma* is led by the local imam, who is sometimes given the honorary title *khatib* (official preacher). This may also indicate a special appointment to larger mosques with the assignment to deliver a public *khutba* and further that the preacher holds a diploma from an Islamic college (*madrasa*). The *juma* prayer follows a subsequent pattern and the delivery of the *khutba* most often ends with the *takbir* phrase '*Allahu akbar*', followed by two *raka*s and the greeting wishing for blessings on Muhammad (*taslim*).

There are a number of titles connoting preachers, instructors, guides and teachers: a preacher (*waiz*) or a popular preacher (*qass*) does not give the formal *khutba*, but offers sermons or lessons (sing. *dars*) in a more broad sense. In this connection, the educational duties of Sufi masters should be mentioned as an example of there being other spaces than the mosque for transmitting religious instruction. Women are also trained in local religious schools and may preach to other women and children and domestic milieus should not be underestimated as spaces for the transmission of both Islamic knowledge, in terms of scriptural traditions and norms, and familiarity with performative and ritual practices.

The contemporary role of the imam may include a variety of duties in relation to the congregation as a formal organization and in relation to administrative authorities and, in the diaspora, also to Muslim or other congregations. The title can denote the imam as the leader of public rituals or be a term for the respected function to lead communal prayer (especially the Friday midday prayer). As the leading person of a community, his opinions on moral and legal matters, and his guidance, often goes far beyond the religious; this is also the case in rural environments with less-educated imams as well in urban congregations facing the need for advice on how to deal with the challenges of modern life.

The educational qualifications of an imam differ. Today, imams have often graduated from a *madrasa* or a theological faculty for Islamic studies. The position of imam can be a formal appointment, but imams are not ordained like Christian clergy; nor do they take vows. There is no tradition of celibacy for imams, or at all in Islam, but traditionally it is not unusual that within families with Islamic educational traditions that several males serve as imams and teachers. Within the structure of the modern nation state there are various examples of administrative bodies that accredit and appoint Islamic officials. The Turkish administrative body Diyanet (see text box below) is an example of how modernization processes in many cases have increased state control over the organization of Islamic practice, and not always recognized regional Muslim minorities.

Diyanet: the Turkish Directorate of Religious Affairs

The directorate was established in 1924 as a means of organizing the public performance of Islam. Hence, all Turkish imams are state employees and their education is organized under the auspices of the state. The role of the modern state has had a regulating impact on the recognition of Muslim groups under the umbrella 'Turkish Islam', which gives the administration a political role.

Diyanet distributes a weekly sermon to Turkish domestic preachers and to those abroad. It is posted on the administration's website and at some Turkish embassies' sites. This is an example of the state not only striving towards homogenization but also providing individual access to theological sources. For the last couple of years, the directorate has been sending out female preachers and teachers to homeland congregations and in the diaspora.

Traditionally, the local Muslim community has been a congregation of believers rather than a formal organization. Islam knows no equivalent of the diocese and it is either established around local authority patterns or ruler/state structures that have given local imams a great deal of power. State regulation of the education of imams in combination with new bases of authority have challenged the role of the imam today, while it has to some extent been strengthened in the diaspora, where formal organizations are needed to interact with the authorities.

The mosque

The mosque has by tradition been an important place for the execution of local religious authority; and it has long served as a meeting place and constituted a nexus for local (mostly male) networks. The question is, whether the mosque and its premises will remain the most important place for Muslim communities and, if so, on what conditions.

The mosque is a highly mono-gendered space (either used by men exclusively or visited by women only in between the canonical prayers). Over the last 20 years, however, women have been conquering more space in mosques for worship and teaching. The mosque is a prime location for Islamic teaching as it is the site for the canonical worship and the issue over who has the right to lead the prayers, deliver sermons and teach the local congregation is here to stay. The leading of the Friday prayers has become a controversial issue today, but that controversy should not conceal the identification of other spaces for women teachers, traditionally and in modern times.

The contemporary mosque faces many other challenges. Other places are now competing with it as the location for devotion, transmission of knowledge and guidance. There are new meeting grounds for new generations (for example, at educational institutions or in leisure areas, which are often mixed-gender spaces, with or without regulation), which can serve as environments for religious instruction, for the mobilization of groups of varying inclinations and for the establishment of civil society groups that run parallel with the established religious institutions. There is also the internet with its innumerable virtual meeting places, where the most unexpected encounters can occur.

The mosque is still an important site for Muslim authority – for mobilization, education, politics and social networking as well as religious performance. However, the construction of new, alternative spaces has caused the mosque to lose some of its traditionally very strong local dominance in many Muslim contexts, especially in the diaspora.

Fig. 7   A prayer rug (*sajjada*). A prayer rug defines ritual space and indicates *qibla*. It is considered improper to walk in front of a person praying on a mat in a mosque or domestic ritual space; some interpreters even say it makes the *salat* invalid, as the line to Mecca is broken. *(Source: Walters Art Museum [public domain], via Wikimedia Commons)*

The mosque as a structure is not mandatory for valid prayer. Beside domestic spaces are 'open-air' spaces (*musalla*) for congregational prayer, an alternative paradigm for how to construct other ritual spaces accepted in compliance with sharia law. The important thing is not the building as such, but the construction of a space that is ritually pure, distinct from ordinary activities and visibly marked as a restricted area.

The call to prayer (*adhan; ezan* in Turkish and Persian) is made by the *muadhdhin* (frequently used in its anglicized form *muezzin*) from the minaret of a mosque for every *salat*. This is a specific task within the community, performed by a special *muadhdhin*, the local imam or *hafiz* or given as an honorary duty at a specific occasion. To master the *adhan* is complex. The wording of the call consists of seven main parts and has the character of a creed, repeating the essentials of the faith five times a day to the believers. *Adhan* is therefore in many Muslim societies whispered in the ear of a newborn to be the first words heard.

Pious exegesis emphasizes the call as being without musical qualities, and the *adhan* is never referred to as being sung, in order for it not to be confused with art or entertainment.

The daily call to prayer (adhan)

> Allah is greater, Allah is greater,
> Allah is greater, Allah is greater.
> I bear witness, there is no god but Allah,
> I bear witness, there is no god but Allah.
> I bear witness, Muhammad is His messenger,
> I bear witness, Muhammad is His messenger.
> Come to prayer, come to prayer.
> Come to salvation, come to salvation.
> *[for the dawn prayer the following lines are added here:*
> Prayer is better than sleep,
> prayer is better than sleep.]
> Allah is greater, Allah is greater.
> There is no god but Allah.

Not only do the words of the *adhan* summarize the central concepts of Islam (monotheism, the role of Muhammad, salvation through prostration in prayer), but the very act of calling it out is a mark of collective identity for a neighbourhood or a village, like Christian church bells. It also marks time and the structure of the day.

The minaret (from the Turkish form of the Arabic word *manara* meaning 'site of light', indicating that minarets were originally lit towers showing travellers the way to shelter) functions in conventional imagery as a symbol for the mosque, though far from all mosques have minarets and far from all mosques are mono-functional buildings; the mosque can be a part of larger premises. A mosque can in principle be any room where Muslims regularly meet for prayer. It can be a room in a basement or a multi-purpose part of the premises of an association that is kept ready to be used for rituals.

A mosque (*masjid*, literally 'place of prostration') constitutes a location for collective prayer, and can be very limited in size, while a *jami* is a mosque, which offers Friday sermons has a pulpit (*minbar*) for the preacher and is, most often, a purpose-built building. Despite considerable architectural variety, there are further features that appear in most mosques. A niche (*mihrab*) in the mosque wall marks the

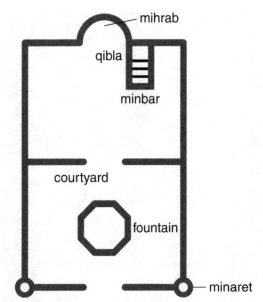

Fig. 8   The basic spatial structure of a mosque. *(Author)*

direction of the prayer towards Mecca (*qibla*). The enclosed area around the *mihrab* and the *minbar* is the space from which the communal prayer is led by the imam and sermons and teaching are delivered. Facilities for ablution are always at hand, as is a more or less visible gender division of the mosque space.

Most mosques are decorated according to local convention, despite the widespread belief that there is a complete prohibition of pictures in Islam. The ban on depicting humans, and in many environments also animals, has been not only an obstacle to artistic creativity but also a source of inspiration. The arabesque pattern is constructed by repeated elaborate ornaments in geometric forms (lines, curves or vegetal branches), which sometimes constitute a figure (a flower or an animal) in their own right. The arabesque is an example of how artistic creativity can blossom within strict limitations on expression.

The mosque is not only a ritual space; it also serves as a social meeting ground outside prayer hours. Spatial separation between men and women is mandatory in the Muslim tradition and the women's part of a mosque has often been in a (semi-)walled area close to the entrance or some kind of balcony construction overlooking the major prayer hall, but protected from unwanted gazes. Women, when

Fig. 9   A sixteenth-century ceramic tile from Iznik indicating the direction of prayer.
(Courtesy of the David Collection, Copenhagen; photo: Pernille Klemp)

serving as ritual leaders, have often chosen spaces other than the
mosque, such as private homes or semi-public spaces, but sometimes
use the local mosque in between prayer times.

Other forms of Muslim prayer and piety practices

In Islam, as in all religions, there is a variety of modes of prayer that
play an important role in the life of individuals. The Qur'an itself
formulates several prayers, and not only the obvious *sura* 1, al-Fatiha.
Four of the final short *suras* (109, 112, 113 and 114) are formulated as
prayers directed to Allah, all of them beginning with the imperative
'Say!' The heavenly voice of the Qur'an hereby instructs humankind
in what mode to approach Allah. These Qur'anic formulations are
often integrated in larger prayer schemes with variations to be chosen
in relation to attitude, type of problem, phase in life, etc. A common
denominator is a personal approach, often embedded in a locally
defined ritual practice. The rituals connected with Sufism are dealt
with in the latter part of this chapter, although when it comes to

gatherings of a general devotional character they are hard to distinguish from Sufi rituals.

The issue of what may be regarded as controversial rituals is strongly connected to modern Islamic reform movements of both radical and liberal inclinations. The radicals deem them as additional to the original religion and the liberals as remains of folklore of the uneducated. None of these theological currents see any value in these often more emotionally oriented practices. Personal communication with Allah is very much emphasized in Sufi traditions. These more emotive rituals are, however, not necessarily an evident part of Sufi theology but are often embedded in the veneration practices of local saints. Pilgrim routes constitute essential parts of healing rituals connected with tombs and shrines, vows and seeking protection from evil spirits or knowing the future by means of various divination rituals. The production and distribution of amulets also belong to this area of contested practices. The conceptual basis for these ceremonies is the blessing or spiritual power (*baraka*) that emanates from living persons and the tombs of saints. The transmission of *baraka* through the touching of the coffin of the venerated, drinking of the water from a nearby fountain, eating of sweets and the distribution of artefacts far beyond the pilgrim site by visitors, who thus bring the blessing back home as a gift and a memory, is an equally important part of the concept *baraka* and its instrumentalization.

Blessing (baraka) – to receive and to transmit

Closely connected to the ritual web of devotional prayers is the central concept of blessing (*baraka*) and the means to transfer it. It is regarded as a gift from Allah received through holy people, places or objects. *Baraka* is supposed to have a healing capacity as well as protective power.

Sharing and distributing blessing received is a major part of pilgrimages, long and short.

There are several genres of spiritual communication to be mentioned and many (local) names of prayers. Many of these prayers are closely linked to the recitation of the Qur'an. *Dua* is a prayer of appeal (supplication or invocation) to Allah expressed in personal formulations, with or without general or traditional phrases or passages from the Qur'an. It can take the form of an established formula or an individual petition for support, and it is not always easy to distinguish from extra (*nawafil*) non-mandatory *salat* prayers. A string of prayer beads (*subha* or *tasbih*; Turkish *tesbih*), most often 33 or 99, can be used as a tool for prayer discipline. Each bead represents a combination of one or several prayers: for example, 33 *Allahu akbar*, 33 *al-hamdu-li-llah* and 33 *subhan Allah*. When repeating the prayers, the number 99 (or three times 33) is associated with contemplative Sufi prayers, but also used as a means for framing the concentration during longer prayers outside the Sufi orders.

A particular point of controversy in veneration is the status of Muhammad and that of the saints venerated at Sufi shrines. Veneration of Muhammad or the saints, whether in commemoration of them or as people worthy of imitation, does not necessarily mean supplication or assuming that they act as a mediator between Allah and humans. It can simply be a question of intercession. The criticism of such practices is formulated with the same arguments as when *mawlid* is rejected by conservative theologians. An example of popular devotion can be taken from the numerous songs that praise Muhammad with roots in the Persian- and Turkish-speaking world. *Naat, qasida, ghazals* and other poetic genres have a long history are cherished in large parts of the Muslim world. *Naat* is a poem of praise in honour of Muhammad popular in South Asia and performed in the mosque at the end of the Friday prayer, and combines recitation and prayer sometimes accompanied by a hand-drum. Jami (d. 1492), a Persian poet whose *naat* poetry is still very much appreciated in Pakistan today, wrote:

> The limits of his praise – who knows them except God?
> Who am I, that I should dare to extol Muhammad?

And the repeated verse says over and over again:

> My speech cannot seek to attain the laudatory description of his perfection –
> Oh my God, bless the Prophet and his family! (trans. in Schimmel 1985:206)

The act of seeking forgiveness (*istighfar*) can be an emotive method of coming closer to Allah (*tawassul*) guided by Muhammad's moral standards and his light. It is a kind of intercession, although many

Muslims find this expression a violation of the concept of *tawhid*. The redemption 'I seek forgiveness in Allah' (*astaghfirullah*) is often repeated as part of *dua* and *dhikr*. Calling down Allah's blessings upon Muhammad (*taslim*) is part of the *salat* prayers, but it is also frequently used in other collective and individual prayers.

Sufism, Sufi orders, fellowship and veneration

Sufism, not uncommonly given a vague definition such as 'the mystical traditions of Islam', is not a faction like Sunni or Shi'i Islam; it is rather an umbrella term that covers a variety of theological and ritual traditions. Neither is Sufism limited to specific social strata or geographical regions. This wide concept covers the ideal of an individual lifelong spiritual quest for the refinement of the soul under the guidance of a master (with or without charisma) by means of intense repetitive prayers performed within a community whose ritual and moral conduct is regulated by the instructions of a living *shaykh* and his deceased predecessors. Although it is true that Sufism has an exclusive (and sometimes even esoteric) side, the social importance of the Sufi orders (sing. Arabic *tariqa*, pl. *turuq*; Persian *tariqat*; Turkish *tarikat*) must also be underlined. The orders constitute the basic ritual and social organization for more formalized Sufi activities under the leadership of a *shaykh* who us understood to continue the teachings of the historic founder of his particular order. The formation of the orders as structures representing various theological and ritual traditions developed in the tenth century. Throughout history, they have constituted important local and trans-regional networks for religious ideas, trade and social change. Sufi-inspired doctrine has always been rooted in popular piety and in large parts of the Muslim world Sufism is a vital part of the texture of everyday Islam as well as in sophisticated philosophy and theology. The organization of Sufi practice and its hierarchical leadership is always embedded in local power structures.

Opposition to what is deemed folk religion has grown since the late nineteenth century and is articulated from conservative Islamic positions as well as by secular modernists. The wide range of rituals and practices connected with Sufism and the Sufi orders has also been targeted by this dual rejection of what is considered uninformed and local, and thus not in tune with 'authentic' and 'grand' tradition. The growing number of revivalist reform movements in search of original (more or less purist) Islam have cracked down on devotional practices in their ambition to rid the contemporary expression of Islam of what they regard as un-Islamic elements and ignorant corruption (see also Chapter 9). This purist endeavour is, however, not a new or specifically modern line of thought in Islamic theology. One medieval thinker stands out as a particular source of inspiration for several attempts at providing an Islamic answer to the demands of modernity: Ibn Taymiyya (d. 1328). His writings are known for their criticism of alterations to the authentic message, especially in the Sufi and Shi'i doctrines, which makes him a point of reference today. The following quotation gives an indication of the kind of reasoning that has been guiding criticism of popular ritual practices. Ibn Taymiyya regarded it as *shirk* when: 'People who turn graves and relics of prophets and saints into sanctuaries intend to pray to, implore for help and revere a personage for whom others have no consideration. Not so with the true believers of God. They serve God alone, without associating Him with anything' (457, ed. and trans. Memon, 1976:324). He emphasized the believers, loyalty to *tawhid* and the trust in they should put the possibility to find a path back to the sources. He opposed any symbolic readings of the Qur'an and instead argued for the firm guide of sharia, which, according to him, leaves no room for concealed meanings.

The major issues of conflict with the supposedly more orthodox have been emphasized in some literature on Sufism to the extent that the many conservative Sufi theologians and orders with quite established members that regard themselves as defenders of tradition and moral conduct (*adab*) have been neglected. The traditional orthodox arguments against local piety are similar to the purism of contemporary Islamism that regard Sufi thinking as innovation (*bida*) that its practices encourage disputable ritual behaviour. As stressed above, Sufis are accused of seeking mediation through their veneration of Muhammad and the saints, and it is argued that their traditions in general have weak support in the Qur'an and the *hadiths*. Nevertheless, Sufi theology and esoteric philosophy have always had defenders, which have to a varying extent been successful in their attempts to argue in favour of the possibility to find hidden (*batin*) meanings of exterior statements or signs, in holy books as well as in events in nature. Contemporary criticism of Sufism can be equally harsh but does not necessarily come from *salafi* positions; there are more general purist trends that reject local traditions and what is then conceived as amendments to the original religion, and therefore a violation against *tawhid*.

> **Ibn Arabi – Sufi philosopher, mystic and teacher given several honorary names by his followers, such as 'The Great Master', 'The Renewer of Religion'**
>
> Ibn Arabi (1165–1240) grew up in Andalusia but travelled to most of the important places of Islamic learning. He is the author of a vast body of texts. The two most influential collections represent a significant legacy of the Sufi golden age in the Middle Ages, *The Meccan Revelations* and *The Bezels of Wisdom*. Here, Ibn Arabi contemplates the limits of conventional knowledge and the necessity of striving towards an inner truth. Ibn Arabi therefore advocated a symbolic reading of the Qur'an that would reveal a cosmic unity of a mystic kind, and he was criticized for this search beyond the observable by conservatives and traditionalists.
>
> Ibn Arabi's work has recently enjoyed a renaissance – even the Sufi critic Ibn Taymiyya, mentioned above, is among its promoters – and the writer holds a special position among converts to Sufism today. His mode of writing apparently speaks to modern readers with its openness to quests for inner truth.

In an attempt to sketch some characteristics of Sufism past and present, four angles could be outlined and taken together as they point towards some fundamentals relevant to most Sufi-orientated milieus past and present.

First, Sufi theology and teachings emphasize individual spiritual progression and the importance of striving towards a greater closeness to Allah. This is expressed in the ideal of the progressive development of the soul, which reaches various stations (*maqamat*) on its path towards perfection. This process is thought to tame the ego and pave the way to unity.

The second angle to shed light on the specifics of Sufi traditions is the social life it is embedded in. To a great extent, the institutions of Sufism constitute the framework for the execution of spiritual authority and the supervision of a guide (*murshid*) or master (*shaykh* or sheik in its anglicized form). The hierarchical structure is the basis of religious and social activities. The disciple (*murid*) is ideally though to serve both the teacher and the order. Literally, the honorary title *shaykh* means 'elder', and it can be used in a broad sense for a respected community leader or a teacher. It also indicates how the framework of a Sufi group is regarded as necessary to secure the proper transmission of teachings and practices – the structure of a Sufi order is therefore not only a question of hierarchies, but also how to build and maintain fellowship.

Rituals constitute a third common feature of Sufi communities and are performed in designated locations, sometimes with elaborate techniques for reaching the spiritual goals charted in local tradition. Specific ritual genres are cultivated within the orders and are often attributed to the founder of the branch; thus, ritual participation is regarded as a means to connect with the lineage of the order.

Last, Sufism has a long tradition of using aesthetic expressions for spiritual purposes and has left a heritage of music, poetry, calligraphy and images that still serves as a major attraction to new followers.

Mausoleums of Sufi *shaykhs* or of founders (sing. *pir*) of sub-branches often constitute the centre of an order's premises and is often the location where a specfic group have resided over a long period. These sites regularly include prayer rooms (but not necessarily a mosque), teaching halls and facilities for food distribution and social activities. Historically, these meeting grounds were the family home of the *shaykh*. Urbanization has enforced changes in these patterns. Not uncommonly, the *zawiyas* are sites of local pilgrimage and votive prayers, and the mausoleums constitute the nexus of these rituals. Touching the green cloth that covers the coffin or bringing clothes from sick people to the saint's grave in order to transfer blessing (*baraka*) prolongs the experience far beyond the actual visit. The veneration of the holy person can take many forms in terms of rituals, readings and prayers. The commemoration of the saint has three dimensions: it visualizes the memory of a life worthy of imitation, it underlines the tactile character of veneration that can transmit *baraka* and finally it points to the sacred environment itself as both an instrument and object for mediation.

Other frequent terms to indicate a Sufi meeting place (sometimes including the mausoleum of a deceased *shaykh* or of a founder of a branch of a Sufi order, or a site where a miracle has taken place) are

Fig. 10   Members of a Sufi order in Pakistan waiting in their ritual red garb for the *pir*
to arrive and the ceremonies to start. *(Getty Images)*

zawiya (Arabic), *tekke* (Turkish), *dargah, khanagah* (Persian), *ribat,*
mazar and *jamaat-khana* (Urdu).

The term Sufism (*tasawwuf*) supposedly derives from the Arabic
word for wool (*suf*). Both speculations on the etymology and the
exegesis of the context of the word have a long history. It is sometimes
taken as a reference to the ascetic practices of the early Sufis and their
use of robes (commonly regarded as a heritage from the Christian
monks of Eastern denominations, who were part of the milieu of early
Islam). The woollen dervish robe (*khirqa*), still worn today in some
orders (mostly at ceremonial events), is in pious discourse regarded as a
reminiscence of humble living.

Sufi sometimes indicates a mystic in the profound sense of the
word, although in other contexts it refers merely to a person
connected to a Sufi group. Dervish (from the Persian word *darwish,*
the Arabic equivalent being *fakir*) literally means 'poor' and suggests a
link to Sufi history and the possible monastic legacy. A dervish is
nowadays a formally initiated member of a Sufi order. Sufi traditions
in terms of both theology and rituals go back to the eighth century and
a movement within the early Muslim communities that sought a more
affectionate relation to Allah by means of a spiritual path with several
stations offering techniques for the progression of the soul.

Many people engaged in Sufi communities today do not use terms
like Sufi or dervish as a self-definition or relate to their worldview as
tasawwuf-oriented, but often employ a rich local vocabulary for ritual
genres, prayer forms and devotional practices; and they put trust in the
authoritative leadership of the *shaykh*. The attachment to the practices
rather than a theological superstructure gives an indication of the
differences in the uses of the term Sufism as a wide descriptive term
and as a self-definition.

Sufism today cannot be discussed without mention of its fusion
with New Age and contemporary forms of spirituality, which have
greatly influenced the general picture of what Sufism is. These new
trends have meant a reformulation of theology and institutions, in
some respects of leadership in groups, whereas ritual patterns appear to
remain largely intact. In these new groups the expressive aspects of
Sufi tradition seem to persist, whereas the traditional forms of
authority are met with more reluctance from new followers. It is not
unusual to hear representatives of the new spirituality claim that they
are not Muslims, but Sufis.

In general, analyses of Sufism have gone in two directions. On the one hand, there are studies that take a comparative perspective, emphasizing similarities in teaching and practice over time and space in terms of theological conception and ritual genres; on the other hand, there are studies that adopt a contextualized perspective, often based on case studies, where cultural practice and social relations play a major part in the analysis. Both perspectives are relevant for a full-fledged picture. Below, the history of Sufism, its theological particularities, and the ritual genres are discussed.

The history of Sufism

The beginning of Sufism is very much part of Islam's early history and its background in the multi-religious environment in which Muslims, with their extensive trading contacts on the Arabian Peninsula, stood out as a distinct group.

By the eighth century there were already movements that emphasized intense piety as a path to a more personal relationship with God. As discussed in previous chapters, many factors influenced the initial development of Islam. Four of these can be seen as conditional for the emergence of Sufism. As in the case of the discussions about the contact zones between the monotheistic religions in the early days of Islam, foreign influences on early Sufism have long since been an ambiguous standpoint. Some take it as an indication that Sufism does not spring from the sources of Islam and is to be regarded as an innovation, while others deem the underlining of these contacts as a proof of the universal qualities of Sufism.

Research has emphasized that Eastern Christianity, with its monastic life, provided the impulse towards ascetic piety, repetitive prayers and contemplation. The Sufi ideal of renouncing the worldly life and its pleasures and committing oneself as a servant of Allah and of fellow human beings is likely to have come from encounters with Christians in the vicinity of the early Islamic communities. The tradition of honouring saints during their lifetimes as spiritual guides and venerating the holy ones after their deaths is supposed to belong to this mode of devotion, too. In the early history of Sufism, spiritual training and self-discipline in poverty went hand in hand with the formulation of the various paths of Sufi theology. Through Greek philosophy, early Islamic theology encountered dualistic tendencies such as neo-platonic thoughts on the gradual refinement of the soul and the striving towards truth and beauty that had appeared before Christianity and developed in various directions. The dualism between this world and the ideal was a central concept in Manichean theology too; and especially emphasized the dichotomy between the physical body tying the individual to the earth and the liberating potential of the spiritual soul. Influences from as far away as India – on breath control and meditation as a spiritual technique – are sometimes suggested, as well as traces of even more distant (Central Asian and shamanic) influences. This is nevertheless highly controversial, as Muslims conventionally regard Hindus as polytheists. Many Sufis would strongly emphasize that repetitive and emotional rituals, like *dhikr* and the contemplation over instrumental music during *sama*, could not be compared to meditation of Indian origin, as they strive towards Allah instead of introspection. A popular custom with a Buddhist background in both Christian and Muslim daily piety practices is the use of the rosary (*tasbih*) as an instrument for keeping pace with long, repetitive prayers as well as for counting the number of prayers spoken. This tool is also described in more esoteric teachings that seek to establish correspondences between the colours of the beads and spiritual organs, between planets, numbers and letters, as a way of reasoning that apparently has Eastern origins.

Discussions of influences from the East always touch upon the core issue in the criticism and defence of Sufism: its Qur'anic legitimacy or, as its critics would claim, the lack thereof. A hint of mystical experience is contained in the description of Muhammad's Night Journey. Legitimacy is also claimed by linking Sufi demeanours to the *sunna* of Muhammad and by finding examples in the *hadith* literature, supplemented by legendary narratives, that tell of the prophet's spiritual experiences. There are ascetic and ecstatic traits in early Sufism and they have lingered as ideal characteristics and tropes in literature, but also developed into expressive modes that have been severely criticized.

The poem overleaf was composed by another of the foremost representatives of the golden age of Sufism, Jalal al-din Rumi (1207–73). 'I have seen that the two worlds are one', he wrote, thereby expressing Sufi theology in poetic form. Originally from northern Afghanistan, Rumi spent the majority of his life in Konya, Anatolia. An encounter with a wandering dervish made Rumi's life take a turn

'I am the Truth'. The mystic and martyr Mansur al-Hallaj (ca. 858–922)

Al-Hallaj was a controversial ecstatic mystic who went so far in his combat with the ego that he experienced the spiritual state of annihilation of the self (*fana*), which made him exclaim in public 'I am the Truth'. This statement was perceived either as a true Sufi's unity with Allah or, as his enemies who executed him claimed, a heresy. Al-Hallaj was not only a man who shared his experiences on the streets of Baghdad; he was also a writer of theological treatises and renowned for a work that interprets the mystic letters that precede some of the *suras* in the Qur'an.

from a sharia-orientated attitude to a more devotional life. The didactic poem *Masnavi-ye manavi* outlines his esoteric commentary on the Qur'an, and since the Middle Ages his poetry has been widely read for both its religious and its literary qualities. His corpus is a good example of the rich contributions in Turkish and Persian to the Sufi legacy. The following stanzas come from his work *Divan-i Shams-i Tabriz*, a collection of poetry in commemoration of his friend Shams. The quotation contains two central tropes in Sufi poetry: the upheaval of contrasts and dichotomies of this world that govern earthly life and the soul's yearning for unity with the One. The voice of the poem uses negation to define his Sufi identity. As Allah is 'greater', the One cannot be described or comprehended but with one quality at a time; human language cannot grasp the greatness in one single mode of representation of Hu, 'Him':

> What is to be done, O Moslems? for I do not recognize myself.
> I am neither Christian, nor Jew, nor Gabr [Zoroastrian], nor Moslem.
> I am not of Nature's mint, nor of the circling heavens.
> I am not of earth, nor of water, nor of air, nor of fire;
> I am not of the empyrean, not of the dust, nor of existence, nor of entity.
> I am not of India, nor of China, nor of Bulgaria, nor of Saqsin;[18]
> /—/
> My place is the Placeless, my trace is the Traceless;
> 'Tis neither body nor soul, for I belong to the soul of the Beloved.

I have put my duality away, I have seen that the two worlds are
one;
One I seek, One I know, One I see, One I call.
He is the first, He is the last, He is the outward, He is the inward;
I know none other except 'Ya Hu' and 'Ya man Hu'.
I am intoxicated with Love's cup, the two worlds have passed
out of my ken; (trans. R. A. Nicholson, 1999:125, whose
translation from 1898 conveys the content rather than the
rhythm)

A core theme in the poem is unity and the striving to abolish the
distance to Allah, represented in a repetitive construction that
resembles the *dhikr* prayers. 'Ya Hu', 'Oh He!' the frequently
pronounced phrases and the repetitive structure are on the boundary
between poetry and prayer, and creation, with its 'circling heavens',
seems to be joining the *dhikr*. The last two lines provide examples of
the sometimes daring metaphors used to express the bewildering
experiences of the dervish. Some Sufi poetry explicitly mentions
wine, and intoxication symbolizes exuberance in the unity with Allah.
The Mevlevi order of 'whirling dervishes' developed from the circle
around Rumi, and to his followers is he known as Mevlana,
'Our Master'.

Sufi orders

The importance of the Sufi orders in the spread of Islam throughout
history, especially from the thirteenth century onwards, should not be
underestimated. Even today, their activities are one of the more
important means of attracting converts. Many presentations of Sufism
are structured around the orders, which thus play a structuring role,
but they should not be emphasized to the extent that other forms of
Sufi fellowships are neglected. Neither should the Sufi orders be
misunderstood as resembling Christian monastic orders, although
convents were not uncommon in early Sufi history. It has also been
customary for devoted disciples to reside for periods in their *shaykh*'s
vicinity to receive intense training and teaching.

The word *tariqa*, which literally means 'path', is often understood to
be an indication of the need for a surrounding strict structure for those
who seek spiritual development and hence to indicate both the

Fig. 11   The turning ceremony (Turkish *sema*) practised by the Mevlevi order is not a dance, but is regarded as a form of prayer that emphasizes the striving towards Allah. The circular movements of the dervishes correspond to the circling heavens in the poem quoted on the previous pages. The rhythm of the turning is likewise regarded as a representation of the pulse of the universe. *(Source: Tomas Maltby [public domain], via Wikimedia Commons)*

organization and the method for spiritual development – the path to be taken under the supervision of the *shaykh* – to lead a life less dependent of worldly lure. The activities of the orders represent various ways of seeking closeness to Allah, as is clear from their ritual traditions. The orders connect the discursive side of Sufism with the social and ritual; a focus on individual spiritual progress in theology and philosophy is balanced with a sense of social cohesion among the devotees and shared collective ritual experience.

Being part of the legitimate chain of authority (*silsila*) provides the *shaykh* with his authority to guide and instruct. An order is by definition hierarchical, as it transmits blessings and insights all the way from the founder of the order (*pir*) and the founder of the sub-branch. The roles of the head of the order, the *shaykh*, are manifold. The idealized close relation between the master or guide and the disciple is not always a reality; nor are the internal hierarchies under the *shaykh* always visible.

Making an oath of allegiance (*baya*) to the *shaykh*, known as 'giving the hand', is a ritual established by Sufi theological literature and oral narratives that confers formal membership of an order. As a token of affiliation the disciple receives a collection of prayers and verses from the Qur'an to be read as a repetitive litany (*wird*) based on a combination of prayers and Qur'anic quotations (*hizh*). This compilation of texts is either personal or significant for a particular branch of an order, and its donation confers full membership along with the right to wear the insignia and vestment of the group (cap, vest, robe) at prayer meetings.

In many orders, however, it is hard to distinguish between formal members and followers, as formal membership is not always important. The importance of initiation differs between the orders. A charismatic Sufi leader, a distinctive set of rituals connected with a place or the celebration of certain festivals may attract large numbers of participants.

Shaykhs are ideally supposed to appoint their successors, often through messages received in dreams or via other signs, in order to secure the lineage. The web of stories about divine messages in the past about who is a true *shaykh* is as important as the formal appointment for the status of a *shaykh*, and in many environments the position of *shaykh* still passes from father to son in families that have dominated a certain sub-branch of an order for a long time.

Some *shaykhs* are venerated as living saints, although this is far from the rule, and most Sufi *shaykhs* are simply community leaders. In his monograph *At the Shrine of the Red Sufi: Five Days and Nights on Pilgrimage in Pakistan* (2012), and the accompanying documentary film of the same name, Jürgen Frembgen conveys the intensity of such a pilgrimage to a holy man and the conflicts attached to living and dead *shaykhs* arises. Many narratives confirm the legitimacy of late *shaykhs* with references to blessing (*baraka*) and the capability to perform miracles (*karamat*) – two traditional characteristics of a 'true *shaykh*' where local narratives about the latter are not so convincing in modern times as they used to be.

The marabouts of North and West Africa can in this context serve as an example of the many functions of a *shaykh*. The marabouts are renowned for their healing gifts and their consultation services based on folk medical traditions in their communities, but they are also educated Islamic teachers and sometimes the formal heads of an order or branch. While alive they are at the centre of celebrations of festivals and commemorations; when deceased many of them remain in the collective memory. The mausoleum and shrine (*qubba*) of a deceased marabout is often the goal of local pilgrims.

Sufi theology has throughout history been expressed in terms of a formally argued discourse as well as oral forms like sermons, hymns and legendary narratives and is part of general Islamic historiography. The expressions of Sufi theology provide a strong flavour to local aesthetic representations (literature, music, art) that has always been part of Sufi heritage. Sufi literature spans a number of genres: theological treatises and Qur'an commentaries, manuals for prayers and spiritual training, poetry and legendary history writing. The capstones of Sufi teaching are said to be four hierarchical concepts. First, sharia and *tariqa*, indicating that no doctrine or practice may be accepted that goes against the law dictated by Allah or the proven experience and insights that are transmitted through the traditions of an order. The two other fundaments are the striving towards transcendental truth (*haqiqa*) and the search for esoteric or spiritual knowledge (*marifa*) beyond formal knowledge (*ilm*). Instructions for the taming of the self or ego (*nafs*) and how to cultivate the spirit (*ruh*) can be found in Sufi philosophy as well as in local song traditions. The human's heart (*qalb*) is the organ where knowledge, insight and conscience should be united in order for a person to be able to experience absolute trust in Allah (*tawakkul*). From this springs respect for and fear of Allah (*taqwa*), which lead to the appropriate devoutness. The goal of Sufi teaching is to support the progression between the stations of spiritual development (*maqam*, pl. *maqamat*). These constitute the seven states (*ahwal*) on the ideal path towards annihilation (*fana*, literally 'going through'), when the human unites with Allah.

Following the instructions of the *shaykh* on how to perform the ritual practices of an order is not only a question of a manual, but to a great extent a mode of transmitting theology by means of bodily movements that are conceived to manifest a number of religious truths. Therefore, the ritual techniques are of equal importance to the conceptual formulations. A well trained *shaykh* has a multiplicity of rituals to select from.

Sufi rituals

Sufism can to a large extent be defined in terms of its rituals. The collective repetition of Allah's name (*dhikr*) under the guidance of a *shaykh* has become the defining ritual of Sufism, but the individual prayers and contemplation such as *wird* and *hizb* can play just as important a role.

The core of the *dhikr* is the 99 'most beautiful' names of Allah (*al-asma al-husna*), which in practice means a lengthy repetition of a selection of names, a ritual that goes back through the history of Sufism and is thought of as an uninterrupted chain of prayers since the days of the *pir*. Some orders even claim a lineage back to Abu Bakr and Ali. To keep the rhythm and the focus on the names, various techniques are taught. A string of beads (*tesbih*) is used to count the names of Allah during individual practice as well as during *dhikr* and, for advanced practices, a special name, adjective or other characterization (*subah*) is connected to each bead.

Allah's 99 most beautiful names

The number 99 indicates that there are innumerable words to describe the qualities of Allah, but only one of them at a time, and the human mind can never grasp them all, but can only contemplate them one by one. The repetition is under the command of the *shaykh* and varies in tempo and intensity during the ceremony. In some orders, the pronouncing of the names is accompanied by rhythmic bodily movements and techniques for breath control, which add to the intensity of the ritual.

Among the most commonly repeated names during *dhikr*, beside *la ilaha illa Allah*, are:

al-Alim – The Knowing or the Wise
al-Haqq – The Ultimate Truth
al-Hayy – The Living
al-Karim – The Gracious
al-Latif – The Benevolent
al-Nur – The Light
or simply Hu, Him, as in the poem of Rumi quoted earlier.

A *dhikr* is not a ritual open to anyone; a disciple needs the approval or consent of a *shaykh* to participate. It is performed at weekly gatherings of a Sufi order, when members and associates, who have not taken the full step to *baya*, meet. The regular participants are known as a circle (*khalka*) in all senses of the word: the ritual is performed in a circle and a strong fellowship is usually developed in the wake of the intensity of the ritual. Listening to poetry or music in a ritualized way (*sama*; Turkish *sema*) may be a parallel activity of the *khalka*.

'Remembrance' or 'recollection' (*dhikr*) is mentioned in the Qur'an, as is the requirement to remember Allah (*dhikr Allah*): 'We indeed created man; and We know what his soul whispers within him, and We are nearer to him than the [his] jugular vein' (50:16) and Allah's presence in his creation: 'In the alternation of night and day, and what God has created in the heavens and the earth – surely there are signs for a god-fearing people' (3:190–191).

The home of the *shaykh* may very well be, and was often historically, a part of the greater compound of a Sufi order, but the lodge is not the only place for Sufi gatherings. Family homes and semi-private locations also serve as ritual settings, especially for women's activities. Collective *dhikr* is led by an imam at regulated times but is not exclusively led by a male *shaykh*. In contrast to collective *salat*, a *dhikr* ceremony (whole or part) can be embedded in other ritual activities and can be led by a woman.

The veneration of deceased masters and saints can take the form of visits (*ziyarat*) to a shrine (*zawiya*) containing the holy person's mausoleum. The visit to such a tomb can include formal rituals as well as more individual prayers in order to sense the closeness of the saint. Physical proximity is a central part of the veneration and the tactile dimensions of blessing and grace are manifested in the relics and are transmitted through sweets brought from the holy place or cloth brought back home after being placed on top of the coffin.

Religious practices in everyday life

Religious activities are always part of social life and are never performed in a realm of their own. The Muslim ritual obligations constitute a daily and weekly web of piety practices. Their correct performance is strictly regulated by specific sections of the *hadith* collections, and the daily prayers are guided by the conception of the *sunna* of the prophet. The correct way is to imitate the impeccable behaviour of Muhammad. All Islamic prayers require that the performer is in a state of ritual (or perhaps better, lawful in terms of sharia) purity, and the steps in the washing process are as detailed as those for *salat*. Furthermore, any ritual performance must be based on the proper intention (*niyya*) in order to be valid.

Beside the prescribed rituals, Muslim tradition includes a variety of greater or lesser devotional practices. Many of them are centred around saints (and their mausoleums) with a more or less clear connection to a Sufi order. Sufi rituals have throughout Islamic history offered more emotionally intense prayers to initiated members and dervishes, as well as to visitors to *zawiyas* and *tekkes*.

When more conservative Muslims criticize Sufism as theological discourse and ritual practice, they are following a line of theologians from the Middle Ages that reject anything they consider to be an innovation in relation to authentic Islam. This rift remains and is, if anything, growing. In the modern period, Sufi traditions have been a means of expressing a liberal Muslim attitude, and yet many Sufi orders defend quite conservative views, despite their emotional rituals.

Further reading

Baldick, Julian, *Mystical Islam: An Introduction to Sufism* (London: I.B.Tauris, 1989).

Banu, Masooda and Hilary Kalmbach (eds), *Women, Leadership and Mosques: Changes in Contemporary Islamic Authority* (Leiden: Brill, 2012).

Bianchi, Robert B., *Guests of God: Pilgrimage and Politics in the Islamic World* (Oxford: Oxford University Press, 2004).

van Bruinessen, Martin and Julia Day Howell, *Sufism and 'the Modern' in Islam* (London: I.B.Tauris, 2007).

Frembgen, Jürgen, *At the Shrine of the Red Sufi: Five Days and Nights on Pilgrimage in Pakistan* (Oxford: Oxford University Press, 2012).

Gilsenan, Michael, *Recognizing Islam: Religion and Society in the Modern Middle East* (London: I.B.Tauris, 1982).

Knysh, Alexander, *Islamic Mysticism: A Short History* (Leiden: Brill, 2000).

Raudvere, Catharina and Leif Stenberg, *Sufism Today: Heritage and Tradition in the Modern World* (London: I.B.Tauris, 2009).

Sirriyeh, Elizabeth, *Sufis and Anti-Sufis: The Defence, Rethinking and Rejection of Sufism in the Modern World* (Richmond: Curzon, 1999).

Werbner, Pnina, *Pilgrims of Love: The Anthropology of a Global Sufi Cult* (London: Hurst, 2003).

Chapter VII

Shi'i Islam: Religious Authority and Remembered Martyrdom

The differences between Shi'i and Sunni Muslims have been touched upon at several points in earlier chapters when discussing the leadership of the Muslim community after the death of Muhammad. The conflicting positions taken on this issue developed into the most serious division among Muslim groups, both in historical times and today. The schism developed along both theological and political lines. Early on it also prompted the emergence of sub-groups among the Shi'i Muslims, and later the discord was used for marks of cultural identity in politics. The establishment of Shi'ism was a process rather than consistently shaped theological stands from the beginning of the history of Islam. From a historical and genealogical perspective, Sunnis and Shi'is have different views on religious leadership, which have had an impact on how their legal traditions have evolved over the centuries as well as their visions of how a good and just society is to be defined. Sunni and Shi'i Muslims also differ in their ritual practices, in both the mandatory prayers and in the more devotional practices promoted in Shi'ism; Shi'i Muslims are known for the elaborate commemoration rituals, with Muhammad's immediate family, saints and martyrs as the focal points. These two traits of thought and practice within the Islamic world, though one is very much a minority in comparison to the other, have been the driving forces of major regional developments in the Muslim world. The political and cultural processes in the Persian world is intertwined with Shi'i Islam, as the Arabic- and Turkish-speaking worlds are predominantly Sunni-orientated; although the Persian influences on the Ottoman world and the importance of the Arabic-speaking Shi'is should not be under-estimated. There are undoubtedly differences in doctrinal positions and ritual focus, but Sunnis and Shi'is also share many fundamental Islamic beliefs, and the main areas of contention are questions related to who has the legitimacy to interpret and formulate verdicts.

Although it is hard to obtain exact numbers, between 10 and 13 per cent of the Muslims in the world are Shi'i and a large group of them (about 70 million) live in Iran, with around 16–18 million each in Iraq, Pakistan and India.[19] The total number of Shi'i Muslims in the world is most likely around 180 million. These figures must, however, be read from the perspective that Shi'i Muslims constitute minorities under pressure in many places. There are political reasons for both over- and under-estimations of their numbers. The recent violent attacks on Shi'i mosques in Iraq and Pakistan are brutal reminders of how religious affiliation is used as a tool in regional conflicts. There are also large groups (over 1 million) of Shi'i Muslims in Turkey, Yemen, Azerbaijan, Afghanistan, Syria, Saudi Arabia, Lebanon, Nigeria and Tanzania. Some count the 15–20 million Turkish Alevis as Shi'i Muslims, while others regard them almost as Sufis with Shi'i influences. In several of these places, the situation of being a minority among Sunni Muslims is problematic, if not dangerous.

A quest for legitimate leadership

The historical background to the break between Sunnis and Shi'is is to be found in the very early development of Islam. There were distinct groups, but they were not necessarily from the beginning theological stands that defined communities. Muhammad had not only been a charismatic religious leader; the community had already during his time started to grow in terms of regional expansion and structure of the *umma*. Political and military leadership was crucial for the continued spread of Islam. Keeping together was a religious as well as a political necessity in order to develop as a distinct faith and tendencies to split were as dangerous as external threats. The leadership of the first caliphs was crucial in these matters, as discussed in the second part of Chapter 2.

Under the first three caliphs, conflicts over what constituted legitimate leadership were not accentuated, but they flared up when Ali ibn Abi Talib – Ali, son of Abu Talib – (d. 661) became caliph in 659. The position of Ali, and his male descendants, is one of the key issues in the diverging positions between Sunni and Shi'i Muslims. After Muhammad's death in 632, Ali was the male who could claim the closest family link to the prophet, being a paternal cousin and son-in-law (married to Muhammad's daughter Fatima and thus the father

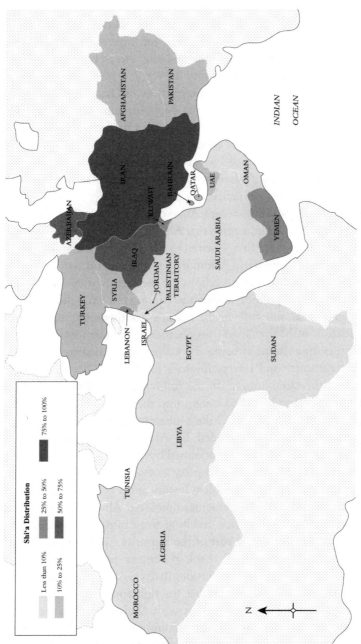

Map 3   The major Shi'i communities of the world.

to Muhammad's grandchildren). Ali's father was not only Muhammad's uncle, but also the foster-father of the orphaned child. It had been a struggle for nearly 30 years for those who supported Ali and the idea that leadership followed the direct bloodline. These rejected the first three caliphs before Ali was accepted (hence *shiat Ali*, 'Ali's group or party'). The Umayyads (who had expanded their sphere of influence under the first three caliphs) immediately contested the claims of Ali and his group. Among Ali's harshest opponents was Aisha, the favourite wife of Muhammad, and Abu Bakr's, the first caliph's, daughter and hence a supporter of the Umayyads. In short: to great extent these conflicts emerged around families seeking both religious and political influence in a growing empire.

Today, Sunni Muslims accept Ali as the fourth rightful caliph and part of *sunna*. All Muslims agree that Ali was among the early converts to Islam, if not the very first, as stated by Shi'i Muslims. Sunni Muslims do not attribute more status to him than to the other three caliphs and the line of the rightly guided caliphs for them ends with Ali; the title thereafter refers to political leadership. Among the Shi'is, however, he is recognized as the first imam because to them he represents a continuation of Muhammad's prophethood; the term imam in Shi'i tradition is understood as being the keeper of an inherited legacy of spiritual authority and refers only to a limited number of historical persons of the same lineage. In the following line of imams in Shi'i Islam, Ali is said to have had insight into the hidden meanings of the Qur'an and the will of Allah. Like Muhammad, Ali too, in Shi'ism, is regarded as faultless and guided by Allah. Furthermore, he was, according to Shi'i Muslims, proclaimed by Muhammad as his rightful heir because of his virtues and piety but was pushed aside by the Umayyads. Shi'i history is a violent history and a point of departure in collective memory is when enemies murdered Ali in 661. Narratives of martyrdom and oppression resulting from unjust Sunni claims to power have formed a vital part of the minority in Shi'i identity, and constitute a core theme in its theology, history and ritual practice.

Parallel to the image of the virtuous martyr, Ali is the picture of the knight engaged in military combat for righteousness. According to general Muslim history, Ali fought with Muhammad in the major battles against the enemies of the early community and he has become a model for the courageous warrior, for strength in armed battle and for chivalry (*futuwwa*). The sword and the lion are therefore his symbols.

Fig. 12   A young man in Baghdad holding a poster of Ali – martyr, mystic and knight
– after a bomb attack in a Shii neighbourhood. *(Getty Images)*

Ali – martyr, mystic and the knight

Shi'ism emphasizes that Ali (and his male descendants) embodied and transmitted the spiritual qualities of Muhammad and had an extraordinary contact with Allah in comparison with other humans. The Shi'i call to prayer includes the phrase 'I testify that Ali is the friend (*wali*) of Allah', which Sunni Muslims regard as a violation of the concept of *tawhid*.

Ali is venerated as a friend of Allah and a martyr, and supplications are made to him. Ali's grave in Najaf in southern Iraq is the goal of a pilgrimage for Shi'i Muslims from all over the world, who invest the journey with as much significance as the *hajj* to Mecca. Early in Shi'i Muslim history, the grave was transferred from its original site in Kufa to protect it from Sunni offence. Ali's mausoleum in Najaf has been attacked and damaged, with considerable loss of life, at several points in history. The political situation in Iraq today, with clashes between Sunni and Shi'i Muslims, have made this pilgrimage complicated, if not hazardous, as the attacks have escalated since 2003.

Due to the Umayyad opposition to Ali's position as caliph, two geographical focal points of the Muslim community developed during the time of Ali's caliphate: Ali and his supporters resided at Kufa and the other node was Damascus, which was to become the nexus from which the Umayyads reigned over a steadily expanding area from 661 to 750.

The role of the imams in Shi'i tradition – the imamate

In Sunni tradition, an imam is the respected man who at stipulated times of the day 'stands in front of' the community, and leads the Friday prayer or any *salat* performed by a group, in a mosque or elsewhere. It is not a formal clerical position, although the term is more and more frequently used for a local leader of a Muslim community or congregation. In Shi'i Islam, imam is a designation given to a limited number of people in history: those who are considered to have been the bearers of blessing and divine guidance which they can transmit to ordinary people. This is based on their link to Muhammad and spiritual qualities, passed on from father to son, after Ali, the first imam. The imams are considered infallible. Early in the Shi'i tradition, there was a split between those who recognized seven imams and those who recognized twelve. The latter group constitute the majority of Shi'i Muslims with its heartland in today's Iran and Iraq.

Muhammad's only surviving child, Fatima (d. 633), from his marriage with Khadija, holds another of the key positions in Shi'i genealogy. Fatima's marriage to Ali produced two sons, Hasan and Husayn, the grandchildren of the prophet. According to the Shi'is, these were the only two males who could claim direct the progeny of Muhammad. One daughter from this marriage, Zaynab, would also play a significant role in Shi'i martyr history.

The elder son of Ali and Fatima, Hasan, served as his father's successor, as imam, only briefly. It was instead his younger brother Husayn who came to play a major part in the Shi'i narrative of the fate of 'the people of the house' (*ahl al-bayt*) and of the continuation of the imams as leaders of the Shi'is. The rift between the two major claims to leadership in the Muslim world, the Umayyad caliphs and the Shi'i imams, at this point grew into a violent conflict.

Members of *ahl al-bayt*, that is, those with a family link to Muhammad, among them the succession of imams, play a key role in early Shi'i history. Sometimes, only a few people of the larger family

are named as having been selected by Muhammad during his lifetime
and referred to as 'the people of the mantle' (*ahl al-kisa*). Pious Shi'i
Muslims ask for their supplications and veneration is performed at
their mausoleums. A *hadith* in the Muslim collection tells the
following story of how Muhammad covered some of his nearest,
Ali and Fatima with their two sons, Hasan and Husayn, with his
mantle, indicating his protection of them and is thought to have
confirmed their purity by this action:

> Aisha reported that Allah's Apostle (may peace be upon him)
> went out one morning wearing a striped cloak of the black
> camel's hair; then there came Hasan b. Ali. He wrapped him
> under it; then came Husayn and he wrapped him under it along
> with the other one (Hasan). Then came Fatima and he took her
> under it; then came Ali and he also took him under it and then
> said: 'Allah only desires to take away any uncleanliness from you,
> O people of the household, and purify you (thorough
> purifying)'. (Sahih Muslim 031:5955)

For Sunni Muslims, this is not only a matter of leadership selection but
also a metaphor for the trust placed in belief and striving for closeness
to Allah, and the imagery plays a major part in popular piety among
Sunnis and Shi'is alike. In Shi'i Islam, however, the view developed
that guided leadership is a necessity for reaching this closeness.

Shi'i history

Shi'i history is to a large extent connected to Persian culture and the
rise and fall of Persian centres of power. The initial split into factions
based on theological views on leadership and authority were soon, if
not immediately, included as vital elements in regional conflicts.
Sunni and Shi'i positions became hallmarks of empires and tools that
defined geopolitical conflicts as well as identity markers for groups
and individuals. In short, Shi'i pre-modern history can be roughly be
divided into the following historical epochs and for periods in
history Shi'i Muslims, although being a minority, dominated the
Muslim world:

The Umayyad dynasty (661–750) was the prime enemy throughout
early Shi'i history and played a decisive role in the martyrdom of the
grandson of Muhammad, and hence became the iconic image of

unjust rule. The Abbasid victory over the Umayyads paved the way for a new dynasty of caliphs (750–1258) who established their base in Baghdad, which became a thriving centre for science and art. In general this is primarily a formative period for Sunni theology, even so Persian cultural influences remained strong. The Shi'is gained political visibility through the Abbasid revolt in 750. The Abbasids were challenged early on by the Fatimids, later by the Turks and finally by the Mongols under Djingis Khan. The Mongol conquest of Baghdad in 1258 meant the end of a long period of intellectual advancement where Persians also played a significant role.

The Ismaili dynasty, claiming ancestry from Muhammad's daughter Fatima but belonging to the Shi'i minority that only accepts seven imams ('the Seveners'), ruled during the Fatimid caliphate (909–1171) governing an expanding empire with its centre in Cairo. It was in conflict with the Abbasids in Baghdad and North Africa from the tenth century and with the Shi'i majority of 'Twelvers' in Persia.

The peak of political influence for the Shi'i dynasties in the Middle East came with the Safavids, 1501–1736. They made Twelver Shi'ism the state religion throughout the Persian empire and it remains so to this day in the Islamic Republic of Iran. The Safavids prolonged the heritage argument when claiming their right to power based on family links to the imams, and it was successful thanks to the bonds to the Safavi Sufi Order and its networks that helped to implement this idea of legitimate political power. This alliance is also a reminder of the historical links between Sufism and Shi'ism, although these are not acknowledged by the rulers of Iran today. A political and cultural peak was reached under Shah Abbas (d. 1629) when he reconquered previously lost land and organized successful campaigns against the Ottomans and the Uzbeks. Shah Abbas made Isfahan the Safavid capital of the empire, and it remained for centuries afterwards a centre for art and literature, leaving a legacy long after the decline of the Safavid empire.

Shi'i theology

When it comes to scriptural traditions, the Shi'i *hadith* collections comprise the sayings of the imams and even contest certain wordings in the standard Qur'an with reference to the imams and their more esoteric interpretations of the meaning of the canonical texts.

The sixth in the line of imams, Jafar al-Sadiq (d. 765), is also the most influential theologian for the majority of Shi'i groups. His writings are an early example of attempts to formulate Shi'i doctrine, which was not finally formalized until some centuries later, and he gave his name to one of the two Shi'i branches of the schools of law, *jafardiyya*.

Jafar is recognized among Sunnis as a transmitter of *hadiths*, but he was also a target of mutazilite criticism. Their rationalistic mode of reasoning in theological matters did not agree with the esoteric tendencies of Shi'ism. Additionally, the personal life of Jafar is significant in relation to the split among the Shi'i groups that took place in the late eighth century and the division between 'the Seveners' and 'the Twelvers' (and later with more sub-groups). The difference between the two groups is not primarily in theological principles, but in the view on where the line of infallible imams ends. Jafar's oldest son died young and some Shi'is consider the imamate completed with him; hence 'the Seveners'. This belief has remained the view of a Shi'a minority, and the largest group among them is the Ismaliya. Though a minority in relation to the other Seveners, this line has had a significant impact on both religious and cultural history, not least since it formed the basis of the Fatimid reign in Cairo, 909/969–1171.

For the Shi'a majority, the imamate lasted to the twelfth imam; hence 'the Twelvers'. As state religion in Iran since the sixteenth century, this denomination has formed the image of what Shi'i Islam is. A significant concept among the Twelvers is their expectation of the so-called hidden imam (*mahdi*). The twelfth imam is believed to have been kept hidden away from enemies and not to have died, but disappeared in 873 or 874. He was represented for a period by deputies, but was eventually thought to have gone into the major occultation that still lasts. It is believed that the *mahdi* is still able to support his followers and that he will return when the end of time approaches. This messianic figure will safeguard the Shi'a community and install divine rule and there are many pious narratives about his support from his hidden position through history. The political power of the eschatological expectations surrounding the *madhi* character has always been strong, as it combines personal piety with a master narrative that explains the present and gives hope for the future.

There is a significant tradition of esoteric interpretation in Shi'a theology, where symbolic readings of normative texts aim at finding hidden meanings. As with the narratives of the *mahdi*, guidance is believed to be needed for the individual believer to receive the correct insights and is thus linked to leadership and interpretative authority. This applies not only to formal leadership and legal authority; the deceased imams are also regarded as intermediaries between Allah and humankind, which is one of the specific theological features of Shiʻi Islam. The imams are considered to be without sin (*isma*) and therefore to be included in *sunna* in Shiʻi theology.

The importance of the line of imams does not mean that the traditional scholars (*ulama* – or, to use the Persian word for a religious executive, *mulla* or *molla*) are without importance. Quite the opposite; the tradition of interpreting hidden meanings in normative texts and the political influence of men of theological learning are perhaps stronger, or at least more represented by narratives outside the institutions, in the Shiʻi world than among Sunnis. Ideas connected with the imamate, and especially discussions about who can act and speak on behalf of the hidden imam, have made the Shiʻi attitude to interpretation different from the general Sunni reluctance to accept *ijtihad*.

The city of Qom in Iran has been the centre for Shiʻi theology for centuries, along with the schools at Karbala and Najaf. It is a popular pilgrimage destination as the mausoleum of the eighth imam's daughter is situated there. The many theological institutions of Qom are connected with the ideas that led to the Islamic Revolution in the late 1970s. The link between spiritual guidance and political leadership has always been strong in Shiʻi theology used in opposition against the shah.

The Shiʻis being the minority in many milieus and the fact that the theological differences in relation to the Sunnis often have been inscribed in political conflicts sometimes made it impossible to openly declare Shiʻi identity. Dissimulation for the purpose of hiding religious affiliation (*taqiyya*, literally 'caution') in times of danger is a general Islamic concept, but especially associated with Shiʻi Islam. *Taqiyya* has been practised in the complicated minority situations Shiʻi Muslims have lived in for long periods. The minorities within Shiʻi Islam likewise take up the *taqiyya* stance in relation to the dominating Twelvers. The concept could be regarded as contradictory to the focus on martyrdom, but it has perhaps functioned more as the other side of the coin. Both angles emphasize exposition, vulnerability and suffering as essential parts of Shiʻi self-definition, themes that have always been significant in Shiʻi history writing.

The role of martyrdom in Shi'i cultural memory, doctrine and ritual

The crucial event in Shi'i history took place in 680 during the battle of Karbala in southern present-day Iraq. The prolonged struggle on the plain was a clash between Husayn, Ali's son – now recognized as the third imam – and Yazid of the Umayyads, who had recently succeeded his father as caliph. The rebellion was against what some groups, among them Shiat Ali, regarded as illegitimate rule, which did not take descent from the prophet into consideration. Consequently claimed that Husayn should be the Muslim leader.

In the battle, a small group from Ali's party were captured and denied water from the Euphrates. Their thirst and suffering are tropes in the Shi'i narratives that emerged from this event. These 72 companions fell in battle, among them Husayn; women and children were taken captive and brought to Damascus. Therefore, the grave of Zaynab (also a grandchild of the prophet) is to be found in the heartland of the Sunni Umayyads, Damascus. A mausoleum in Cairo, once the Fatimid capital, is competing to be the site of Zaynab's final resting place. Both sites have for centuries been cherished by Shi'i pilgrims. Likewise, Husayn's head is contained in a shrine in Cairo, while his body is buried at Karbala. All these shrines are popular sites for pilgrimage and physical closeness to the venerated martyr is not only a ritual matter, but also a lasting connectedness between the devotee and the sources of the supplication.

Husayn's grave at Karbala

At the site where Husayn's body was found after the battle, a grave was dug, but his head was later brought to Cairo and a mausoleum built around it. Husayn's grave at Karbala has been destroyed several times, but it has always been rebuilt and never lost its attraction as the prime location for Shi'i pilgrimage. In 1802, the grave was demolished by *wahhabis* from Saudi Arabia and, because of the conflicts in present-day Iraq, several attacks on the grave have been conducted in anti-Shi'i campaigns, many during Shi'i festivals when large crowds gather, and with major casualties.

The revolt in 680 against Yazid and the Umayyads at Karbala – righteous, but lost – provides the matrix for the narratives about suffering under an unjust ruler, repeated yearly in the Shi'i calendar of holy days and serving as a force of resistance for those living as suppressed minorities.

Many Shi'i practices are close to Sufi customs, but the relationship between Shi'ism and Sufism is a complex matter in terms of historical development and piety genres like rituals, narratives and art. Ali plays a part in both traditions, as he combines the roles of the unremitting defender of belief and the modest mystic. In Shi'ism, the concept of esoteric knowledge (*irfan*) functions rather like the Sufi quest for spiritual insight along a path with several stations of enlightenment.

Shi'i rituals are known to be emotional in their representation of historical events. The expressed closeness to Muhammad, Ali, Fatima, Hasan and Husayn is significant. Pilgrimage (*ziyara*) is organized for the annual commemorations of the members of *ahl al-bayt* at their shrines and mausoleums. All the graves of the imams are shrines (sing. *imamzadeh*) and are connected with the same kind of requests for intercession and belief in received blessing (*baraka*) as those of *ahl al-bayt* and martyrs. Manuals are distributed to visitors explaining the rituals and the litanies to be spoken. In addition to the already noted shrines at Karbala, Najaf and Qom, some other important Shi'i pilgrim sites could be mentioned, including Hilla, Kazimayn and Samarra in Iraq, Mashad in Iran and Mazar-i Sharif, in Afghanistan, is competing with Najaf to keep the grave of Ali. The place of female characters in Shi'i sacred history is notable, and the women of *ahl al-bayt* are also objects of supplication.

The major event in the Shi'i ritual cycle is Ashura, the tenth day of Muharram, the first month in the Islamic calendar. On this day, some of the emblematic rituals in remembrance of the battle of Karbala are carried out and the basic narratives of Shi'i doctrine are manifested in public performance and enactment. Ashura is a day of voluntary fasting among Sunni Muslims, though the mourning and commemoration is also part of Sufi traditions in previously Ottoman regions. For Shi'i Muslims the first ten days of Muharram provide an opportunity to contemplate one's own shortcomings, repent and start anew in preparation of the culmination during Ashura.

The stories of martyrdom and injustice have been kept alive in Shi'i communities throughout history by means of artistic representations, commemorative rituals, the recitation of elegies during Muharram retelling the story of Karbala and pictures of the fate of *ahl al-bayt*.

Muharram processions include public re-enactments of the Karbala in dramatic form (*taziyeh*). These 'passion plays' are unique in the Muslim world; recitations of the martyr narrative in rhythmic verses are accompanied by drums and flutes, while the men beat their breasts with their hands or perform self-flagellation with chains. The representation of the Karbala drama reaches its aesthetic highpoint during the Ashura processions that include standard-bearers and carriages with the key scenes of the battle narrative staged with miniature replicas of Husayn's grave. The professional or semi-professional actors/reciters are all men, even in the representation of the women's parts of the story. The colour scheme of the performance is highly symbolic: green is the colour of Islam and the heroes of Karbala; white is used to indicate the innocence of martyrdom, while red is for the villains.

This event, displaying a combination of drama and public ritual performance with its strong emotions, loud recitations and blood-stained men, is often used to illustrate Shi'i Islam, frequently in more or less explicit contrast to the allegedly more sober Sunni Islam. Similar celebrations are also held in private and semi-public premises (of more or less permanent character), and named after who is at the centre of the commemoration: for example, the place of worship could be called *husayniyyeh* (Husayn), *fatemiyyeh* (Fatima) or *zaynabiyyeh* (Zaynab). Parts of larger homes may be redecorated for these events. When not in public, these rituals constitute important religious arenas for women, who act as performers/reciters, guests and co-performers.

It is not only in the commemoration of historical events that divergences between Sunni and Shi'i are emphasized. Some *salat* (in Persian and Turkish *namaz*) customs are significantly different in Shi'i communities. Among Shi'is it is common to concentrate the five daily prayers to three times a day and to place a piece of clay from Karbala between the forehead and the prayer mat to connect the praying person with the location of the narratives of martyrdom. These tablets (*turbah* or *mohr* in Persian) usually have short texts and symbols pressed into them. It is said to have been the custom of Husayn's son, the fourth imam, to keep soil from the place of his father's martyrdom with him. It is not mandatory for a Shi'i Muslim to use a *turbah*, but it is recommended and is of emotional importance to people who are unable to visit Karbala, so that they have physical contact with the epicentre of the Shi'i world.

Fig. 13   *Turbah*, a clay tablet that connects the Shi'i fellowship over time and space. *(Courtesy of the David Collection, Copenhagen; photo: Pernille Klemp)*

Shi'ism in contemporary Iran

Ever since the Safavid era, Persian culture has been interwoven with Shi'i characteristics. Although symbols from the pre-Islamic Zoroastrian religion (still practised by a minority in Iran today and by the Pars communities in Bombay) have previously been used to point to an ancient civilization and to provide elements of a national narrative, the Shi'i identity has nevertheless been crucial in how differences between Persian and Arabic culture have been articulated.

The political rhetoric before and after the Islamic Revolution in Iran made use of the Karbala matrix that provided easily communicated slogans: the ruling shah was seen as the usurper Yazid, and the supporters of the Revolution were ready to face martyrdom for the just cause. What international media reported as demonstrations in 1978/ 79 turned out to be enacted religious drama in the streets for some of the participants. Various groups, driven by sometimes conflicting interests, brought about the Iranian Revolution. There was not only a divide between secular and Islamic groups, but also substantial differences among the religious activists about how to relate to the emerging theocratic leadership in relation to individual freedoms.

The way Shi'ism has been formulated in Iran over the last 35 years has formed the image of Shi'i Islam outside the country. One word more than any other is connected with the rule of the Islamic Republic: *ayatollah*. It is a title indicating authority to communicate the will of Allah above any decisions by earthly powers. This concept of supremacy has complicated the governance of administrative and social institutions, as has been evident since the Revolution.

An *ayatollah* is regarded as a righteous leader who rules in the absence of the hidden imam (*velayat-e faqih*) and is understood as the guardian of the clerical authorities. From this point of departure, opinions expressed by ordinary people can never be anything but fortuities in relation to *tawhid*, the sovereignty of Allah communicated through his deputy. Ayatollah Khomeini was successful in his strategy of combining theological speculation with modern politics; even before he came to power in Tehran, he was able to mobilize supporters for the uprising from his exile. The Islamic Republic is therefore waiting for the return of the *mahdi* and eschatological themes are to be noted in the political discourse of the theocratic rulers of the country. Some of Khomeini's followers regarded (and still regard) him as the returning *mahdi* or a sign that the return is imminent.

Shi'i Islamists

The media image of Shi'i Muslims as being more prone to fanaticism than other Muslims has its basis in the Iranian Revolution, and the Iranian position as an ideological nexus and provider of support to extreme groups is undeniable. Shi'i radicalism shares general features with Islamism, the political vision of sharia norms as the absolute foundation for society. No matter how esoteric the theological references made by the rulers in Tehran may seem, Iran has a direct influence on groups and movements far beyond its national borders: on Hizbullah in the Israel–Palestine conflict, on groups and militias in Iraq and Syria, on groups in Central Asia and on the situation in Afghanistan.

The present situation in Iraq, with its impact on both regional and global politics, has brought attention to the population balance between Shi'i and Sunni Muslims in the country and the tense situation between the groups. During the rule of Saddam Hussein, the

Ruhollah Khomeini (d. 1989) – referred to in international media by his clerical title Ayatollah Khomeini and also known to his followers as imam Khomeini – was the religious and political leader of the Islamic Revolution in Iran 1979. He became the symbol of the definitive change from popular uprising to theocratic rule. Born in Iran, Khomeini went into political exile in 1964, first in Turkey and then for many years in Iraq, where he served as a cleric and teacher in Najaf. He had by then already received the title Grand Ayatollah and thereby took his place among the highest leaders of the Twelver Shi'is; he was an early critic of shah Mohammad Reza Pahlavi (d. 1980) and combined anti-Westernism with ideals of 'the perfect man' (actually a Sufi concept) and the apocalyptic themes in Shi'i beliefs in the returning *mahdi*. Khomeini was a charismatic leader and some followers saw the returning *mahdi* in him. When Khomeini was called imam, it had connotations to Shi'is of infallibility and the correct interpretation of the will of Allah. After the establishment of the Islamic Republic, the Khomeini regime soon sullied or completely broke relations with Western states and institutions, especially after the long occupation of the American embassy in Tehran and the *fatwa* against the British novelist Salman Rushdie – a situation that has so far not been resolved. Iran's support of militant groups (see Chapter IX) and its development of nuclear devices are today major obstacles in the country's foreign relations.

The rhetoric during the Revolution and the later long war with Iraq made use of the Muharram paradigm in inscribing enemies, injustices and revolt in a historical narrative in order to mobilize crowds and soldiers. Khomeini's mausoleum in southern Tehran has become a site of veneration in a mode that mirrors traditional Shi'i pilgrimage.

Shi'is of Iraq constituted a suppressed majority, as the dictator favoured Sunni groups, to which he himself belonged. Regional conflicts inscribed in the Shi'i–Sunni divide linger on today in the civil and paramilitary violence.

More recently, Islamist Shi'i leaders have exerted control over Shi'is in Afghanistan and Pakistan through their visions of the implementation of sharia and religious governance. Among the most influential of these was Muhammad Sadeq al-Sadr (d. 1999), killed by the Saddam Hussein regime and regarded as a martyr by his supporters. Sadr's ideas undoubtedly had an impact on the Iranian constitution drafted after the Revolution and the transformation of the administration of the country. According to him, the Qur'an and the *sunna* (the latter including the twelve infallible imams) cannot be questioned by humans and are to be obeyed by believers and non-believers alike – a position unaffected by any arguments or claims. The Sadr family continues its influence over Shi'is in Iran and Iraq. His son, Muqtada al-Sadr (b. 1973), is currently the leader of the Mahdi militia, which is especially strong in the suburb of Baghdad known as Sadr city, inhabited by 2 million Shi'i Muslims. This settlement was constructed in 1959 as 'Revolution City' and a monument over Arab Nationalism, only to be converted a few decades later to 'Saddam City'. The area has remained poor and has been the scene of escalating sectarian violence and with hideouts for militant groups.

Martyrdom and memory in Shi'i Islam

In her study *An Enchanted Modern* (2006), Lara Deeb analyses public Shi'i piety in Lebanon after the civil war of 1975–1990, when the political conflicts were partly structured along the Sunni–Shi'i divide. Deeb shows how communication through and interpretation of Shi'i narratives, pious practices and theological concepts shifted with context and speaker. No matter how unpretentious the stories and rituals may seem from a structural point of view, they have the potential to guide in complicated situations. In their rich variety, the references to religion, legacy and good deeds turn out to be most useful tools in defining how a modern pious life can be lived. Instead of being understood as deficiency, Shi'i tradition is turned into the main argument for women's public appearance as performers of good deeds and teaching.

The difference between Shi'i and Sunni Islam is mainly depicted by the media in terms of the political conflicts in Iraq, Lebanon, Syria, Pakistan and Afghanistan or with reference to transnational groups such as Hizbullah and Hamas. As this chapter has indicated, the division has throughout history been a tool to pronounce national and ethnic particularities or represent minority positions, and continues to do so today.

From a theological point of view, the division grew out of a conflict over the legitimate leadership of the *umma*, but this discord was not formalized in doctrinal terms until later centuries. In Shi'i thought, the twelve (or seven) imams continue the infallible sovereignty through divine guidance. Interrelated by family and thereby transmitting the prophet's extraordinary insights, the imams and the contemporary mullas who act as keepers of their legacy constitute the fundament of Shi'i theology and history writing.

The rituals are perhaps the most significant Shi'i feature – especially the veneration of *ahl al-bayt* and the imams, who are thought to be able to respond to supplications. The celebrations during the month of Muharram, and especially on the tenth day, Ashura, are organized in commemoration of the martyr-death of the grandson of Muhammad, Husayn, his family and his loyal followers and are manifested in processions through the streets.

Two of the most important Shi'i pilgrimage sites, Karbala and Najaf, are situated in present-day Iraq and have been the targets of continuous bombings and suicide attacks. This violence is a result of the often tense relationship between Sunni and Shi'i Muslims throughout history.

Further reading

Aghaie, Kamran Scott, *The Martyrs of Karbala: Shi'i Symbols and Rituals in Modern Iran* (Seattle, WA: University of Washington Press, 2004).

Chelkowski, Peter and Hamid Dabashi, *Staging a Revolution* (New York: New York University Press, 1999).

Deeb, Lara, *An Enchanted Modern: Gender and Public Piety in Shi'i Lebanon* (Princeton, NJ: Princeton University Press, 2006).

Flaskerud, Ingvild, *Visualizing Belief and Piety in Iranian Shiism* (New York: Continuum, 2012).

Friedl, Erika, *Women of Deh Koh: Lives in an Iranian Village* (Washington, DC: Smithsonian Institution Press, 1989).

Halm, Heinz, *Shiism*, 2nd edn (New York: Columbia University Press, 2004).

Khosronejad, Pedram, *Saints and their Pilgrims in Iran and Neighbouring Countries* (Wantage: Sean Kingston Publishing, 2012).

Mottahedeh, Roy, *The Mantle of the Prophet: Learning and Power in Modern Iran* (London: Chatto, 1986).

Ridgeon, Lloyd, *Shi'i Islam and Identity: Religion, Politics and Change in the Global Community* (London: I.B.Tauris, 2012).

Torab, Azam, *Performing Islam: Gender and Ritual in Iran* (Leiden: Brill, 2007).

Chapter VIII

Muslim Ethics: Ideals, Responsibilities and the Challenges of Modern Life

There is no set of rules in the Qur'an that corresponds to the Ten Commandments of the Old Testament, although the tablets given to Moses are referred to in the normative literature of Islam. The Qur'an itself expresses very few systematic regulations. The principles of what is judged to be Islamic in everyday life are established by local tradition and the large corpus of legal interpretations that constitute sharia, as discussed in Chapter 4. The framework for the implementation of sharia is the theological standpoints argued from statements in the Qur'an and the *hadith* literature. Islamic ethics in general have a universal character, as its fundamental concept is Allah's unity (*tawhid*), and its basic norms are regarded as eternal and therefore unalterable. Furthermore, Islamic ethics does not make any distinction between religious and civil regulations. These methods of interpretation developed in the legal schools affect the understanding of how practical ethical concepts are to be considered in a variety of situations when sharia is put into practice. The regional differences are therefore considerable.

The scope of this chapter is to map some of the rules and standards governed by Islamic ethics, such as ways of organizing life, the ideals of how life should be conducted and how legitimate interaction between people is to be carried out. The concept of ethics in general refers to a more or less coherent system of right and wrong, and ethical matters in the Muslim world have been touched upon in previous chapters: *sunna, muamalat,* the consequences of *tawhid, ibadat* and the prescribed modes of ritual obligations. But it should not be forgotten that the moral choices of today are equally affected by modern living conditions, which influence lifestyles and social patterns.

Stances taken on ethical matters have been major issues of conflict in the history of Islamic theology, and ethics as a philosophical science (*ilm al-akhlaq*) has a large literature, whose aim is to systematize regulations and assess demands in relation to each other. Yet *akhlaq* also connotes efforts to reach what is required by sharia. Islamic theological anthropology regards humans as capable of comprehending what is good, but pride and greed make individuals fail nevertheless. There is no equivalent to the Christian concept of original sin in Islamic theology. The human predicament is to have been granted the capability to intellectually grasp the difference between good and evil while still being morally imperfect. From a philosophical point of view, the Mutazilites in the eighth century took a position emphasizing objective and absolute ethics, whereas the opposing philosophers and theologians argued for no limitations to Allah's freedom to constitute the world according to his intentions. The Mutazilites thereby underlined the consequences of individual choice: humans are committers of evil deeds, despite the conception of Allah as the origin of everything, and they therefore have to face the consequences of the freedom of the human will. There is in general a trust in knowledge and a strong emphasis on individual responsibility to achieve what is demanded.

Islamic ethics and Greek philosophy

Abu Nasr al-Farabi (ca. 870–950), held in high esteem as one of the major Islamic philosophers, developed Muslim ethics and applied Greek philosophy to Islamic issues. He discussed matters beyond the religious and claimed trust in logic and reason as the capstone for the governance of an ideal state founded on moral principles. Greek philosophy also influenced his views on ethics, in which the goodness of Allah pervades the human soul and acts as a resource in the pursuit of personal and societal fulfilment.

Two concepts have always been central to the ethical debate. *Adab* refers to correct manners and etiquette, but also to the educational background to know and understand the imperatives of religion, while *akhlaq* connotes character or a person's moral disposition. They point to the poles of opinion on how moral judgements should be made: with reference to an individual's innate character or with an emphasis on the capacity to repent, improve and develop as a human being.

The central concepts in Islamic ethics are:

good deeds (*al-khayrat*)
virtue or the endeavour to perform at one's best (*ihsan*)
justice (*adl*) – fairness in a broad sense
taqwa – the respect for Allah that motivates the practice and
implementation of the central concepts of belief (*iman*)

Sin (*dhanb*) is defined in traditional *fiqh* as a shortcoming or a wilful
transgression of the rules provided by Allah (sharia). Sins are acts that
contravene the fundamental principles of Islam: the belief in Allah
(*iman*) or the acceptance of his unity (*tawhid*). Therefore, sins like
apostasy (*ridda*), acceptance of any transcendental being beside Allah
(*shirk*, i.e. polytheism) and infidelity (*kufr*), which indicates pride or
arrogance (*kibr*), are considered severe offences. Thus, sins are defined
as attitudes as well as actions that either diminish the superiority of
Allah or reflect immoral attitudes in relation to other humans. The
concept of temptation (*fitna*), with its connotations corruption and
disorder, is an umbrella term for conceptions and deeds that represent
the wrong path and constitute the opposite of the harmony in Allah's
creation: immorality, contamination and wickedness. Temptation is
the antithesis of the harmonious religion of the natural order (*din
al-fitra*).

The image of Allah in the scriptures and in Islamic piety is far from
always judgemental. For those who have taken the wrong turn there is
always the possibility of repentance (*tawba*), and being forgiving is one
of Allah's major qualities in Qur'anic discourse and traditional
preaching. The call for repentance and forgiveness by Allah are
intertwined with promises of mercy (*rahma*), irrespective of the
shortcomings of mankind. One of the central aspects of Allah, as
repeated daily in rituals by the *basmala* 'In the Name of Allah, the Most
Graceful and the Most Merciful', is that his forgiveness is greater than
any sin. The conventional interpretation of this phrase is that any sin
committed by a human can be forgiven by Allah, except *kufr*, which
connotes not only rejection of the truth but also ungratefulness. The
Qur'an states:

> If you avoid the heinous sins that are forbidden you, We will
> acquit you of your evil deeds, and admit you by the gate of
> honour. (4:35)

The *hadith* literature similarly reports:

> Al-Agharr al-Muzani, who was one amongst the Companions
> (of the Holy Prophet) reported that Allah's Messenger (may
> peace be upon him) said: 'There is (at times) some sort of shade
> upon my heart, and I seek forgiveness from Allah a hundred
> times a day'. (Sahih Muslim 12:35)

Believers are supposed to keep their covenant (*ahd*) with Allah, which
is what links them to the norms of sharia with the same intention
(*niyya*) as in ritual conduct. The understanding of evil deeds and moral
corruption is linked to contemplation of the relation between
predestination or destiny and the free will of humans. The normative
literature and traditional practice are not univocal on this issue. There
are two major paths of reasoning that run in parallel through Muslim
history. One of them emphasizes the free human will as a vital
component in the tropes of conversion and repentance as the path to
Allah with an emphasis on individual choice, as when the Qur'an
states: 'those who believe, and do righteous deeds; they shall have a
wage unfailing' (95:6). The other line of reasoning emphasizes fate and
the limitations of free will, but nevertheless puts emphasis on human
responsibility.

The ethics of any religion or ideology is always based on an
anthropology that explicitly or implicitly stipulates the conditions for
human nature. Islamic anthropology expresses the ideals for the
relationship between Allah and humans as well as that between
humanity and nature. Certain parts of the human body and mind are
identified as symbolic sites where ethic reflection takes place. These
are corporal symbols for spiritual cultivation and improvement. The
various aspects of the individual 'mind' are known as heart (*qalb*), soul
(*nafs*) and spirit (*ruh*), and all play a vital part in Muslim, and especially
Sufi, anthropology. To battle selfishness and open the heart to Allah is
known as the greater *jihad*, literally 'effort' or 'endeavour', whereas the
lesser *jihad* is to take arms against the enemies of Islam.

In contrast to the notion of free will is the thought/idea of the
creation as complete, with a full plan for every individual. Allah is
the origin of everything, and the concept of *tawhid* does not give
space to more than one originator. This idea opens up the classical
problem of the origin of evil. Belief in fate (*taqdir*, literally 'to
measure') is one of the six *aqaid* discussed in Chapter 1, belief in

divine predestination. Providence is, according to a traditional interpretation of a statement in the Qur'an, written down. *Sura* 83:9 speaks of 'a book inscribed', where there is a list of the lost souls. During Laylat al-Qadr ('the Night of Power', the name it is given in the Qur'an (97:1), on the twenty-seventh of Ramadan the sending down of the Qur'an is commemorated. Ceremonies and vigils take place all night with Qur'an recitations and prayers to make the coming year a good one. Both the beliefs in destiny and rituals to seek the future are deeply embedded in local culture and during the celebrations the line between well-wishing and active divination is sometimes hard to draw.

The normative sources of Islamic ethics

The emphasis in the Qur'an and other normative sources on the fact that Islam is a matter of embracing the correct belief and leaving heresies behind has ethical consequences. There is a central obligation on believers to keep to what is lawful (*halal*) or at least accepted (*maruf*) and fulfil the mandatory (*fard*). In practice the concerns of Islamic ethics are, to a great extent, built on the concepts and classifications of sharia. The Qur'an states in its second *sura* that the fulfilment of religion is more than exterior behaviour and that belief in the broad sense of the concept is a contract (or covenant) between Allah and the individual that must have consequences:

> It is not piety, that you turn your faces to the East and to the West.
> True piety is this:
> to believe in God, and the Last Day,
> the angels, the Book, and the Prophets,
> to give of one's substance, however cherished, to kinsmen and orphans,
> the needy, the traveller, beggars, and to ransom the slave,
> to perform the prayer, to pay the alms.
> And they who fulfil their covenant
> when they have engaged in a covenant,
> and endure with fortitude misfortune, hardship and peril,
> these are they who are true in their faith, these are the truly god-fearing. (Qur'an 2:177)

Several of the fundamentals of the Islamic religion are mentioned in this quotation. Here the Qur'an emphasizes individual responsibility for correct belief and encourages followers to practice in accordance:

> So do thou fight in the way of God; thou art charged only with thyself.
> And urge on the believers; haply God will restrain the unbelievers' might; God is stronger in might, more terrible in punishing. (4:84)

The Qur'an is quite straightforward when it comes to the consequences of misdeeds, and it provides vivid imagery of the judgements and punishments that will be executed by Allah. It should be noted that moral responsibility in the Qur'an is not based on a collectivity such as a family or ethnic group, but on the individual in terms of confession, commitment and practice.

> As for the orphan, do not oppress him,
> and as for the beggar, scold him not;
> and as for thy Lord's blessing, declare it. (93:9–11)

Certain groups are identified as being in special need of care and protection and the treatment of them stands out in normative and legal texts as a test of righteousness and justice. It is repeatedly stated that slaves should be treated well and efforts made to free them. To release a slave can also be an act of penance. Slavery was a common practice in Muhammad's day and remained so in large parts of the Muslim world until modern times. Some debaters link contemporary inhuman working conditions with the urge to treat slaves well and find arguments for improved workers' rights. Orphans are also cited, along with widows, as worthy of special protection in their vulnerable position (93:6). These statements reflect an ancient society and its ways of solving social problems, but they are also the images that have guided Islamic ethics in history and that are adapted in contemporary times to argue in favour of social engagement.

References to the *hadith* literature, the descriptions of Medina, the historical utopia of the good society and the implementation of this vision in the contemporary world have been put forward as the ideal for the *umma* of how a fair community is organized and how its hierarchical relations are legitimized. The presence of other religions and their followers is also a prevalent theme, with topicality for the modern world with its frequent encounters with other beliefs and other forms of worship, morals and rules.

The *hadith* literature moulds the concept of correct behaviour (*adab*) into narrative form and a broad range of instructive literature in many genres gives advice on how to cultivate *adab* and live a virtuous life. Didactic texts dealing with *adab* include not only stated rules or moralities, but also pious narratives, poetry and songs to exemplify and to provide moralities to be remembered. Guidance in Islamic ethics has a long history that crosses several genres of various length and sophistication, but they all build on the principle of building the argument around the transmission of tradition to reach answers to issues of immediate concern.

Islamic ethics as a theological and philosophical concept is closely connected to the principles of sharia and *fiqh*, as well as to conventions (*urf*) and local rules of good behaviour.

Although a comparative perspective shows up variations in practice, there are central demands that are stipulated in the normative texts, and most theological tradition expresses discourses on ethical matters as valid irrespective of time and place, and without exceptions for rich or poor. The absoluteness in traditional arguments is challenged today by interpretations that historicize the Medina model as well as contesting local traditionalism and instead putting moral issues in changing living conditions into focus. This endeavour to contextualize also applies to discussions about individual human rights in relation to unconditional religious claims, as will be discussed below. The idea that Muhammad's *sunna* constituted the norms for behaviour, especially as represented in the *hadith* literature, has received new attention in modern times in discussions about what constitutes a good, just and Islamic social order. The historical utopia as the matrix for an ideal society will be further discussed in Chapter 9. The concept of *fitra* – connoting not only the primordial harmony between Allah and his creation, but also the potential and predisposition of humans to return to this state – is central in Islamic ethics as it relates to *tawhid*.

In all three Abrahamic religions, Adam has a special status in the account of the creation as the first human and the ancestor of mankind. According to the Qur'an (2:30), humans were created as Allah's custodians or 'keepers' (sing. *khalifa*) on earth and therefore had an important responsibility: to fulfil Allah's intentions. Consequently, they were created with the capacity to absorb knowledge and make ethical judgements. The narrative about Adam's fall is also the story of mankind's complex relationship to an all-knowing and infallible God. This is the case in the Islamic representation of the Adamic theme, but with no original blame on Adam's wife, Hawwa, as she is not a distinct character in the story until later traditions. Adam is accorded full knowledge during the process of creation, as described in the Qur'an (2:30–38).

Adam and the Fall of Man

The Qur'an tells the story of the fall of Adam at several points. The narrative comes fairly close to the version in Genesis. A particular Islamic trait, however, is the emphasis on the breaking of the contract between Allah and Adam, which has served in Islamic thinking as a master image for the gap between the human world and Allah that only religion can provide the tools to bridge.

> And We made covenant with Adam before,
> but he forgot, and We found in him no constancy. (20:115)

As in the Jewish and Christian traditions, the fall defines the relationship between God and humans.

The narrative of the fall and expulsion of Adam, who is under the influence of Shaytan, illustrates the crack in the harmony of the creation and the distortion of its original intention. Adam's fall is a difficult theological theme, as the story is symbolic of the relationship between Allah and humans. The prophets of Islam, of whom Adam is one, are considered to be without sin. This scene requires a third party with other intentions than Allah that can explain how evil came into the world. Iblis, the devil, who also appears in the Qur'an and in many narratives under the name Shaytan, is a fallen angel and has at least three aspects. Iblis/Shaytan is a figure of cosmological dimensions, a metaphysical force acting as Allah's enemy (although not inscribed in a theological system with dualistic tendencies, as is the case in some Christian philosophy), and a concrete actor in folk belief, where, with the help of djinns, he takes control of people's lives. The 'stoning of Satan' is a highly emotional part of the *hajj*. And Iblis's pride made him refuse to fall down in front of Adam, which is traditionally interpreted as an indication of the devilish origin of any rejection of the prophets' message. Satan is the reason why unacceptable old religious customs, such as divination with arrows connected to the worship of the pre-Islamic deities, still linger. The Qur'an states:

> O believers, wine and arrow-shuffling [divination]
> idols and divining-arrows are an abomination,
> and some of Satan's work. (5:90)

It thus identifies a specific force behind all evil and immoral deeds.

The limits not to be transgressed

Several *suras* summarize the central ethical demands, although no single list of commands or systematic outline of requirements is presented in the Qur'an. The many vices indicated in the Qur'an are hindrances to correct knowledge, as humans forget, are lazy and are easily tempted. When the Qur'an asks humans to remember Allah (*dhikr*), it is not necessarily an encouragement to perform a repetitive, Sufi-style prayer, but a statement on the human predicament of having being expelled from the primordial Garden. The Qur'an is not a systematic collection of rules and demands. The comparative scarcity of direct prescriptions of punishment in the Qur'an that relate to human misdeeds underlines the fact that the text is less legalistic than is generally assumed by non-Muslims.

The will of Allah is represented by both imagery underlining that humans can better themselves under the supremacy of Allah, as well as suggestions that the events in the life of a person are part of a greater plan that aims for the better good. At the same time, the Qur'an states several times that every human has a destiny, which in Islamic ethics is balanced against encouragement to endeavour and attempts to change wrong to right. Speculation over individual destinies is a sensitive issue, as it touches on the legitimacy of seeking to affect the future – frequent in many Muslim environments and embedded in local ritual life, but strongly condemned by conservative imams and theologians. The quotation above states clearly that divination rituals are forbidden.

For some categories of crime, however, definitions and penalties are stipulated in the Qur'an. These are the limits (*hudud*) that cannot be transgressed without the punishment as deliniated. Among them are theft, adultery, false accusations of adultery, wine consumption and gambling.

The limits (hudud) *as stipulated in the Qur'an*

A few severe crimes are defined explicitly in the Qur'an as transgressions of 'the limits' (*hudud*, sing. *had*, meaning 'rule') which are sometimes used to name the transgressions. The stipulated punishments are correspondingly harsh. The following quotation from *sura* 24 has often dominated the general picture of Islamic ethics:

> The fornicatress and the fornicator –
> scourge each one of them a hundred stripes,
> and in the matter of God's religion
> let no tenderness for them seize you
> if you believe in God and the Last Day;
> and let a party of the believers witness their chastisement. (24:2)

The *sura* continues:

> And those who cast it [accusations] up on women in
> wedlock, and then bring not four witnesses,
> scourge them with eighty stripes, and do not
> accept any testimony of theirs ever. (24:4)

Theft is also among the *hudud*:

> And the thief, male or female: cut off the hands of both,
> as a recompense for what they have earned,
> and a punishment exemplary [warning example] from God'.
> (5:38).

Today, these punishments are still partially implemented in Iran, Pakistan, Saudi Arabia, Sudan, Yemen and northern parts of Nigeria, while a majority of Muslims do not approve of a literal reading of these verses.

Dietary laws

A specific strand of Muslim ethics is the dietary laws that regulate what can be eaten and how food should be prepared. The prohibition against alcohol is generally known to non-Muslims, as is the apparent similarities with Jewish law against the consumption of pork. In religiously motivated dietary laws more than nutrition is at stake. As will be shown in this chapter the Islamic dietary laws, in many respects, summarize the character of the relationship between humans and Allah and they reflect an Islamic anthropology in theological discourse. Furthermore, they are also good examples of how modern living conditions not only challenge traditional life patterns, but also bring about solutions that make it possible to consent to Islamic demands in a contemporary context. When it comes to the consumption of food, the words of the Qur'an are certainly not simply negative and prohibiting. The Qur'an also encourages the enjoyment of food as a gift from Allah: 'Eat of what God has provided you lawful and good; and fear God, in whom you are believers' (5:90).

The central concept is what is deemed permissible or lawful (*halal*). It is a legal category used in contrast to what is considered to be if not directly forbidden (*haram*), at least discouraged (*makruh*) – on the scale of legal qualities as discussed in Chapter 4. The term *halal* is usually associated with food, but it can be generally applied to conduct, apparel, clothing and spaces in terms of which are regarded as being pure and proper. It also ultimately forms the basis of trust in distribution systems and local shopkeepers. Throughout history, *halal* has had political and theological implications, as the locus of the authority for determining what is *halal* has been disputed.

The pig is the only animal specifically mentioned in the Qur'an as prohibited, though tradition declares beasts of prey, dogs, monkeys and donkeys also to be unclean and therefore *haram*. The prohibition against pork consumption has become emblematic of *halal* and is not only an issue of what meat to eat. Commonly offered and generally available products can contain porcine residues, including gelatine in sweets and puddings, capsules of medicine and certain emulsifiers, flavourings and animal fats in processed food. These residues are invisible and hard to acquire correct information about and consequently dominate Muslim advice sites on the internet. As in Judaism, dishes made from animals or the blood of animals that have died naturally are prohibited by the Qur'an:

> Forbidden to you are
> carrion, blood, the flesh of swine,
> what has been hallowed to other than God [animals sacrificed to pagan goods],
> the beast strangled, the beast beaten down,
> the beast fallen to death, the beast gored,
> and that devoured by beasts of prey –

excepting that you have sacrificed duly –
as also items sacrificed to idols,
and partition by diving arrows [fortune seeking];
that is ungodliness. (5:3)

In the examples given improper purposes can also contaminate
foodstuff and this underlines the fact that *halal* is both an issue of the
innate qualities in a substance, but to an equal extent how it is treated.

A significant part of the dietary regulations relates to the Islamic
practices for the slaughter (*dhabihah* or *zabiha*) of permissible animals,
that is, the sometimes controversial methods of butchering according
to *halal* regulations. These acts do not require a ritual specialist,
although a professional butcher is the standard in Muslim societies.
Any adult Muslim can perform *halal* slaughter and it should start with
the pronouncement of the *basmala*. Thereafter, the jugular vein of the
animal is slit, but the head should not be severed. The most critical part
of the procedure is that the blood should be drained from the animal's
body as quickly and completely as possible, since any consumption of
blood is strictly forbidden. Furthermore, *dhabihah* is only valid if the
slaughter is performed strictly separately from any processing of pork
meat by non-Muslims, and ideally sold from special counters if not for
sale in a specialist *halal* shop. The appropriate intention and blessing
are as important as the correct procedure.

Another contemporary dilemma in relation to ritual slaughter that
has caught a great deal of media attention is that of animal rights versus
religious freedom. The criticism of Muslim butchering methods as
cruel and prolonged is sometimes turned into a counter-argument,
where *halal* slaughter is emphasized as respectful of the animal,
guaranteeing a quick death under absolute control, and small-scale
religious slaughter is sometimes advocated in favour of industrial meat
production. Again, the religious argument works in parallel with the
organic perspective.

Wine (*khamr*) is also explicitly forbidden in the Qur'an, and the
prohibition is commonly extended to any substance that causes
intoxication, such as spirits and drugs: 'O believers, wine and arrow-
shuffling [a reference to divination practices], idols and divining
arrows are an abomination, some of Satan's work; so avoid [them];
haply so you will prosper' (5:90). According to this quotation, wine-
drinking is as severe a sin as falling away from Islam into polytheistic

beliefs and illegitimate rituals. The wine prohibition has throughout history been an identity marker in relation to Judaism and Christianity, as wine is a ritually significant beverage in both those religions. Early Islamic tradition is also clear on its rejection of the intoxicating beverages (*nabidh*) that were produced at the time in Arabia.

Muslim dietary laws are fairly straightforward and clear, and are generally strictly adhered to in Muslim communities (though with varying cultural attitudes to intoxicative practices). However, following the *halal* regulations in the contemporary world means being an observant customer and a conscientious parent when selecting groceries. Socializing in private or business life can become an ethical dilemma, and choices have to be made: how to be loyal to tradition and at the same time wish to blend Muslim lifestyle with other ways of living and still be able to keep to the Islamic essentials. Some Muslims refuse to patronize restaurants that serve forbidden food or alcohol, or sit at a table where such things are served, while other Muslims emphasize the importance of cross-cultural contacts and that each individual takes responsibility for how he or she behaves in accordance with his or her tradition. There is no tradition of vegetarianism as a religious choice in Islam, but to eat only non-animal food, and thereby avoid any meat or blood, can be a contemporary solution that can also be regarded as a positive choice or a healthy alternative rather than simply observance of a prohibition. To many young Muslims, vegetarianism is the optimal way of keeping *halal*; it is consumer-conscious and does not require a lot of explanation.

In principle, anything people eat, touch, inhale or come close to can be declared *halal* or *haram*. Therefore many contemporary *halal* discussions focus on substances that come into contact with the body, such as toothpaste, lotions and perfumes (the latter two often contain alcohol). There are large economic interests in the multinational food and health industry, and businesses have to take diverging consumer patterns into consideration; *halal* production is a large global business. Today, companies that can guarantee *halal* sweets and sodas as well as other kinds of fast food and mass consumer foodstuffs have the potential to reach new users, and *halal* has become a brand in itself. Global consumption is also showing a trend towards what is 'healthy'. Beside the religious dimension of purity, *halal* has a strong image among Muslims of being proper and sound. Choosing *halal* is not necessarily a question of personal piety, but may very well be a Muslim way of avoiding the food scandals that have repeatedly occurred from the point of view that *halal* means controlled production.

It is easy to reproduce an image of the Qur'an as a text that promotes prohibitions and fasting, but there are also stanzas praising Allah as the provider and where food is identified among the good things in life:

> It is He who produces gardens
> trellised, and untrellised,
> palm-trees, and crops diverse in produce,
> olives, pomegranates, like each to each, and each unlike to each.
> Eat of their fruits when they fructify, and pay the due thereof on
> the day of its harvest; and be not prodigal; God loves not the
> prodigal. And of the cattle, for burthen and for slaughter, eat of
> what God has provided you; and follow not the steps of Satan; he
> is manifest foe to you. (6:141–142)

In this passage cattle are presented, along with fruit and vegetables, as a gift from Allah. The slaughtering of animals and the consumption of meat – especially as part of the festival Id al-Adha and the pilgrimage to Mecca (*hajj*) – also have an iconic status that does not necessarily correspond to everyday eating habits. Generosity during these celebrations is brought forward in pious discourse and the slaughtering is regarded as void if part of the meat is not given to charity. Before too much emphasis is put on issues dealing with meat and slaughter, however, it is essential to underline that a majority of the world's 1.5 billion Muslims live in poor circumstances where meat is a rare luxury – hence the perception of meat as something to be consumed at special events and festivals. Certain food has the status of festival food, as seen in the quotation above; dates and honey are also thought to represent authenticity as they are mentioned in the Qur'an: 'Shake also to thee the palm-trunk, and there shall come tumbling upon thee dates fresh and ripe. Eat therefore, and drink, and be comforted' (19:25–26).

Abstaining from food has religious connotations. Fasting – abstaining from food and drink, sexual activities and smoking, from dawn till dusk – is a topic closely related to the dietary laws. The fast during the month of Ramadan (see Chapter 5) is mandatory, but there are also rich traditions of voluntary fasting, with regional variations and a multitude of 'causes'. These abstentions are traditionally practised on Mondays and Thursdays, and fasting is not desirable on Fridays or religious festivals, in preparation for a holiday or before a pilgrimage.

The rules of *halal* have been followed by Muslim communities since the early days of Islam. Norms of this kind are always both a form of ethical guidance and an identity marker. Things that are deemed forbidden and impure in themselves, such as wine (and other intoxicating substances), dogs, pigs, blood and milk from forbidden animals, also carry an aspect of moral contamination, so that observance becomes a social signal associated with the pure and the proper. In more religiously homogeneous societies with local food production distributed in tight and stable networks, there are fewer opportunities to diverge from the dietary laws, since that social control forms the limits for eating habits and the religious institutions are likely to have a more direct impact on everyday life. Large urban environments with complex multicultural patterns offer various options of food, goods and lifestyles and thereby put *halal* issues to the forefront. Islamic jurisprudence, based on the Qur'an and the *hadith* literature, has formulated strict prohibitions against the consumption of specific foodstuffs.

In differing contexts, such as being in a minority situation or in an ecological environment very dissimilar from the Arab ideals in the normative literature, Muslims have faced different problems when striving to apply the regulations and interpret how to regard substances not mentioned in the normative scriptures. Modern lifestyles and the spread of the diaspora have led to debates on health, cultural colonialism and overconsumption in relation to the *halal* agenda as well as ethnic belonging.

Health, responsible consumption and environmental consciousness have become strong identity markers in contemporary middle-class discourses worldwide. Islamic food regulations are not necessarily only a question of being a practicing Muslim, but *halal* could be a means for ethical and organic consumption. Other contemporary trends in dress codes and *halal* lifestyle might include modes of representing a Muslim identity in everyday practice and not necessarily connected to conventional piety, but opening up for individual ways of expressing stands and opinions.

In order to fulfil *adab*, Muslim ethics requires that both men and women dress decently and follow the exhortations in the Qur'an to

Fig. 14   Muslim women in Oxford Street, London. The style and shape of Muslim women's head coverings has varied over time and space, dependent on environment, social and marital status – and the position women hold in various communities.
(Source: Alfredo Borba [public domain], via Wikimedia Commons)

lower their gaze and guard their modesty. The proper covering of most body parts is therefore to be counted as part of a *halal* lifestyle. Urbanization and growing groups of Muslim middle class people have developed the Islamic fashion industry into a major global market. The *hadith* literature mentions Muhammad's beard and his contempt for ostentation, while the mention of his not letting his robe drag in the dirt has been the point of departure of a recent fashion among more radical Muslim men to wear notably short trousers. But it is the dress code of women that has caught most non-Muslims' attention, in older travel literature as well as in recent political debate.

Few things in the Muslim world have caught the attention of non-Muslims more than the way women been required and/or chosen to cover themselves in various contexts. Veiling has been a major trope of difference in Western popular writing since the eighteenth century and pictures of women in varying costumes have often been used to illustrate distant and exotic places.

The 'veiling issue' has since the beginning of the twentieth century been at the core of secular ideologies and authoritarian modernization projects as well as in various modes of formulating a Muslim mode of modernity. Over the past century, governments in Muslim countries have tried to forbid head covering in order to liberate women as well as demanding mandatory covering for their protection. Men's and women's opportunities to choose clothing is a privilege that requires both economy and social space, and is a quite recent phenomena in the Western hemisphere, too. The Islamic fashion industry has taken off during the last two decades and immediately raises ethical questions among its consumers about modesty, custom and individual choices – as well as fair trade and organic production.

Attitudes towards images and representations of living creatures

The publication of the so-called Muhammad cartoons in a Danish daily paper in 2006 and the conflicts that followed have raised many questions in the public debate on the use or prohibition of imagery in Islamic tradition. Polarized positions are often sketched where absolute rejection stands against appreciation of the variety, richness and complexity of imagery that is to be found in the Muslim world. Among the many current stereotypes of Islam and Muslims, one of the most ingrained is that there has always been a total prohibition against images. This is not to deny that many religious authorities have indeed opposed all kinds of representations of Allah, as well as of living creatures (humans and animals), and in particular the prophet Muhammad irrespective of whether the picture has a religious or profane purpose. It is the bodily form of creatures with souls that throughout history has caused the most offence in theology and jurisdiction, and plastic forms (statues and bas-reliefs) have occasioned greater opposition than two-dimensional images. This crossroads between ethics and aesthetics says a lot about the variety within the Muslim world, but also about the eye of the non-Muslim beholder.

The Qur'an contains no unequivocal or general prohibition against images, but one of the fundamental concepts of Islamic faith is that nothing exists that can be equated or compared to Allah. The central conflict relates to the concept of figuration (*tawsir*); it is Allah only who gives form. It has therefore been claimed that visual representation in itself is an expression of pride, setting up humans in competition with Allah the creator. Theological disagreement in debates over imagery has been whether it is possible to manifest the divine or the created, or if it is in conflict with the axiom, 'God is greater'? The final verses of *sura* 59 read:

> He is God; there is no god but He.
> He is the knower of the Unseen and the Visible;
> He is the All-Merciful, the All-Compassionate.
> He is God; there is no god but He.
> He is the King, the All-Holy, the All-Peaceable,
> the All-Faithful, the All-Preserver,
> the All-Mighty, the All-Compeller,
> the All-Sublime.
> Glory be to God, above that they associate!
> He is God, the Creator, the Maker, the Shaper.
> To Him belong the Names Most Beautiful.
> All that is in the heavens and the earth magnifies Him;
> He is the All-Mighty, the All-Wise. (59:22–24)

The theological issue has therefore been how any human can claim to be creative. A closely connected theme in the Qur'an is the rejection of idolaters and their idols. To worship or honour pictures is from this point of view a rebellion against God, the originator of all things. But, as seen in the quotation above, the canonical text is not at all explicit, whereas interpretive tradition has taken clear positions throughout history and has taken its arguments from the *hadith* literature. The expression 'Angels do not enter a house where there is a dog or a picture' is found in several *hadiths* from various contexts. The same goes for the testimony that Muhammad said that Allah would punish anyone who produces pictures. The prophet's wife, Aisha, states that Muhammad saw her playing with dolls when she was small and said that it was tolerable for little girls to play with dolls, even though the dolls with their plastic character were close to idols (Sahih Bukhari 8:151). Other versions of the narrative relate that Muhammad asked Aisha to tell him about the dolls and laughed in amusement at her stories. Yet another *hadith* refers directly to Aisha, who says that she had covered a cushion with animal motifs in order to please Muhammad. She had the best of intentions with her embroidery, but he was incensed and said that angels do not enter houses where there are dogs or pictures (Sahih Bukhari 4:47). The latter, often repeated, phrase refers to a combination of filth and idolatry that makes the argument a strong one. The attitude to the portrayal of living creatures in these and similar early narratives is clearly negative, but it is not until the later theological and philosophical literature a few centuries later that we find more principled and theoretical discussions on aesthetics and pictorial art. The view of idolatry in Islamic normative literature is much harsher, as discussed in Chapter 2.

The use of visual representation in the Muslim world

In certain interpretative traditions, any depiction of human beings or animals is an improper and blasphemous competition with Allah as sovereign creator. At the same time, Muslim history reveals numerous examples of pictorial art. The various legal traditions that have developed over the centuries have provided various explanations for these, and local traditions have developed different attitudes on how to use imagery, from a strict rejective to a conviction that creativity and beauty are for the greater glory of Allah. The subject has remained loaded, however, and has had consequences for all artistic representation in painting, writing and music – whether sacred or profane.

It is true that Islamic theological literature has been dominated by a negative view of imagery – or at least by a hesitation over representing living creatures. But within two major traditions, images have been used extensively: Sufism and Shi'i Islam.

A significant theological issue throughout the history of Sufism has been the trust in the possibilities of the intellect and imagination to represent fragments of Allah's greatness. These reflections have left their mark on artistic forms such as poetry, music and painted miniatures. The golden age of Sufism produced many masterpieces that tried to grasp and transmit features of God's greatness, and this pictorial and literary tradition has lived on in popular Sufism around the Muslim world. Sufi traditions have always been met with criticism from orthodox theologians. Nonetheless, over the centuries, many Sufis have claimed that such personal testimonies and attempts to reach divine reality through art have both a theological and an existential significance.

Within Shi'i Islam there has long existed a broad, popular use of pictures, with the circulation of depictions of events in Muhammad's and Imam Ali's lives and, not least, pictures of the martyr Husayn and the battle of Karbala. Posters, postcards and decorative objects are sold in the markets and streets of present-day Iran without the governing theocracy's interference. Other pictorial forms are also deeply

Is there a 'Muslim art'?

The frequently used concept 'Muslim art' is to a great extent misleading, especially if used as an umbrella term for arts and crafts in countries where a majority of the population are Muslim. There are two reasons why the concept is problematic. First, the consumers, producers and vendors of these objects may profess a religion other than Islam; numerous urban environments in the Muslim world have been multicultural throughout history. Second, a complex area such as art production cannot be reduced to solely religious terms. The consequence of such a way of reasoning would be that the ethical, social and political motifs become secondary to the analysis of how a specific piece of art was designed, produced, used and appreciated. Nor can art in the Muslim world be discussed exclusively as a question of a univocal ban. There are many examples of aesthetic programmes in how to interpret the human condition in stylized and repetitive forms. Arabesques, transpositions and repetitions of simple motifs are the fundaments of Islamic art, poetry and music.

embedded in popular Shiʻi faith. During the festival of Ashura, a popular drama is acted in public areas, bringing the question of representation very much to the fore. The drama is far more aesthetically and socially complex than the images of black-clad flagellants in disciplined processions normally shown on TV. For centuries, the story of the 72 martyrs has been performed by amateur actors: Husayn's white horse with green decorations, military standards and copies of his mausoleum in papier-mâché are carried in the processions. Informal competitions take place as to who is the finest storyteller, and in private homes song cycles are recited. The whole event is a blend of profound individual religious emotion, public drama and festival entertainment. Entire local populations are engaged in the preparations and the production, and even though it is only men who actually act in the public spaces, the performances are collective events for the whole community. The forms that this annual commemoration of martyrs has assumed are the closest thing to traditional theatre in the Muslim world. The representation of these historical events in public performances has been contested by stricter interpretations of Islam, as well as by political rulers who have always feared the emotional potential of such rituals. The words and images describing the battle of Karbala constitute part of a collective emotional discharge that more than once has had political consequences.

In large areas of the Sunni Muslim world there are popular narratives linked to Muhammad's Night Journey (*isra*) to Jerusalem and his subsequent ascent to heaven, which is briefly hinted at in the Qur'an and in the *hadiths*. In addition, a multiplicity of local stories and pictures tell in rich detail the beloved story of how Muhammad rides through the heavens to pray with Moses and Jesus. When disparaged as un-Islamic, the content, elaborated in detail in folk narratives, is defended as the epitome of Islam's central message: that Muhammad is the messenger of the definitive revelation, and Jews and Christians are offered this knowledge, as their prophets were the predecessors of the final prophet. But the forms that the representations of this commonly shared Muslim view take, in words and pictures, are based on local aesthetics.

The technological development of the past 150 years has meant that the world has gradually been flooded with images, in both the public and the private domains. Naturally, this is also the case in the Muslim world and it has raised new questions of whether it is permissible or unacceptable to depict living creatures, be the purpose functional or decorative. Photographs and postage stamps were among the first modern pictures to be discussed from a pious point of view. Later, it was human voices on the radio, and then films, TV programmes and other media innovations that gave rise to theological discussions. Each time, the arguments returned to the canonical sources mentioned above. But the texts, which form the basis of sharia, are open to various interpretations. Far from surprisingly, no consensus has been reached on a theological view of the triangular relationship between function, decoration and seduction.

As early as the 1950s, new reproductive techniques were becoming an effective instrument for spreading religious messages, and this development has become increasingly pronounced ever since, as has the missionary potential. The criticism of the making of pictures has remained, though, even if the illustrations form an important part of the most radical groups' promotional materials. Muslim groups that historically have not participated in publicly articulated interpretation (young people, women) have acquired access to new media, which is a

challenge to the established power elites, be they traditional
theologians or world rulers. Private citizens are challenging the
media world, long dominated by professionals. New media creates
domains where people can test their arguments and voice their
opinions. The internet has thus become a significant opening for
Muslims living under authoritarian and undemocratic regimes. Blogs
written by people subjected to dictatorships send out topical
information about local conditions, young people in Pakistan can
listen to Islamic hip-hop from the USA, Muslims from regions where
Islam is the dominant religion can encounter the conditions of being
in a minority position and get in touch with a variety of Muslims who
represent other local traditions and lifestyles and women can enter
feminist discussion groups. However, the major question about Islam
and new media is not immediately concerned with the use of images,
even though the internet offers innumerable opportunities for
pictures, picture manipulation and animation to promote religious
messages. The challenge is rather the theological diversity and the
question of how local religious leaders are to deal with the fact that
people are encountering such a variety of interpretations of the
Muslim tradition through new media. An artistic combination of text
and images is taking place not only on the internet. Pious instruction
books and films have for several decades been produced in large
quantities, and must relate themselves to the aesthetics and technology
of the day if they are to achieve success. There is enormous
inventiveness with regard to the representation of Muhammad: in
traditional fashion without a face, as a silhouette or as a voice only.
The depiction of other living people is apparently less problematic in
contemporary didactic genres. The prohibition against imagery in the
Muslim tradition is not just a closed door – a cultural blocking
mechanism. From the perspective of art history it has proven to be the
opposite too: a source of creativity.

Traditional values and new lifestyles

Sharia and Islamic ritual practice is gender-divided when it comes to
spaces as well as social interaction. In relation to modern living
conditions, religious or traditional rules are challenged by changed
views on sexual morality, the introduction of secular family law and
women's access to professional life. Contemporary lifestyles and family

patterns can be provocative in relation to traditional customs as well as to conventional interpretations of Islam. Most Islamic theology expresses a strict view on sexual relations, since adultery is explicitly mentioned as one of the limits (*hudud*) not to be transgressed. The space for sex is within wedlock and female sexuality has been traditionally identified as the cause of disorder (*fitna*) and in some Muslim environments connected to 'the sharia punishments'. The *hudud* punishment for adultery is the same for men and women: whipping (or stoning, although this is not mentioned in the Qur'an). But this is far from generally practised or defended even by all traditionalist *ulama*. Instead, analogies can be used as a way of reasoning and the statements in the Qur'an about harsh punishments are taken as an indication of the seriousness of such sins, but not necessarily as a compulsory form of punishment.

There is no tradition in Islam of celibacy or monastic life, and celibacy does not carry any moral value as such. Asceticism was rarely practised even in medieval times and, if it was, only late in life after marital commitments had been fulfilled. Alongside references to *adab* and the rules of *sunna*, the moral conduct of individual believers is put forward as part of *dawa* (especially in minority contexts), where each Muslim represents Islam with his or her behaviour. Gender relations therefore play a significant part in the mobilization among conservative Muslims groups.

Same-sex relations are hardly ever accepted in traditional Muslim environments. Some sharia-orientated contexts accept medical changes of sex, but homosexuality is strictly forbidden. The Qur'an refers at several places to the prophet Lot and his warnings to his hometown and the indecent life among its inhabitants: 'See, you approach men lustfully instead of women; no, you are a people that do exceed' (7:81). The open 'rainbow mosques' that are starting to appear in diaspora environments are not only an indication that difference is considered tolerable but also conscious attempts to raise theological arguments that accept homosexuals as honourable Muslims.

Property and prosperity

An important aspect of intra-human relations in the Islamic canonical literature is the handling of various forms of property. The historical background of Muslim ethics and sharia in a world of traders at the time of Muhammad is apparent in the regulation of economic transactions and property. The relationship of humans to Allah is depicted by an image of a covenant in *sura* 2. The Qur'an, which can be so inexact in other regulations, describes a contract with the following precise wording, linking it to divine justice:

> O believers, when you contract a debt one upon another for a stated term, write it down, and let a writer write it down between you justly, and let not any writer refuse to write it down, as God has taught him; so let him write, and let the debtor dictate, and let him fear God his Lord and not diminish aught of it. (2:282)

The text continues with detailed instructions for the proper wording of loans and other agreements. Tradesmen and people used to economic transactions form an important group of those who first received the message Muhammad brought forward. The Qur'an is definitively set in a community of traders.

Acquiring wealth is not a sin according to the Qur'an or the *hadiths*, but valuables should be handled with high morals. The prohibition against usury (*riba*), which includes taking interest from economic transactions, deriving profit from loans and unjust exploitation, has both symbolic and practical importance. The Qur'an states in strong words:

> Those who devour usury shall not rise again
> except as he rises, whom Satan of the touch
> prostrates; that is because they say,
> 'Trafficking [trading] is like usury.' God has
> permitted trafficking [trading], and forbidden usury. (2:275)

The moral statement is clear, but the regulation is difficult to observe strictly, as its causes practical problems when economic values are transferred in business. But the theme is frequent both in the Qur'an and in the *hadiths* in various wordings. Sahih Bukhari's collection contains the following:

> Narrated 'Umar bin Al-Khattab: Allah's Apostle said, 'The bartering of gold for silver is *riba* (usury), except if it is from hand to hand and equal in amount, and wheat grain for wheat grain is usury except if it is from hand to hand and equal in amount, and dates for dates is usury except if it is from hand to hand and equal

in amount, and barley for barley is usury except if it is from hand
to hand and equal in amount'. (Sahih Bukhari 3:34:344)

The message is clear although the examples the text provides have
distinct features from its original context, 'dates for dates'. During and
after the expansion of the oil industry in the 1970s, an insistent need
became apparent in the Gulf States to find forms of investment of the
income that were in accordance with sharia. Several of the leading
international Islamic banks derive from this period: the Islamic
Development Bank, the Faisal Banks and the Dubai Islamic Bank. In a
global economy, Islamic banks are constructed to function in parallel
with conventional monetary institutions. The methods for transactions with non-Muslim enterprises have steadily become more
integrated with the world economy. Over the following decades,
businessmen in favour of a sharia-observant economy found many
ways to support competitive businesses in more complex economies.
Today Islamic economy is not isolated to particular regions, but an
option in most part of the world, for small and large businesses alike. In
practice entrepreneurship and wealth building in trading through
investments could be organized in a way acceptable to sharia. From a
philosophical point of view Islamic economy is further developed to
include business ethics for investments beyond the discussion of
interest and commission.

Today, Islamic banking works both at the global level and for local
initiatives for investments and loans. It is sometimes considered to be a
non-Western alternative for economic development, and can
certainly not be regarded to be a Middle East phenomenon only.
Malaysia, Indonesia, other emerging economies in Asia and, not least,
the worldwide Muslim diaspora and trade via the internet are now part
of the Islamic economy on a large or small scale. The transnational
distribution of *halal* goods serves as one example.

The major moral mission for Islamic economy is the avoidance of
riba and to steer clear of any business that is involved with alcohol,
gambling or pork. The arguments in favour of this broad concept can
come from several, sometimes contradictory, points of view. It can be
part of a strictly sharia-oriented attitude that tries to find Islamic
solutions to most aspects of life; it can be related to the formulation of
justice claims in favour of a sustainable micro economy and to support
small-scale entrepreneurs who struggle to break away from local

Fig. 15   A halal counter in a modern supermarket. *(Getty Images)*

usurers; or the argument could be anti-colonial and striving towards an alternative to Western capitalism, while yet others take the opposite position in favour of a free, unregulated market where Islamic morals are regarded as a winning concept.

Riba is sometimes contrasted with its moral antithesis *zakat* – to share, whether wealthy or poor – and the Qur'an states:

> And give the kinsman his right,
> and the needy, and the traveller;
> this is better for those who desire
> God's Face; those – they are the prosperers.
> And what you give in usury,
> that it may increase upon the people's wealth,
> increases not with God; but what you give in alms,
> desiring God's Face, those – they receive recompense manifold.
> (30:38–39)

Discussions of economic frameworks in accordance with sharia often bring forward positive concepts instead of prohibitions. Trust (*amana*) is one of the central ethical concepts that are contrasted to *riba* and declared a norm for transactions as well as claiming the lack thereof could be a tool when formulating criticism and reprobation. The concept of mutual help (*takaful*) can also serve as an alternative to the practices of market economy and refers to the moral ideal of solving problems through negotiations within the local community.

A traditional way of organizing good deeds is through a trust or endowment (*waqf*) with stipulated objectives (sometimes highly detailed): often charity and education are formulated in a charter and thus protected from misuse. The initiative to create such a foundation could come from a will or the memory of a deceased person. Women have been visible in connection with trusts throughout Islamic history, both as objects of remembrance and as agents establishing memory sites. In the compounds around the larger mosques in the Ottoman Empire, soup kitchens (sing. *imaret*) provided various forms of welfare and charity. In their immediate vicinity, schools, libraries, hospices and travellers' lodges were established.

Muslim ethics in a world of change

What is properly Muslim or Islamic today is the subject of comment and criticism from many angles. Migration and urbanization, mass education and the professionalization of work life have led to new encounters and exposure to many modes of living 'a modern life'. The classical law schools are still influential, but the scope of themes for their consideration has broadened to include topics such as human rights, democracy, women's position and environmental issues.

Islamic ethics are always based on sharia as the governing principle, but there are in individual cases links to local Muslim custom (*ada* or *urf*), as well as to regional theological traditions. The implementation of sharia therefore, dependent on every specific context and the discussions among the *ulama* on how to reach a righteous verdict, can follow its own set of local norms of what proper Muslim ethics are.

There is no concept of original sin in Islam. Stipulated mandatory practice and the exemplary behaviour of Muhammad define a good deed. Rules in relation to the obedience to Allah and regulations for social interaction between humans cover civil, criminal and commercial issues.

Markers of Muslim identity in everyday life, principally based on sharia and the verdicts of its interpreters, such as dietary rules, dress codes and modes of social interaction, are mostly taken as evident in Muslim majority societies. Life in minority contexts both challenges the habitual and promotes references to tradition; it also connects to the narratives of the early *umma* when Muslim identity was underlined in public performance.

Further reading

Bonner, Michael et al., *Poverty and Charity in Middle Eastern Contexts* (Albany, NY: State University of New York Press, 2003).

Clark, Janice, 'Islamist Women in Yemen. Informal Nodes of Activism', in Quentin Wiktorowicz (ed.), *Islamic Activism: A Social Movement Theory Approach* (Bloomington, IN: Indiana University Press, 2004).

Cook, Michael, *Commanding Right and Forbidding Wrong in Islamic Thought* (Cambridge: Cambridge University Press, 2000).

Kuran, Timur, 'The Provision of Public Goods under Islamic Law. Origins, Impact, and Limitations of the Waqf System', *Law & Society Review* 35 (2001), 841–898.

McChesney, Robert, *Charity and Philanthropy in Islam: Institutionalizing the Call to Do Good* (Indianapolis, IN: University of Indiana Press, 1995).

Metcalf, Barbara, *Moral Conduct and Authority: The Place of adab in South Asian Islam* (Berkeley, CA: University of California Press, 1984).

Scott, Joan Wallach, *The Politics of the Veil* (Princeton, NJ: Princeton University Press, 2007).

Singer, Amy, *Starting with Food: Culinary Approaches to Ottoman History* (Princeton, NJ: Markus Wiener Publishers, 2010).

Chapter IX

Political Islam: Visions and Nightmares

Violence in the name of belief has been evident in all world religions, and Islam is no exception. Cultures and societies have been built and developed in the name of religion, but have also been destroyed. All religions have representatives that advocate peaceful as well as violent means for change. Still, it is apparent that the religious repertoire of narratives and symbols has both emotional and intellectual potential when it comes to impacting on arguments of how to change the world. Markers of religious belonging and religious narratives have often been used in conflicts and have turned out to be forceful tools when defining the enemy in dichotomized worldviews. Though religion in politics is not only related to questions of religious truths and morals of right and wrong; it is to a large extent also an issue of authority of leadership, as discussed in Chapter 7 in relation to Shi'i Islam. Other examples will be given in this chapter that indicate various forms of community building where Islamic norms meet contemporary living conditions.

The meeting points of religion and politics are never uncomplicated, even when the intentions are democratic. A decisive distinction seems to be between making politics in the name of religion and engaging in politics based on religious values leaving space for moral inducements of others. The modus operandi of modern politics is negotiation – parliamentary, economic or legal – and this pragmatic attitude is always at risk of causing conflicts between individual genuine religious conviction and the conditions on which politics works where compromises are necessary.

Islamism, in its broadest definition, is a religious and political ideology that regards Islam as the ultimate foundation of governmental administration, social life and religious practice. The common image of political Islam is associated with radical positions, acceptance of violence and holy war (one of the meanings of *jihad*) as a rightful means to further the just cause, and the term *jihad* has become part of non-Muslim vocabulary. Jihadists or *jihad*-oriented propagators can refer to militant (more or less formal) groups and to individuals who execute or defend violence with an Islamic motivation. 9/11 affected Muslims and non-Muslims alike as direct victims or in loss of trust. No discussion about the relationship between Islam and political engagement today can fail to point to this event as marking the fundamental shift in the conditions for commitments in the name of Islam, be they civil or political. Global terrorism has left its mark on inter-faith communication. Both the terror attacks themselves and Islamic defence of the use of violence also put moderate Muslims in situations where they feel that their faith is associated with aggression and destruction and where their opinions tend to come in the background of the violent attacks. The world today can offer many examples of when religious ideology rules over life and death, irrespective of the victims' faith. It should nevertheless be remembered that most conflicts in the name of religion and most Islamist violence claim local victims.

The consequences of religiously motivated violence have had a wide impact long after the atrocities. After 9/11 and 7/7, the conditions for Muslim communities and individual lives in non-Muslim environments changed dramatically. Individuals with a Muslim background were either directly approached or experienced pressure to take positions on radical interpretations of Islam far from their own convictions and traditions. The post-9/11 conditions have also caused internal schisms with a long-term impact on Muslim communities far from the sites of terror attacks.

The terminology for defining the violence-prone groups is often confusing. The frequently used term 'radical Islam' is an even broader term than *jihadist* and can imply a strict interpretation of Islam for an individual's lifestyle, but mostly refers to acceptance of violence as a political tool. It is a relational term and hard to use, as it presupposes some kind of mainstream the radicals have moved away from.

International terrorism, more often than not with state support, as a political tactic operates without borders or boundaries and strikes blindly among its victims, but sometimes with highly symbolic targets and on a scale of violence that has immediate global consequences. These attacks are not limited to the regional conflicts that were often the background to the Islamist movements taking shape during the

---

The greater and lesser jihad, and the construction of martyrs

Jihad means 'effort' and has had a double meaning throughout the history of Islamic theology. It can refer to the individual's striving towards spiritual fulfilment and resistance against infidelity and deviations from the primary principle of *tawhid*. But this commitment can have another meaning: to go to war to defend Islam following the Qur'an: 'And fight in the way of God with those who fight with you, but aggress not: God loves not the aggressors' (2:190) and 'struggle for God as is His due, for He has chosen you, and has laid on you no impediment in your religion, being the creed of your father Abraham' (22:78).

Jihad can furthermore imply holy war in a most concrete sense: the willingness to die for Islam and the expectance of reward for those who die fighting: 'If you are slain or die in God's way, forgiveness and mercy from God are a better thing than that you amass; surely if you die or are slain, it is unto God you shall be mustered' (3:157–8) and the fighters are promised a place in Paradise (3:169). To the jihadists, the ultimate contribution to holy war is martyrdom. The word for martyr (*shahid*, literally 'witness') comes from the same root as *shahada*, to bear witness – the name of the Muslim proclamation of faith. To those who advocate the second meaning of *jihad* and acts of terrorism, suicide attacks are deemed to be a way of bearing witness.

---

twentieth century. The enemy might be narrowly defined, but more often widely, such as the West, the USA, Israel or the Zionists. Focus is often on the operations as such; there is not always a coherent programme explicated, but an emphasis on slogans. Religiously motivated attacks are mostly executed by comparatively small and isolated groups, but with devastating effects, causing immediate atrocities as well as long-term disruption.

There are difficulties in finding proper concepts to characterize the various inclinations of those who criticize the shortcomings of present societal order and seek to build a vision of an Islamic alternative. Several terms are used in the media and academia: Islamists, radicals, radicalized, jihadists, fundamentalists, revivalists, (neo-)orthodox Muslims, (neo-)traditionalists, *salafis* and *wahhabis* – terms that mostly obscure rather than clarify. Islamism is here used as an umbrella term covering a range of organized activities from Islamic civil society welfare to violent groups. Rather than referring to a specific ideology, the term covers a range of organizations and modes of mobilization that share some common ideological features. It is also used to indicate general conservative attitudes where religion plays a vital role when deeming lifestyle, family values and morality.

Politics is not necessarily only to be defined as state administration or formal decision making. In the context of political Islam, part of the attraction of the utopian visions presented is the emphasis on new possibilities for the involved to participate in communal activities. Radical individuals and groups have often been vocal and caught media attention where more liberal interpretations of Islam tend to be transmitted among intellectuals. The organization of Muslims of a more moderate orientation as a public stand against militants is a comparatively recent phenomenon. The media focus on vociferous radicals following crisis and conflicts has provoked the public appearance of other Muslim voices, but not necessarily the formation of mass-mobilizing liberal groups. Such views are regularly expressed from a point of departure where religion and piety are regarded as a private matter and a personal commitment, and an opinion that social and political projects should extend religious boundaries. These positions should not be excluded from the concept 'political Islam', allowing the radical alternatives a monopoly.

Islamism can only to a limited extent be regarded as a coherent ideology. Ideas of what a society based on Islamic principles should be like have differed over time, and spokespersons have had conflicting political orientations or visions. One common denominator could be that Islamic values should form the basis of society. There are visions of a morally clean and just society, and lawful implementation of the rules given by Allah. But when it comes to how this should be done and the role of sharia in the formulation of such a society, the answers differ. In her study *Rethinking Islamist Politics* (2003) Salwa Ismail discusses the successes and failures of political Islam during the last decades and concludes that the paradox of Islamist politics lies in the discrepancy between the rhetoric of unity and the complex variety of contexts in which small groups as well as mass movements try to mobilize for action and ideological support. Engagement in local politics and social issues does not necessarily evoke loyalty to large-scale Islamist state projects, but it paves the way for a number of interpretations of the normative sources formulated by lay people who want to tackle fundamental problems in the Middle East and the Muslim world: poverty, inequality, global economic challenges and environmental issues.

The conflicting positions within contemporary Islam necessarily not only have political implications in the conventional sense, but also raise questions about what the political can be beyond ideology. Who is then political in the global situation with access to information and forums for communication? Radical groups mostly recruit among people who have not been politically involved before and offer arenas for engagement. Politics in this sense includes social networks and activities designed to obtain power or influence and based on shared values; the term then will cover not only parliamentary politics but also a broad spectrum of people who regard religious values as the basis for their engagement, from liberal Muslims to militant groups, and who regard welfare and educational programmes as both a religious and political commitment.

This chapter will initially present some of the influential thinkers whose ideas formed the ideological basis of what could broadly be defined as Islamism, some of them advocating radical interpretations of religion and acceptance of violence. The second part will focus on activities with a civil society orientation, where commitment to a better society is founded on Islam. These are far from always politically proclaimed, but are frequently political in their consequences. There is an ongoing academic debate over whether Islamism has failed, as it has not come up with any sustainable political alternatives for the Middle East and other Muslim majority areas, and whether the present is a post-Islamist era with on the one hand local civic activities other than the conventional involvement in politics and global militancy on the other. The groups and organizations with roots in the early twentieth century are sometimes today overrun. New social movements attract young people, who master social media in all its forms that connect to a broad spectrum of interpretations of Islam and communicate far beyond what the conventional elite can reach. Young people and women have also found more space and alternative modes of action in the more recent forms of mobilization.

Religious leadership is always based on authority and legitimacy, and it differs from other forms of leadership as it draws these from transcendental references and often monopolizes access to interpretation. In one way or another, mediating and judging are part of the execution of religious leadership.

Authority could briefly be defined as the consequences of certain speech acts and certain social behaviour; authority is inherently performative. Authority is an impact that indicates an assurance of accuracy, reliability and power in the more conventional understanding of the word. The special importance of authority in religious contexts has not only theological but also institutional implications. The cohesion of a group or community is always challenged when new claims to authority spring up. This is the situation for many women when claiming the right to leadership. Religious leadership has traditionally been executed in domestic and semi-public spaces. Through the various modernization processes in the Muslim world, visibility in the public sphere has increased, which brings the issue of new agents as independent intellectuals into focus. Access and presence are first steps, which can be promoted by reform and regulation, but the acceptance of arguments is perhaps a greater challenge.

Legitimacy could be defined as a locally understood lawful right (for example, to lead prayers). From the perspective of this chapter, the concept could be further specified in terms of claims to access to sources, of being publicly regarded as based in tradition instead of as a novelty, of the right to issue a call or a spiritual demand. In short: to be conceived as a leader is to be able to demonstrate lawful authenticity, credibility and validity in forms acceptable to a local community or group. The step from legitimacy to implemented power is often short.

If power is understood as impact and control within certain religious institutions, as possibilities to have access to certain discursive arenas, and as how the relationship between ability and capability is locally defined, then leadership of new Muslim actors is a political issue. Any discussion of power will in the end open up questions touching on what is political and who is political. No religious leadership can be anything but political. Additionally, it should be noted that Muslim leadership today is almost always mobilizing. Few, if any, examples can be provided where new agents' theological interpretations, interests and visions are put forward to a larger audience without having implications in terms of regional and national politics – not only at the local level (where we usually find discussions of young people's and women's activities).

Islamist visions: theorists and some groups

The Islamic political movements and groups founded in the first part of the twentieth century all relate to the modern nation state, positively or negatively, both in their visions and in the character of their activities. The background to the formation of groups advocating Islamic alternatives to societal problems can be sought in the decline and fall of the Ottoman Empire and opposition to colonial rule.

At the beginning of the twentieth century, large parts of the Muslim world were still British, French, Belgian or Dutch colonies. The processes of independence were complicated and still today many countries with a Muslim majority population lack stable democratic structures. Other factors have increased instability in the Middle East, North Africa and Indo-Pakistan regions. Authoritarian regimes have for a long time used religious institutions and pious discourse for control, and the differences between denominations have been used to prevent unified opposition, while military conflicts have caused waves of migration to and between Muslim countries. This has both aroused suspicion against the religious institutions as being corrupt as well as giving tailwind to those who have preached a path to authentic Islam. In the struggles against the colonial powers, a split between secular nationalists and Islamists soon became apparent. The latter emphasized unity (*tawhid*), invoking the oneness of Allah and the *umma*, and stood in sharp contrast to the awakening secular Arab nationalism that received most of its support from the educated elite with ambitions for large-scale modernization projects and mass education clearly inspired by Western ideals of enlightenment and progress. These ventures were closely connected to the hetero-geneous reform (*islah*) movement(s) known as awakening or revival (*nahda*), with its roots in Egypt at the end of the nineteenth century. These groups should not be regarded as anti-religious per se; they paved way for Islamic reformers like Jamal al-Din al-Afghani (1839–97) and Muhammad Abduh (1849–1905).

A complicated picture emerges, already recognizable among the nineteenth-century Islamist writers: disgust at modern/Western lifestyles and colonial exploitation is combined with appreciation of technical progress and the distribution of welfare and education. Early Islamism during the colonial era often had a supranational perspective and strove towards the unification of the *umma*, split by underdevelopment and Western hegemony. This Islamic universalism often came into conflict with the parallel development of nationalist movements, whose ideologists strove for the liberation of a specific nation and must be characterized as secular nationalists, often having a negative attitude – not always to religion as such, but critical of the traditional religious institutions. The split between Islamic universalism and a nationalist focus on the particular problems of a nation or a region is evident still in today's conflicts in the Middle East and the Muslim world.

In the post-colonial era, after World War II many of the old colonies in the Middle East instituted campaigns for mass education based on an optimistic trust in reform and development, only to face serious political and economic problems. A backlash against these secular ideologies came from the recently educated middle class: civil servants, engineers, doctors, teachers and lawyers who saw work in the name of Islam as a platform for societal development. The failures of Arab nationalism became apparent: inability to deal with corruption, weak political leadership and military interventions in large parts of the Middle East, North Africa and Indo-Pakistan regions. There are many dimensions to the Islamist response to the colonial encounter. Here, only the impact of the educational system will be emphasized, as mass education had an impact on students' attitudes to their religious tradition in a complex way. With higher education came a critical understanding of history, new modes of reading canonical texts and ways to relate to the religious authorities. At the same time, education provided the intellectual tools for formulating resistance against colonial rule as the rejected aspects of modernity.

Visions of an original society based on divine instruction as a trope in criticism of the present can be traced back a long way in Islamic thinking. Here, however, the focus will be on the reactions to colonialism and subsequent developments. The Islamic alternative in general looks to the reconstruction of a golden age (the Medina model) and uses history as a mirror to define and suggest solutions to contemporary problems based on studies of the Qur'an and *hadith* reports. Islamism stands in contrast to visions for a good society built on human reasoning, as in the case of modernist ideologies such as liberalism or socialism, which dominated political debates during the nineteenth and twentieth centuries, not only in Europe and North America but also among the elites in the Muslim world. The returning themes in these clashes are the role of sharia and what religious rules may be imposed on individuals.

In his book *Holy Terrors: Thinking about Religion after 9/11* (2003), Bruce Lincoln distinguishes between two major tendencies in attitudes that are observable in contemporary religious discourse when it comes to the role religion should play in personal and public life: maximalism and minimalism. He defines maximalism as 'the conviction that religion ought to permeate all aspects of social, indeed of human, existence' and minimalism as a perspective which 'restricts religion to an important set of (chiefly metaphysical) concerns, protects its privileges against state intrusion, but restricts its activities and influence to this specialized sphere' (Lincoln, 2003: 5). Both positions are highly visible in contemporary Muslim life; maximalism is perhaps a better concept to cover what is otherwise referred to as radicalism, fundamentalism, etc., while minimalism covers more or less secularist attitudes and thus avoids any misunderstanding as to whether secular refers to ideological or constitutional viewpoints. A minimalist position may well be pious; the concept refers only to a position taken on the place of religion in society.

The variations of radical Islamism fit into this understanding of maximalism as organizing life at all levels according to Islamic norms. *Salafi* and *salafiyya* are broad terms that do not indicate any specific type of activist or any coherent ideology. A common feature is to search the roots of Islam in the formulation of the Medina model as a political alternative and the ideal to follow is defined as that of the pious predecessors. A contemporary *salafi* is then a person who claims to follow these role models in belief and practice. The *salafi* vision expresses a trust in the forefathers, or predecessors (*salaf*) of the first generations of Muhammad's followers and selected individuals from the early history of Islam. Their pious examples are regarded as constituting a way of coming closer to an authentic form of Islam. This search for authenticity emphasizes the role of Muhammad as a founder of a new form of society – just and laid out according to the intentions of Allah for mankind – and goes back to those forefathers who organized Muslim life in accordance with the instructions from prophet.

The narratives and statements of the normative literature are read as explicit directives. A *salafi* position does not accept any symbolic or historicized interpretations of the holy scriptures, but finds direct instructions in the Qur'an and in *sunna* as expressed in the *hadith* literature. Anything else would be a promotion of the on-going corruption and decline of religion in the modern world. The reforming tendencies in radical interpretations of Islam and their resistance against innovation (*bida*) and amendments to the original message have been discussed in previous chapters.

Renewal (*tajdid*) has been a vital concept in Islamist discourse when urging for a restoration of the Islamic institutions by means of returning to the sources. The ambitions to purify Islam are often accompanied by a reference to a *hadith* telling of Allah's promise to send a renewer of the Islamic faith (*mujaddid*) every century to restore the *umma* to its authentic state. The historical mirror and the eschatological are hereby intertwined.

Therefore, conflicts, then and now, between modernist reformers – who often take radical courses – and the more traditional *ulama* in the regional educational institutions are often harsh. Many of the early Islamist writers defined themselves as reformers and showed reluctance to engage in *taqlid*, considering it an unacceptable ground for legal and moral verdicts. In that sense, they were modernists, as they saw the need for interpretation in times of change. The main concern for most Islamists was the corruption of the original message. The return to the Medina model was a means to encourage reflection on the Islamic message in order to make it relevant and their search of authentic Islam was supported by the method to go back to the holy scriptures to find answers. This implied on the one hand an emphasis on interpretation (*ijtihad*) as a means of navigating in new circumstances rather than following what had been established as custom (*taqlid*), and on the other the conviction that the sources have the answers for all time.

The founders of maximalist Islamism and other voices that advocate reform from within Islam

The genealogy of Islamism as a set of ideas is complex. *Wahhabism* and *salafism* have been used as both descriptive and analytical concepts in attempts to analyse the arguments in favour of Islam as the solution to contemporary problems. These terms occur as both self-definitions and pejoratives. A more common use of both these terms go back to the late nineteenth century, and their theological and ideological origins go even further back in history, as a reaction to certain aspects of modernity. At its core, Islamism is focused on the application of what is defined as authentic religion to contemporary social and cultural issues. It has directed criticism since its early days externally against colonial rule and general Western influences as well as internally in order to pronounce Islam as the intellectual basis of (various) reform movements. This double target of criticism is present in most Islamist discourse. *Salafiyya* can therefore be regarded as a multi-faceted reform movement with its main roots in Egypt in the late nineteenth and early twentieth centuries.

Before the founding fathers of Islamism from the early twentieth century are discussed, two forerunners, mentioned in previous chapters, will be discussed further, Ibn Taymiyya and Ibn Abd al-Wahhab. They both refer back to Hanbal (ninth century), the founder of the law school attached to his name, discussed in Chapter 4, as the model for arguing religious verdicts. The Hanbalis are known for their strict interpretation of sharia and the rejection of any political or legal decision going against this conservative view of sharia.

The desire to purify Islam from illegitimate influences goes back a long way in Muslim theological history. In the Middle Ages, Taqi al-Din Ahmad ibn Taymiyya (1263–1328), mostly active in Damascus, raised some arguments developed in later Islamism (where his legacy is a recurring reference): trust that the return to the holy scriptures will provide both the diagnosis and the solution and follow the line of argumentation advocated by the Hanbali school of jurisprudence along with a steadfast rejection of anything that could possibly contradict *tawhid*. There is an emphasis on *jihad* in Ibn Taymiyya's terminology, indicating the efforts to stay true to *tawhid*, which was further developed in later Islamism. In the execution of sharia, the Qur'an and *hadiths* provide the answers, not consensus (*ijma*), local custom or tradition (*adl* or *urf*). In an attempt to stop the spread of his ideas, his opponents imprisoned Ibn Taymiyya on several occasions, and he even died in prison. Even if he was not a martyr in the strict sense of the word, his death consolidated the image of a man prepared to suffer for his convictions and adapted in later Islamist ideology.

Ibn Taymiyya has been one of the prime references in Sunni Islamism, dominated by Hanbali standpoints and with more or less direct links to Saudi Arabia (although an Islamist opposition in the country today should be noted) since the nineteenth century, portrayed as the forerunner of the Muslim reform. His argumentation against Shi'i was as severe and forceful as against Sufism. The criticism of folk religion (veneration practices, making vows, visits to graves and shrines) and of Sufism – both as theology and as ritual – was built on personal experience during *hajj*, when he witnessed the practices at the grave of Muhammad, and this imagery of popular customs has remained significant in the Islamist quest for purity.

The theological background to the thinking of Muhammad Ibn Abd al-Wahhab (1703–92) can be traced to the writings of Ibn Taymiyya, who went back to the *hadiths* rather than following later jurisprudence to find guidance as to the interpretation of Qur'an. In al-Wahhab's sermons, given in Najd, absolute monotheism and unity (*tawhid*) stood in sharp contrast to the defined opposite: polytheism (*shirk*), comprising ignorance, heresy and local tradition. Like Ibn Taymiyya, al-Wahhab argued against Sufi, Shi'i and popular forms of veneration and piety such as asking for intercession (*tawassul*). In line with Hanbali purism, the role of Muhammad and the saints was questioned – especially the *mawlid* celebrations. Al-Wahhab was not only a theologian and a philosopher, a community grew around him which expanded to form the beginning of Islamism as a movement.

As a concept related to Islamism, Wahhabism refers to the early movement that grew from the spread of Wahhab's writings. To a great extent, Wahhabism rejected modernity, in contrast to many later *salafiyya*-oriented groups, which embraced the improvements of modernity but used them within an Islamic context. Wahhab's ideas became the ideology of the modern kingdom of Saudi Arabia, but he also had considerable influence during his lifetime. Followers continued in his spirit and even engaged in military campaigns for the just cause. In 1801, the Shi'i imam Hasan's mausoleum at Karbala was attacked and in 1803, the tombs of the early companions of Muhammad were ruined by Wahhab's followers.

Wahhab's ideas were institutionalized with the establishment of the kingdom of Saudi Arabia in 1932. *Fiqh* according to the Hanbali interpretation of sharia was implemented as law in a contemporary state construction and the kingdom became the emblem of an Islamic state. The anti-modernism expressed by Wahhab and his early followers made Saudi Arabia initially hostile to technology, something which changed rapidly after the oil boom in the 1970s and with the resulting economic prosperity in the Gulf States. During recent decades, Saudi Arabia has instigated extensive missions and aid to the Muslim world and has thereby supported a variety of revivalism – by means of education and economic investment that has also spread the Hanbali interpretation of Islam far beyond the homeland of wahhabism.

Most of the early Islamist theorists and mobilizers came from the Arab part of the Muslim world. An important exception was the Deobandis in the Indo-Pakistani area. Their ideological roots are to be found during the British colonial period of the region, but today the Deobandis are a global network. The Dar-Ul-Ulum ('The House of Learning') School was founded in 1867 in the city of Deoband (in today's India) as a traditional and conservative *madrasa*. The school was from the beginning under influence of the Wahhabi conceptions of how to get back to an authentic Islam freed from any traits of folk religion or influences from 'the West', as developed in al-Wahhab's writings, although its teaching was also based on the region's strong Hanafi traditions. The city has given its name to a movement of purist Islamic thinking over more than 100 years in Pakistan and India as well as in the British diaspora and in a worldwide network of Muslim scholars. The Deoband School and its branches have remained in charge of influential educational institutions, and the network has served as a hub for mobilization in various ways.

Several of the Islamist writers throughout the twentieth century have had a different educational background from the traditional *ulama*; they have been engineers, doctors, schoolteachers and journalists who have drawn from other insights when formulating Islamic answers to modern issues. The foremost Deobandi thinker was Sayyid Abul al-Ala Mawdudi (or Maududi) (1903–79), who more than anyone else formulated this Indo-Pakistani version of Islamism. He was a journalist and writer who had by the 1920s developed ideas on the relationship between Islam and governance, and had been active in the Muslim separatist groups opposing British colonial rule in India. Mawdudi produced a large body of Qur'an exegesis (*tafsir*) and an extensive body of books and other texts. Although he was part of the Muslim opposition against the British, he could not see a Muslim identity included in the national Indian platform (the Congress). He regarded it by definition as Hindu, secular and democratic, and saw no space for Islam in any of these concepts. Mawdudi instead introduced the concept of 'theo-democracy' as an alternative to democracy and constitutional secularism, a concept that would instead revive what he conceived was already in the holy scriptures. Based on a view of division of political responsibilities, a link was to be developed between religious authorities and political rule. In Mawdudi's complementary line of thinking, this division puts stress on the primacy of religious knowledge that could never be replaced by government by the people.

In 1941, Mawdudi founded Jamaat-i Islami (the Islamic Assembly or Group) as a network to counteract against Western influences and it became a strong organization. As a journalist and an experienced writer, Mawdudi knew how to use media for effective mobilization. In many ways Jamaat-i Islami could be compared to the Muslim Brotherhood in Egypt, especially in its early non-nationalist strivings for a universal *umma*. Mawdudi had ambitions for an Islamic state when Pakistan parted from India in 1947, with visions of a larger Muslim state beyond the Indian sub-continent. After the partition, Mawdudi found himself in opposition to the national regime in Pakistan and was repeatedly imprisoned. Although he represents a version of Sunni revivalism in the Indo-Pakistani area, the book *Towards Understanding Islam* (1932) has had an international influence far beyond revivalist circles. Together with the mobilization behind the revolution in Iran, Jamaat-i Islami is one of the two major Islamist movements outside the Arab Sunni world (although loyal to the Saudi regime) with influence over a large part of the Muslim world.

To a large extent Egypt was the centre of the development of Islamist thought during the early twentieth century and two of its most important representatives were born there in the same year – 1906. Hasan al-Banna (1906–49) epitomizes the reaction against the British presence in Egypt and against Jewish nationalism in Palestine. He was an elementary schoolteacher who, in 1932, moved to Cairo and was shocked by the colonial presence and the urban lifestyle. Al-Banna produced only a small number of texts: letters (or tracts) on various issues and his memoirs. Instead, he gained influence as the founder of the Muslim Brotherhood (al-Ikhwan al-Muslimun, literally The Society of Muslim Brothers) in 1928 and was known within the organization as the leader, or the 'Guide General'. If the *salafiyya* theorists Muhammad Abduh, al-Afghani and especially Rashid Ridda, with his journal *al-Manar*, were his intellectual predecessors, al-Banna was very much more an organizer than a writer.

In his early days, Banna was active in a Sufi order and realized the importance of a cohesive institution, authoritative leadership and well organized activities. The local cells so characteristic of the Brotherhood were inspired by the Sufi orders as well as the military. No matter how well organized the Brotherhood was, al-Banna did not underestimate the importance of a strong sense of community and religious guidance. As in the Sufi orders, members took oaths of allegiance and mobilization was consciously transformed into fellowship.

The Muslim Brotherhood began on a small scale and was more of a social club that grew larger and more influential under Banna's efficient leadership, mobilizing among workers and the lower middle classes. It took advantage of the ongoing urbanization, but did not appear as a political party. The Muslim Brotherhood built parallel institutions (a kind of Islamic alternative) for schools, hospitals, trade unions and publishing houses, thereby showing its followers that Islam was capable of meeting the challenges of modernity. In its early days, the Brotherhood was one of several Islamic grassroots groups, influencing people through local networks: imams, teachers, doctors and important families. All this supported swift growth and secured the movement a position in civil society that provided infrastructure such as schools, medical clinics and even a kind of workers' 'union', which also spread the religious message. Soon it drew sympathizers from all social strata in Egyptian society and could be characterized as a mass movement with influence over Egyptian politics and beyond. Al-Banna saw himself as a reformer; Islam had the answer for a post-colonial society and the Brotherhood presented its activities to secular Muslims as *dawa* (literally 'invitation') to return to their faith through insights into the Islamic religion and culture – and to discover how it could match the challenges from the West. Soon the Muslim Brotherhood was battled by the British as well as by the Arab nationalists.

In its 1935 charter the Muslim Brotherhood declared:

Allah is our objective
the Prophet is our example
the Qur'an is our law
the Jihad is our life
Martyrdom is our goal

The five formulated purposes have since been taken up by several other Islamist groups as the definition of their aims and methods. The concept of *jihad* in the meaning of 'holy war' is frequent in Banna's vocabulary as an appeal for action and as a means of inscribing the ruling regime in terms of being infidel or heretic, strengthened by the fact that he communicated his message of *jihad* from prison. Martyrdom and the readiness to die for a just cause were combined with calls for resistance against anything that worked against the establishment of an Islamic society. He followed other Islamic revivalists when claiming that it was righteous to oppose unjust and infidel (*kafir*) rulers, and he declared General Nasser an apostate. The restoration of the caliphate was proposed as an anti-Western alternative to the modern nation state with its colonial roots, and has remained a central trope in global Islamist rhetoric as well as attempts to establish sharia-governed rule in state-like forms.

Eventually, the Brotherhood became more explicitly political, with strong networks expanding early on into Jordan, Syria, Sudan and Palestine. It took to armed action in the 1940s and was by that time regarded as an international organization; it was directly involved in the fighting against Israel in 1948 and was banned in Egypt the same year. In 1949, Hasan al-Banna was murdered, but by then the Muslim Brotherhood had already established a strong social and political position.

After al-Banna's death, Sayyid Qutb (1906–66), much more of a theorist, became the most powerful voice of the movement. In fact, Qutb was perhaps the most influential Islamist ideologist of the twentieth century. Born in the same year as al-Banna and also from the countryside, Qutb was not really active in Islamist circles until the death of al-Banna and dedicated the first part of his adult life to literature. Qutb had a different public persona from al-Banna. Trained as a teacher, later a school inspector, Qutb represents the potential for upward social mobility of the time. He had started to turn to Islam when he was in his early 40s, but it was after a visit to the USA in 1948–51, that he was to formulate what he perceived to be an Islamic alternative to the development he witnessed, politically and in terms of lifestyles.

The experiences are described in his autobiography *Milestones* and made him identify materialism, pro-Zionism and liberal lifestyles as the main threats to an Islamic way of life. Qutb returned to Egypt to work as a school inspector, but resigned and joined the Muslim Brotherhood in 1952. Concepts proposed by al-Banna and Mawdudi are further developed in Qutb's writings, which are probably still today the most widely known Islamist texts. They have been an important source of influence for subsequent Islamist groups, in Arabic and in translation.

Qutb was a spokesperson for the Muslim Brotherhood in Egypt in the 1950s and 1960s, though never the formal leader of the organization. He had been disappointed by the vision of a modern society modelled on colonialism argued for by the Arab nationalists and their foremost representative, General Nasser. For him, Arab socialism and the new national elite stood in contrast to the eternal values of Islam. At the time, the Muslim Brotherhood represented a minority discourse in conflict with the administration, and members of the Brotherhood were imprisoned.

Social Justice in Islam (1949) was written while Qutb was still in the USA and is a spontaneous response to his encounter with a new environment. He shared the same sources of inspiration as al-Banna and both could be said to be *salafiyya* reformers in that they sought to define social and political alternatives to the decay of modernity. A commentary (*tafsir*) on the Qur'an in 30 volumes, *In the Shade of the Qur'an*, began to appear in 1954. Qutb wrote it not as the teachings of *alim*, but encouraged individual readings of the sources of *sunna* from which, he had no doubt, an image of authentic and unified Islam would stand. This extensive corpus was written during Qutb's long periods in prison. Qutb has been the inspiration of both violent and non-violent groups. Much of his argumentation is built on polarization. Qutb characterizes his time as an era of ignorance (*jahiliyya*), a term he picked up from Mawdudi. The state of ignorance, injustice and barbarism was conceived the very antithesis of Islam. Furthermore, contemporary *jahiliyya* is established both as a social fact and as a spiritual condition. This classical theological term became one of the most frequently used metaphors in modern Islamic preaching. Qutb builds other medical metaphors around illness, diagnosis and cure with the aim of showing how society can be restored. Secular law based on parliamentary decisions and negotiations is placed in contrast to the demands of sharia. Sharia is based on *tawhid*; it is eternal and a constitutive aspect of *din al-fitra*. It is furthermore regarded as consistent and without contradictions and therefore is in sharp contrast to democracy. But no more specific details of the nature of Islamic governance are provided by Qutb.

Sayyid Qutb's In the Shade of the Qur'an, a tafsir *in 30 volumes*

Sometimes, the title of this work is translated as *In the Shadow of the Qur'an*, but Qutb refers to the protection and comfort he argues is to be found in the scripture.

> I have listened to God the exalted conversing with me through this Qur'an – with me, a small little slave. What a sublime and heavenly honour this is for the human being! To what high rank one is raised by this revelation! What a noble station the human being is granted by his generous Creator! I have lived, in the shade of the Qur'an, looking from an elevation at the pagan ignorance [*jahiliyya*] raging in the land and the petty concerns of its people. /—/ Why is it that they are stuck in this infested mire, and why can they not hear the sublime and heavenly call – the call that elevates life and blesses and purifies it? (translated in Euben and Zaman, 2009: 133f.)

After the attempted assassination of General Nasser in 1954, Qutb was detained, accused of being part of the plot. During his ten years in prison he added several books to his already extensive list of published works. Among his work known in English is *Milestones* (or 'Signposts along the Road') from 1964, which was translated into several languages and is still read today. Sayyid Qutb was arrested again in 1965, taken to military court and executed the following year. He had already as a prisoner gained an indisputable status as a martyr (*shahid*) within the Brotherhood, which was now emphasized.

After a general amnesty in 1971, the Muslim Brotherhood was allowed to work in public, but not to form a formal political party. In 1977, when President Sadat signed a peace agreement with Israel (at Camp David), new waves of radicalism emerged as a response to what was conceived as betrayal and abandonment to anti-Muslim forces. Groups with their roots in the Brotherhood carried out violent attacks on tourists, assassinated Anwar Sadat in 1981 and went underground.

Since the late 1970s, the development of radical Islamist movements in general has taken other directions. The jihadists recruited radical Egyptian students and executed terror attacks in Egypt and abroad. The radical offshoots of the Muslim Brotherhood include groups such as al-Jamaat al-Islamiyya and al-Jihad (mostly known in the media as Islamic Jihad).

Many of the Islamist groups have their roots in regional conflicts, some are involved in national politics and parliamentary work and are still very effective in local recruitment. They have also found new global means to recruit and spread the message. Through new media, new forms of mobilization are established. Hamas – an acronym for The Islamic Resistance Movement that forms the Arabic word for 'enthusiasm' or 'zeal' – is an organization founded in 1987, during the first Palestinian Intifada against Israel. This militia based in Gaza is a continuation of activities among Palestinians previously organized by the Muslim Brotherhood. Under the leadership of the charismatic Sheikh Yassin (who died in 2004 during a targeted Israeli strike against him, which gave him the status of a martyr within the movement) Hamas launched waves of suicide bombings against Israeli targets as part of the Intifada, and Hamas has since been declared a terrorist organization by several countries and international organizations.

As the Hamas Charter of 1988 indicates, its goals are inscribed in regional conflicts, but at the same time it pleads allegiance to the universalist Islamic cause. *Jihad* is mandatory, according to the Charter, for every man and woman, and the third article states that those who offered their loyalty to Allah 'knew their obligation towards themselves, their people, and their country. They achieved *taqwa* [devoutness, piety] of Allah in all [of their obligations]. They raised the banner of *jihad* in the face of the transgressors to free country and folk from [the transgressors'] filth, impurity, and evil' (trans. in Euben and Zaman, 2009: 366). Whereas article 7 emphasizes universality:

> Muslims throughout the world adopt the system of the Islamic Resistance Movement; they work towards aiding it, accepting its stands, and amplifying its *jihad*. Therefore, it is an international movement /—/ whoever closes his eyes from seeing reality, unintentionally or intentionally, will one day awake to find that the world has left him behind, and the justification will wear him down trying to defend his position. The reward is for those who are early. (trans. in Euben and Zaman, 2009: 367f.)

Hamas defines itself as a branch of the Muslim Brotherhood but one that is focused on immediate action and with the Palestinian cause as its prime platform for mobilization, whereas earlier Islamists had been opposed to nationalist campaigns. Today, Hamas has several sub-divisions. There are militia brigades and cells but also a well-developed structure for social welfare, education and religious instruction that includes effective media. Since 2006, a political wing has successfully fought secular nationalism in the Palestinian parliament.

Hizbullah (or Hezbullah) is a Shi'i group founded in southern Lebanon in 1982 in the aftermath of the Islamic Revolution in Iran and is fervent in its anti-Israeli and anti-Western discourse. It has since then been part of the violent conflicts in Lebanon, with support from Iran and Syria. Like Hamas, Hizbullah has over the last two decades developed social programmes and its use of media as new means of recruitment. Hizbullah has also been a political party since 1992 and is today represented in the Lebanese parliament.

There were few early female voices in public defence of Islamism or women theorists, but Euben and Zaman give two interesting examples in their anthology of influential Islamist texts (2009: 275ff.). Zaynab al-Ghazali (d. 2005), a contemporary of al-Banna and Qutb, describes in her memoirs of a long life the formative years of Islamism in Egypt and her work organizing women despite political difficulties. Al-Ghazali's engagement for Muslim Women's Association associated with the Brotherhood was the cause for which she was imprisoned. She was highly controversial to both practising Muslims, who found her too demanding, and secular women's rights advocates, who could not see her arguments as primarily in favour of women but governed by a religious agenda. In general Islamist approaches to issues regarding women's rights and living conditions have often been in conflict with liberal equality discourses. The term feminism is mostly rejected by Islamists as being too closely associated with liberal egalitarianism and when an Islamic alternative is promoted is it often founded on a complementary view on the role of men and women.

In Malaysia, the NGO Sisters in Islam (SIS) have argued in favour of women's rights on Qur'anic grounds since 1990. Following the principle 'If Allah is just, the laws cannot be unjust', the Sisters have protested against several new state-imposed Islamic laws, the traditional sharia court system and the position taken by the state mufti. SIS teaches the method to distinguish the words of Allah as found in the Qur'an from later interpretations and encourages women to go back to the sources themselves in order to form an opinion. But the results are very different from *salafis'*, who actually also advocate a return to the wording in the sacred scriptures. The clash is apparent. SIS emphasizes the right of people other than the *ulama* to discuss and interpret religion. Its leading members are well educated, though not theologians, and are therefore able to provide knowledge resources on their website and offer training programmes. Their emphasis on individual choice and responsibility challenges the traditional interpretations of the local *ulama* and conservative national laws, and these new perspectives break socialization in *madrasas* that build up the trust in the traditionalist religious authorities. As Malaysia is increasingly influenced by radical groups, SIS has caused controversy with its focus on family law, domestic violence and space for women in public debate. Both the organization and its leading members have been attacked by Islamic officials for not being true Muslims, causing a split, lacking knowledge and not being trained in Qur'anic interpretation. The SIS spokesperson for a long period, the lawyer Zainah Anwar, connects women's rights to civil rights in general and finds equality and justice for women in the Qur'an (2001). Today, SIS is a global organization and the American Islamic feminist Amina Wadud has been closely associated with Sisters in Islam since its inception.

Women's rights defenders are not attacked by radicals only. All over the Muslim world, groups with conservative positions on moral values and family issues have an impact on the everyday lives of individuals and communities.

Small groups with mostly moral and religious agendas far away from international politics can nevertheless have a long-term political impact, in a broader understanding of the word. The varied voluntary civic contributions to Islamic civil society may share an Islamic ideal vision for the future as a goal, but they still differ significantly when it comes to methods.

Most contemporary Islamist mobilization in Muslim majority areas is based on an identification of (local) need and the shortcomings of the state and is executing charity work on the fringes of what is conventionally regarded as political. In the diaspora, Islamist groups have established and maintained influence through educational institutions run by their own imams and teachers and through their aid activities. This kind of charity is often very visible in local contexts, but not always taken into consideration when political Islam is discussed if they are not involved in radical activities.

Two very different contemporary preachers, both born in Egypt, can serve as examples of the global impact those who master digital modes of communication can have. In both cases, they have gathered large crowds of followers.

Yusuf al-Qaradawi (b. 1926) is a controversial Islamic scholar (*alim*) with a doctoral degree from al-Azhar. He is known as the writer of numerous books and for his television shows giving sharia guidance, broadcast by al-Jazeera. The best-known of these is called 'Sharia and Life'. Qaradawi is also one of the front-figures of the website Islam Online, established in 1997, which provides *fatwa*s on issues submitted. In 2011 during the ongoing 'Arab Spring' demonstrations, he returned to Egypt after 30 years abroad. As a global actor, Qaradawi is controversial in many respects because of his conservative views on family values and vagueness on the use of violence by radical groups. He was among the first Islamists to gain worldwide global attention thanks to the use of popular media. Qaradawi has many young followers, but he represents a traditional way of establishing authority, and his argumentation is based on conventional *fiqh* methodology.

His antithesis in many respects is Amr Khaled (b. 1967), who has been described as a Muslim television evangelist. His TV shows are widely distributed and his popular website has given a large global audience access to interpretations in accessible language, with a focus on contemporary issues directed at the young and middle-aged. An accountant by profession, Khaled is in style and appearance very different from the traditional clerics, who fiercely contest this layperson's right to preach and give guidance on how to live a decent Muslim life in a changing world.

The Taliban of Afghanistan and Pakistan – from resistance movement to terrorists

The Taliban have become emblematic of Islamist rule. The Taliban, literally 'students [of Islam]', in some respects an organized network based on the region's tribal structure, grew out of Deobandi *madrasas* in the Pashtun-speaking areas of Afghanistan and Pakistan. The Taliban have their background in the *mujahidin* (those who practise *jihad*, literally 'who struggle the most') during and after the Soviet occupation of Afghanistan in 1979. Based in Kandahar, they appeared on the political scene in 1994 as a religious militia under the leadership of mulla Omar (b. 1959). Trained in Pakistan, the Taliban operated in Afghanistan and in 1996 captured the capital, Kabul, where they installed strict rule based on their interpretation of sharia, as they have done in all the areas they have dominated. US intervention made the Taliban leave the city again in 2001, but their understanding of Islam nevertheless dominates Afghanistan and large parts of north-western Pakistan.

Among the Taliban fighters were international recruits, who in many cases moved to other areas of conflict in the 1990s such as North Africa and the former Yugoslavia. At the time of the Soviet occupation, the fighters were supported by the USA, Saudi Arabia and Pakistan, but this backing came to an end long before 9/11, when Taliban-ruled areas started to constitute a base for groups associated with al-Qaida.

The Taliban introduced a harsh Islamist rule despite the fact that the region had traditionally followed the Hanafi law school, rather than the stricter Hanbali, and had been characterized by ethnic and religious diversity for centuries. Taliban maximalist governance displayed hostility towards artistic expression, limited women's public appearance and access to education and work outside the family, adopted an aggressive stance towards other interpretations of Islam (especially Sufism and Shi'ism) and destroyed the country's cultural heritage, leaving no space for other Muslim traditions.

Over the last 30 years, the *mujahidins* and the Taliban have changed from being regarded as freedom fighters against communism to become some of the key players in global *jihad*.

There is a general problem in inscribing political positions taken on an Islamic basis on the right–left axis and it is difficult to find suitable labels to categorize Muslim thinkers and writers who object to radical and violent positions but still regard Islamic values as the foundation for a virtuous society. Some of them are liberals in a Western understanding, focusing on the civil liberties of the individual, while the majority must be characterized as conservatives, with a focus on family values and public morals, but at the same time emphasizing social welfare as a capstone for an Islamic society. Writers of a liberal Muslim orientation often are neglected in overviews of political Islam. One obvious reason is that the violent acts performed by radical groups tend to dominate the concept of 'political Islam' because of their atrocious consequences. Another is that liberal thinkers often base their arguments on an understanding of religion as a private matter, while politics belong to the public sphere, very much in contrast to the maximalist vision of a just society. Islamic liberals do not define their positions as political in the same explicit way as some radicals do, and their reflections on personal freedom and responsibilities tend to be read as belonging to the philosophical sphere.

Visions of an Islamic society

Islamism as an ideology is not only about how the future is envisioned; it is equally an issue of evoking a righteous past (a historical utopia) as a model for a just society. The Medina model hailed as the authentic prototype fits well with the use of contemporary communication technologies. The hallmark of many Islamist groups is a purifying ambition and a demand to return to the holy scriptures that will act as a guide to an authentic version of Islam. Many Islamic revivalists have been critical of traditional regional religion, but for other reasons than the secular nationalists – even if both have their roots in anti-colonial mobilization. The Islamist reformers have seen decline and inappropriate accretions, especially in religious practice and public activities that contradict what they regard as authentic Islam.

Early Islamism was part of a resistance against colonial rule and in its rhetoric targeted Western influences, but it was at the same time in opposition to secular nationalism in the Arab world and other Muslim countries. Some Islamist groups were prepared from the beginning to accept violence as a means to achieving their goals, others developed into radicalized wings during the 1970s, while yet others, less visible in the media, rejected the use of violence and sought parliamentary solutions. The terror attacks of global jihadist groups with little connection to regional conflicts are an indication of a spread at a global scale and the choice of symbolic targets. Parallel with these transnational action-oriented radicals today, national conservative Muslim groups are gaining parliamentary success and influence; they do not necessarily argue in favour of a general implementation of sharia, but when confronted with claims of individual rights liberal attitudes are often highly provocative to their own concepts of moral standards. The confrontations in connection with the demonstrations for the protection of the Gezi Park in Istanbul in 2013 turned in the eyes of many Turks into a clash of lifestyles and an issue about the conditions for liberal public life in a country governed for more than a decade by the pro-Islamic AK Party.

No doubt, processes such as globalization, world migration, transnationality, urbanization and the development of social media have all had an impact on groups that previously have not been particularly visible when it comes to theological interpretation. No one can deny the continuous influence of *ulama*, Islamic educational institutions, local custom and charismatic preachers, but the very access to differing views on the canonical texts has changed the scene. It has promoted radical as well as liberal understandings of what constitutes tradition and, perhaps more importantly, it has raised questions related to contemporary Muslim everyday life, from *halal* toothpaste and dating morals to relationships in multicultural environments and Islamic environmental consciousness. These challenges to the old interpretive domains are certainly not something unique to the Muslim world; they can be observed in all world religions today. Visions of a better society based on Muslim values are certainly not an aim for radical groups only.

Further reading

Abu-Lughod, Lila, *Local Conflicts of Islamism in Popular Media* (Amsterdam: Amsterdam University Press, 2008).

Anwar, Zainah, 'The Struggle for Women's Rights within the Religious Framework. The Experience of Sisters in Islam', in *Modern Malaysia in the Global Economy: Political and Social Change into the 21st Century*, ed. Colin Barlow (Cheltenham: Edward Elgar, 2001), pp. 178–88.

Black, Antony, *The History of Islamic Political Thought: From the Prophet to the Present*, 2nd edn. (Edinburgh: Edinburgh University Press, 2011).

Eickelman, Dale F. and Piscatori, James, *Muslim Politics*, 2nd edn (Princeton, NJ: Princeton University Press, 2004).

Euben, Roxanne and Muhammad Qasim Zaman (eds), *Princeton Readings in Islamist Thought: Texts and Contexts from Al-Banna to Bin Laden* (Princeton, NJ: Princeton University Press, 2009).

Hafiz, Sherine, *An Islam of Her Own: Reconsidering Religion and Secularism in Women's Islamic Movements* (New York: New York University Press, 2011).

Ismail, Salwa, *Rethinking Islamist Politics: Culture, the State and Islamism* (London: I.B.Tauris, 2006).

Kurzman, Charles (ed.), *Liberal Islam: A Sourcebook* (Oxford: Oxford University Press, 1998).

——, *Modernist Islam.1840–1940* (Oxford: Oxford University Press, 2002).

Mandaville, Peter, *Global Political Islam* (London: Routledge, 2007).

Taji-Farouki, Suha (ed.), *Islamic Thought in the Twentieth Century* (London: I.B.Tauris, 2004).

White, Jenny B., *Islamist Mobilization in Turkey: A Study in Vernacular Politics* (Seattle, WA: University of Washington Press, 2002).

Wiktorowicz, Quentin, *Islamic Activism: A Social Movement Theory Approach* (Bloomington, IN: Indiana University Press, 2004).

Epilogue

This introductory volume has emphasized the uses of history in Muslim tradition and how the past is present in contemporary debates in terms of ideals to follow and models for a just society. There is, of course, not one singular Islamic collective memory, and history can furnish events for argument in many directions. While the role of early Islam as an ideal model to follow has always been a significant feature in Islamic theology, albeit with many understandings of the community Muhammad established in Medina and Mecca as depicted in the *hadith* literature and early history writing, there is an apparent clash in contemporary interpretation as to whether these representations of the early *umma* constitute a model to be followed in precise detail or whether the model needs to be contextualized in relation to the ancient world of the Arabian Peninsula.

These ideals of proper behaviour and regulations for societal life are based on narratives about the early Muslim communities during the time of Muhammad and under the leadership of the four caliphs after him, who were also decisive in shaping Islam and Muslim identity. New customs – prayers towards Mecca, dietary laws, the mosque and the Friday sermon – distinguished these early Muslims of the seventh and eighth centuries from their neighbouring Jews and Christians and remain today public manifestations of Islamic identity.

The concept of *umma* has always had a double meaning as it indicates the worldwide, unified fellowship of Muslims as well as the immediate local congregation. The idea in both understandings of the term mirrors the very first community established by Muhammad as the undisputable moral norm. The Islamic faith states that unity (*tawhid*) is the most fundamental characteristic of Allah and the local and universal fellowship of Muslims.

Even if in the majority in many countries and regions, many Muslims throughout history have had contact with non-Muslims. The presence of other faiths has therefore been part of everyday life for many Muslims, past and present. Multi-religious communities were present in large parts of the Middle East until after the end of World War II. Such relations should not be idealized, however, and although regulations between majority and minorities have shifted, they must still be borne in mind when observing contemporary conflicts.

The Islamic world has always been characterized by mobility and long-distance communication between groups, although the impact on large groups of Muslims of increasing world migration over the last three or four decades cannot be overestimated. Large-scale processes such as urbanization, globalization and work migration, along with geo-political conflicts, have led to rapid changes in terms of both settlement and living conditions. While world migration and transnational life is not an issue that belongs only to the contemporary Muslim diaspora in Europe and North America, it has changed the Islamic map in Asia and Africa as well as in the Middle East. The development of transnational Islam with changed conditions for religious authority and legitimacy has paved the way for new positions and possibilities for young people and women to voice interpretations of religion. Muslim groups and individuals respond to changes and trends facing all contemporary religions and ideologies, which are challenged to provide answers to secular lifestyles, multiculturalism, new media and the seemingly endless possibilities of interpretation circulating on the internet and in social media.

In the contemporary world, the concept of *umma* has acquired a yet broader meaning of Muslim diversity, visible in everyday encounters as a consequence of national and international migration. Globalization, increased transnational migration and refugee flows over the last decades have created large Muslim diaspora communities worldwide, especially in countries with a Muslim majority. The challenge is less to live in a minority situation than to cope with Muslim diversity in a global world. Social media can offer virtual fellowships irrespective of great geographical distances and differing living conditions among those in communication. They provide access to sources, interpretations, opinions and events to interactive users whose activities can very well grow into mobilization for particular causes, the establishment of new small communities and groups, or young people who simply bring Muslim dimensions to existing forms of youth culture such as music, computer games or sport. This has been a source both for cultural and social development and, in some cases, fear of introducing illegitimate innovation (*bida*) to the Islamic faith.

Even if only 20 per cent of the Muslims of the world are Arabs, the Arabic language has a special status among Muslims as a sacred language and constitutes a unifying factor as well as an important missionary tool. The Qur'an refers to itself as a book with a message from Allah in Arabic, the language of the daily prayers. Despite all other differences, all practising Muslims have a relation to the Arabic tongue as it is embedded in their everyday piety.

Local and regional leadership has traditionally been conducted by imams, who in most cases share a cultural background with their communities. By leading prayers, preaching and guiding they fulfil the expectations of their role and follow the given modes of executing religious as well as social authority. Basic Islamic education in local Qur'an schools provides proficiency in reciting a few *sura*s, some of them embedded in canonical and local prayer genres, and knowledge of the proper way of performing the daily prayers. But this form of training does not necessarily provide discursive access to the holy text. Reciting the Qur'an in Arabic is as much a mode of prayer as it is a way of extracting religious knowledge from the text. The words of the Qur'an are regarded as infallible and eternal; the very sound of the recited words is conceived as carrying blessing.

Belonging to institutions for higher Islamic training, *ulama* are educated to have the authority to interpret the Qur'an and the *hadith* literature and to formulate verdicts of what conceptions and manners are in accordance with sharia. There has never been a central Islamic administration that has codified dogma or governed the interpretation of sharia. The regional *madrasa* institutions have instead played a significant role in the transmission of *kalam* and *fiqh*, while the implementation of sharia has always been connected to the political power, be it an Islamic state or secular governance with space for the religious communities to provide verdicts on civil matters. In the absence of a supreme institution for the provision of general guidance on moral and theological matters, al-Azhar in Cairo has for centuries offered higher education and the services of a cadre of men of learning within all Islamic disciplines. The normative influence of al-Azhar, both in the past and today, cannot be overestimated. A verdict from its leader, the shaykh al-Azhar, has a clear impact on the Muslim world and often echoes in non-Muslim media as well. Al-Azhar is a large-scale university that trains *ulama* and imams for service across large parts of the world, and a diploma from this institution means both prestige and influence.

Being Muslim can mean a variety of things to an individual. It can be an indication of family and community belonging, it can point to the experience of being connected to a particular cultural heritage or a specific political inclination where religion formulates the basic norms (not necessarily only Islamist view points) and it can, of course, be a matter of personal piety. And all this in a number of combinations. Far from all people who identify themselves as Muslims practise, but few of them would disagree that the five daily *salat* prayers are mandatory both as an expression of personal piety and as a public marker of Islamic identity. To fulfil the prayer demands is the ideal; but, as in all religions, there is a gap between perfection and the realities of individual lives.

The Friday midday prayer with its sermon (*khutba*) constitutes the backbone of Muslim communal ritual gathering, although in most cases it is a mono-gendered one as most women tend to perform their ritual duties at home or in other private spaces. The *khutba* has been the major tool for the imam to teach, correct and guide the local community; today sermons are disseminated through all kinds of media and the preachers are interchangeable from week to week. This has not diminished the importance of the Friday midday prayer, but has made alternative modes of pious fellowship visible and accessible.

Even to those Muslims who do not practise Islam on a daily basis the festivals spread across the year can be an opportunity to connect to family traditions. The lunar calendar provides the basic structure for the ritual cycle of Islamic festivals; the Ramadan celebrations, together with Id al-Fitr (at end of the long fasting period) and Id al-Adha (the feast of sacrifice), are the most important. In these celebrations cultural and strictly religious dimensions are intertwined, and Islamic reformers of the modern era have sometimes strived to purify the ritual activities from what they conceive as un-Islamic elements.

The poetic and ritual traditions surrounding the celebration of the prophet's birth (*mawlid*) have a special status in the criticism of innovation (*bida*) as well as being popular in most parts of the Muslim world. The annual festival commemorates the birth with public events, but the associated songs, narratives and prayers also form the repetoire for domestic gatherings for commemoration of the dead, celebrating births or returns from hajj or as protective prayers for the sick. In private piety such devotional practices play an important role and the sense of cohesion they bestow should not be underestimated. To many Muslims these performances, in private homes or public spaces like the mosque, constitute the very nexus for the expression of religious emotions. The same goes for prayers at the mausoleums of saints, or 'friends of Allah', especially in Sufi-oriented environments and in Shi'i Islam. In some respects the commemorations and venerations can be contrasted with the canonical rituals of the mosque, especially in terms of authority and leadership. Ritual activities of this kind have always had space for women as ritual leaders and, through this, also as religious instructors.

The teaching of Islam and the ways in which Muslims practise their faith is a growing field at academic institutions and one viewed with increasing interest among students; but studies of Islam no longer belong exclusively to the curricula of Religious Studies or Middle Eastern Studies. To mention but a few: theoretical fields such as political science and anthropology as well as more practically oriented education such as teacher training colleges, schools of social studies and journalism, and even nursing schools. This has implications for what aspects of Islam are accentuated. A substantial change can be observed in textbooks and research. The focus has shifted from studying Islam as an unproblematic entity to a growing interest in the variety of Muslim cultures, from the Balkans to China, from Russia to South Africa. Where previously an archaic image of Arab cultures dominated the narratives, the trends today focus on the diversity of diaspora communities, the role of Islam and Muslims in the media and radical political Islam and jihadist ideology.

There can never be a single description of a religion which is true for all; there will always be diverging images in the hearts of different believers. This introduction has tried to depict some commonly shared features of belief and practice among the 1.5 billion Muslims in the world today.

Notes

1   The figures are from the Pew Forum report *Mapping the Global Muslim Population*; see Lugo et al. (2009). The report also gives a short introduction to the methodological problems in bringing different types of statistical material together. The countries with the largest Muslim minorities after India are Ethiopia, China, Russia and Tanzania.

2   Ethnographic material from specific Muslim cultures and communities has been published and disseminated since medieval travellers reported back – both belles-lettres and more systematized knowledge. After World War II, area studies developed as a specific academic field at universities, where the study of Islam and Muslims to a large extent became integrated in Middle East studies. The last decades have seen an increasing number of works that discuss the relationship between the variety of local practices and interpretations of Islam on the one hand and the concept of how Islam is used in both Islamic theology and academic analyses on the other.

3   All quotations from the Qur'an in this book are from Arthur John Arberry's translation, but as this translation does not indicate the number of the verses, these have been added from the Egyptian standard edition to enable the reader to more easily compare with other translations of the Qur'an.

4   The following verses in the Qur'an refer directly to the name Muhammad (literally 'the praised'): 3:144, 33:40, 47:2 and 48:29. He is referred to as Ahmad (literally 'the most praised') once, in 61:6.

5   For a thorough introduction to the source-critical aspects of early Muslim history see Stephen Humphreys' *Islamic History: A Framework of Inquiry* (1999) and Herbert Berg's (ed.) *Method and Theory in the Study of Islamic Origins* (2003). See also Alexander Knysh's *Islam in Historical Perspective* (2009) and Chase Robinson's *Islamic Historiography* (2003).

6   The pre-Islamic gods and goddesses worshipped at the Kaaba and elsewhere were most presumably of a character similar to the

pantheons of the Near East known from archaeological and textual sources from both before and after the emergence of Islam.

7   For academic accounts of the life of Muhammad and discussions of the sources that form the basis of his biography see Michael Cook's *Muhammad* (1983 and later editions), Clinton Bennett's *In Search of Muhammad* (1998), Harald Motzki's (ed.) *The Biography of Muhammad* (2000) and Uri Rubin's *The Eye of the Beholder* (1995).

8   The quotations from the *hadith*s are from the translations published by Centre for Muslim-Jewish Engagement at the University of Southern California at http://www.usc.edu/org/cmje/religious-texts/hadith/. This website offers translations of Sahih Bukhari, Sahih Muslim, Sunan Abu-Dawud and Malik.

9   All quotations from the Qur'an in this book are from Arthur John Arberry's translation, but as this translation does not indicate the number of the verses, these have been added from the Egyptian standard edition to enable the reader to more easily compare with other translations of the Qur'an. There are numerous translations of the Qur'an into English made from historical, philological and literary points of view, as well as translations emphasizing theological interpretations.

The first translation of the Qur'an into a European language was made into Latin in 1143 by Robert of Ketton, an English astronomer and traveller in the Byzantine Empire and Arab lands (Palestine and Damascus). The first English translation of the Qur'an was published in 1649. Throughout the Middle Ages, the Renaissance and the early modern era, there was significant interest among European scholars in the holy book of the Muslims. Systematic academic interest from linguistic, historical and theological points of departure developed at European universities from the second half of the eighteenth century.

Two classical academic translations have appeared in numerous printings: Richard Bell's from 1937 and Arberry's from 1955. The latter is still often quoted because of its ambition to retain the literary quality of the original Arabic. Two other English translations often used by Muslim communities are Yusuf Ali's from 1934 and Muhammad Marmaduke Pickthall's from 1930 (both translators were converts to Islam). These two are available online at www.usc. edu/org/cmje/, together with two other translations. The site is administered by the University of Southern California and provides a search engine for the Qur'anic texts and the four standard collections of the narrative traditions from the time of the prophet Muhammad (sing. *hadith*).

The varying systems of numbering the verses of the Qur'an might appear slightly confusing, but no numbering is to be found in the original manuscripts and the numbering systems are the result of later editorial work. The German scholar Gustav Flügel produced an edition of the Arabic Qur'an (1893) that dominated academic work for a long time, but it was challenged by the Cairo edition, published in 1923, which most contemporary translations follow. The two systems, the so-called Syrian and the Egyptian, can differ within some few verses when references are compared, but are fairly easy to sort out.

10   Sura 6:83–90 provides a longer exposition on the previous prophets and the Book.

11   Or, in Arberry's translation of the full *aya*: 'Let there be one nation of you, calling to good, and bidding to honour, and forbidding dishonour; those are the prosperers'. It will be seen that the phrase begins with an emphasis on unity as the point of departure for sharia.

12   Marriage as a social institution is, for example, as referred to in *sura* 2: 221, 226–233, 236–237 and *sura* 4 (called 'The Women'): 15, 20, 22–25, 35; and, in the Bukhari collection of *hadith* texts, volume 7, book 62 is entirely devoted to the issue of wedlock and marriage.

13   The contrast to *sahih* is when a marriage is considered void, without legal validity (*batil*) or irregular (*fasid*).

14   In some legal texts is it referred to as *sadaq*, the Qur'anic term for 'bride wealth'.

15   *Ikama* has the same phrasing as *adhan* and is pronounced when the *salat* begins.

16   In some places, a name is given to the baby directly after its birth.

17   The waiting time is argued for with reference to the words in the Qur'an 2:234: 'And [for] those of you who die, leaving wives, they shall wait by themselves for four months and three nights; when they have researched their term then it is no fault in you what they may do with themselves honourably'.

18   The region of west central Persia between the Tigris and the Euphrates rivers.

19   The figures are from the Pew Forum report *Mapping the Global Muslim Population*; see Lugo et al. (2009). Various attempts to estimate the number of Shi'a Muslims in the world have been made and the figures vary significantly. Some sources claim that there are well over 300 million worldwide.

Sources and References

These sources and references complement the further readings suggested at the end of each chapter.

Abdullahi Ahmad an-Naim, 1990. *Toward an Islamic Reformation: Civil Liberties, Human Rights and International Law* (Syracuse, NY: Syracuse University Press).

——, 2010. *Muslims and Global Justice* (Philadelphia, PA: University of Pennsylvania Press).

Anderson, Benedict, 1983. *Imagined Communities* (London: Verso).

Arberry, A. J., 1955. *The Koran Interpreted* (London: Allen & Unwin).

Asad, Talal, 1993. *Genealogies of Religion: Discipline and Reasons of Power in Christianity and Islam* (Baltimore, MD: Johns Hopkins University Press).

Bennett, Clinton, 1998. *In Search of Muhammad* (London and New York: Cassell).

Berg, Herbert (ed.), 2003. *Method and Theory in the Study of Islamic Origins* (Leiden: Brill).

Bowen, John, 1993. *Muslims through Discourse: Religion and Ritual in Gayo Society* (Princeton, NJ: Princeton University Press).

——, 2012. *A New Anthropology of Islam* (Cambridge: Cambridge University Press).

Deeb, Lara, 2006. *An Enchanted Modern: Gender and Public Piety in Shi'i Lebanon* (Princeton, NJ: Princeton University Press).

Doumato, Eleanor, 2000. *Getting God's Ear: Women, Islam, and Healing in Saudi Arabia and the Gulf* (New York: Columbia University Press).

Euben, Roxanne and Muhammad Qasim Zaman (eds), 2009. 'Hamas charter', in *Princeton Readings in Islamist Thought: Texts and Contexts from Al-Banna to Bin Laden* (Princeton, NJ: Princeton University Press, 2009), pp. 364–86.

Frembgen, Jürgen, 2012. *At the Shrine of the Red Sufi: Five Days and Nights on Pilgrimage in Pakistan* (Oxford: Oxford University Press).

Humphreys, Stephen, 1999 (rev. edn.). *Islamic History: A Framework of Inquiry* (London: I.B.Tauris).

Irwin, Robert, 2006. *For the Lust of Knowing: The Orientalists and their Enemies* (London: Allen Lane).

Ibn Ishaq, Muhammad, 1955. *The Life of Muhammad: A Translation of Ibn Ishaq's Sirat Rasul Allah*, trans. A. Guillaume (Oxford: Oxford University Press).

al-Kalbi, Ibn, 1952. *Book of Idols: Being the Translation of the Kitab al-Asnam*, ed. Nabih Amin Fares (Princeton, NJ: Princeton University Press).

Knysh, Alexander, 2009. *Islam in Historical Perspective* (Upper Saddle River, NJ: Pearson Prentice Hall).

Manger, Leif, 2009. *Muslim Diversity: Local Islam in Global Contexts* (Richmond: Curzon).

Mawdudi, Sayyid Abul al-Ala, 1960. 'The Islamic Law', in Euben, Roxanne and Muhammad Qasim Zaman (eds), 2009. *Princeton Readings in Islamist Thought: Texts and Contexts from Al-Banna to Bin Laden* (Princeton, NJ: Princeton University Press), pp. 86–106.

Lincoln, Bruce, 2003. *Holy Terrors: Thinking about Religion after 9/11* (Chicago: University of Chicago Press).

Lugo, Luis et al., 2009. *Mapping the Global Muslim Population: A Report on the Size and the Distribution of the World's Muslim Population* (Washington, DC, Pew Forum).

Malik, Abd al, 2009. *Sufi Rapper: The Spiritual Journey of Abd al Malik* (Rochester, VT: Inner Traditions).

Motzki, Harald, 2000. *The Biography of Muhammad: The Issue of the Sources* (Leiden: Brill).

Qutb, Sayyid, 1954, 'In Shade of the Qur'an', repr. in Euben, Roxanne and Muhammad Qasim Zaman (eds), 2009. *Princeton Readings in Islamist Thought: Texts and Contexts from Al-Banna to Bin Laden* (Princeton, NJ: Princeton University Press), pp. 144–52.

——, 1964. 'Signposts along the Road', repr. in Euben, Roxanne and Muhammad Qasim Zaman (eds), 2009, *Princeton Readings in Islamist Thought: Texts and Contexts from Al-Banna to Bin Laden* (Princeton, NJ: Princeton University Press), pp. 136–44.

Robinson, Chase, 2003. *Islamic Historiography* (Cambridge: Cambridge University Press).

Rubin, Uri, 1995. *The Eye of the Beholder: The Life of Muhammad as Viewed by the Early Muslims* (Princeton, NJ: Darwin Press).

Rumi, Jalal al-din, 1999. 'Divani-i Shams-i Tabriz', ed. and trans. R. A. Nicholson in *Selected Poems from the Divani Shamsi Tabriz* (Cambridge: Cambridge University Press).

Said, Edward, 1978. *Orientalism* (New York: Pantheon).

Stetkevych, Suzanne Pinckney, 2010. *The Mantle Odes: Arabic Praise Poems to the Prophet* (Bloomington, IN: Indiana University Press).

Süleyman Çelebi, 1943. 'Mevlidi-i şerif', trans. in F. Lyman MacCallum, *The Mevlidi Sherif* (London: s.p.).

Taji-Farouki, Suha (ed.), 2004. *Modern Muslim Intellectuals and the Qur'an* (Oxford: Oxford University Press).

Index

Abbasids, 54, 174
Abd al-Malik, 11–12
Abdullahi Ahmad an-Naim, 102
Abraham, 15, 45, 46, 49, 116, 128
Abu Bakr, first caliph, 43, 51, 54, 68,
   164, 170
Abu Huraira, 138
Abu Talib, Muhammad's uncle, 39, 46,
   170
adab (correct manners), 25, 152, 186,
   191, 199, 207
Adam, 57, 103, 128, 191
   Adam's fall, 15–16, 191–2
adultery, 101, 193, 194, 207
aesthetics, 201–206
   imagery, prohibition against, 201–3,
      205–6
   Muslim art, 204
   Shi'i Islam, *171*, 179, 203–5
   Sufism, 154, 203
   Sunni Islam, 205
   see also poetry
al-Afghani, Jamal al-Din, 219, 226
al-Agharr al-Muzani, 188
ahl al-bayt (family of the Prophet), 39, 51,
   172–3, 178
ahl al-dhimma (protected peoples), 7
ahl al-kisa (people of the mantle), 173
ahl al-kitab (People of the Book) 7–8, 98
Aisha, Muhammad's wife, 51, 115, 137,
   170, 202
akhlaq, see Islamic ethics
alcohol, 92, 194, 197, 209
   see also wine

Ali b. Abu Talib, fourth caliph, 40, 51,
   53–4, 113, 173
   Shi'i Islam, 39, 168, 170, *171*
Amina, Muhammad's mother, 39, 113
amulet, 78, 119, 149
analogy (*qiyas*), 87, 91
Anderson, Benedict: *Imagined
   Communities*, 4
angel, 20, 34, 42, 202
   Jibril/Gabriel, 20, 25, 41, 42, 44, 66,
      115, 116, 137
ansar, 48
Arab nationalism, 219–20, 229
Arabic language, 1, 6, 241
   Qur'an, 6, 59, 62, 66, 76, 81
Asad, Talal, 16, 26
Asharites, 69
authority, 13, 16, 218
   no central authority, 6, 17–18, 72
   religious authority, 3, 74, 93, 144,
      217, 218
   see also imam; *ulama*
al-Azhar University, 92, 93, 241–2

Balkans, the, 6, 54, 91, 111
al-Banna, Hasan, 226–8
baraka (blessing), 81, 129, 149, 154, 162,
   178
basmala, 18, 63, 64, 124, 140, 187, 196
battle of Badr, 49, 111, 115
battle of Karbala, 54, 111, 177, 203, 205
battle of Trench, 49–50
battle of Uhud, 49
belief, *see iman*

belonging:
  ethnic belonging, 12, 199
  religious belonging, 1, 135, 213
  see also identity
Bowen, John, 26
al-Bukhari, Muhammad, 73
  Sahih Bukhari, 15, 18, 72, 118, 138,
    140, 141, 202, 208, 209
Buraq, 44–5, *46*

Çelebi, Süleyman, 56–7, 112, 120
celibacy, 94–5, 143, 207
children:
  birth and naming, 118–20
  circumcision, 120
China, 2, 54, 159, 239 n.1
Christianity, 5, 7, 15–16, 47, 62–3, 136,
  192
  creed, 17
  and Sufism, 157–8
  see also Jesus
Companions, 48, 71
consensus (*ijma*), 87, 104, 223
creation, 23, 191
custom, *see* tradition/custom

dar al-harb (the house of war/non-
  Muslim world), 6, 92
dar al-islam (the house of Islam/Muslim
  world), 6, 91
Day of Judgement, 20, 43, 67, 122, 125
death and funerals, 121–6, 136
  differences between men/women's
    rituals, 121, 124, 125
  funeral prayer, 125
  funeral ritual, 109, 123–5
  grieving period, 126
Deeb, Lara: *An Enchanted Modern*, 183
democracy, 100–1, 102, 213, 229
  shura, 102
  theo-democracy, 225
Deobandis, 225–6, 234
  see also Mawdudi, Sayyid Abul al-Ala
diaspora, 2, 3, 4, 10–11, 240
  transnational lifestyle, 2, 10, 11, 123
  see also migration

dietary laws, 194–9
  halal, 195–6, 199, *210*
  haram, 195
  pork, 194, 195, 209
  slaughter, 196, 198
  see also alcohol
divination, 24, 33, 149, 189, 193, 196
divorce, 99–100, 126
Doumato, Eleanor: *Getting God's Ear*,
  13–14
dress code, 92, 199–201
  women's veiling, 121, 200–1, *200*

economy, 207–11
  economic transactions, 100, 208
  Islamic banking, 209
  see also usury
education, 3, 219–20, 237, 241
  see also madrasa
Egypt, 2, 93, 219, 226–30
endowment (*waqf*), 100, 211
ethics, *see* Islamic ethics

falsafa (philosophy), 74, 76
al-Farabi, Abu Nasr, 186
fard (obligatory), 19, 88, 121, 189
fasting, 117, 198–9
  Ramadan, 14, 19, 25, 114, 116, 198
  siyam, 108, 136
Fatima, Muhammad's daughter, 40, 51,
  70, 172, 173
Fatimids, 174, 175
fatwa, 90, 93–4
  European Fatwa Council, 89
  mufti, 90
festivals, 109–17, 129–30
  Id al-Adha, 110, 111, 116–17, 128,
    129
  Id al-Fitr, 110, 111, 116, 117, 129
  mawlid, 112–13, 130, 224
  see also Muslim calendar
fiqh (jurisprudence), 69, 75, 86, 89, 108,
  224
  faqih, 89, 90
fitra (primordial harmony), 191
  din al-fitra, 23, 187, 229

four rightly guided caliphs, 51, 53–4, 68,
    168, 170
Frembgen, Jürgen: *At the Shrine of the
    Red Sufi*, 162
Friday prayer (*juma*), 49, 107, 142, 133,
    142–4
    khutba, 107, 142
    see also prayer; *salat*

gambling, 193, 209
gender issues, 13–14, 85, 206
    differences between men/women's
        funeral rituals, 121, 123, 125
    gender relations, 206–7
    homosexuality, 207
    housing, 135
    mosque, 144
al-Ghazali, Zaynab, 232
globalization, 9, 13, 14, 127, 237, 240
God, 15, 21–3, 83–4
    Allah, 21–2, 23, 25
    al-asma al-husna, 22–3, 164
    as Creator, 23, 201
    as legislator and judge, 84, 89
    qualities, 17, 22, 187
    takbir, 22
    taqwa, 21–2
    will of, 193
    see also tawhid
good deeds, 25, 103, 187, 211

hadith, 1, 15, 17, 19, 25, 36, 71–4, 80
    collections of, 37, 57, 72–3, 75
    definition, 70–1
    as foundation for juridical and
        theological arguments, 60
    hadith qudsi, 73–4
    importance of, 70–1
    Islamic ethics, 190–1
    isnad, 71, 74
    as source of sharia, 87
    see also al-Bukhari, Muhammad;
        Muslim b. al-Hajjaj
Hagar, Ismael's mother, 49, 128
hajj, 19, 25, 32, *34*, 50, 108, 126–9, 130,
    136

rituals, 127–8
women, 126–7
see also Kaaba
halal (lawful), 88, 104, 108, 189, 199
    definition, 195, 197–8
    dietary laws, 195–6, 199, *210*
    see also dress code
Halima, Muhammad's nurse, 39, 57
al-Hallaj, Mansur, 159
Hamas, 231–2
haram (forbidden), 88, 98, 108, 195, 197,
    199
    dietary laws, 195
Hasan b. Ali, 51, 172, 173
Helpers, 48
heretic, 7, 24, 277
hijra (migration), 47, 48, 112
Hira, mountain, 40–1, 57, 66
Hizbullah, 232
hudud (limits), 101, 193–4, 207
human rights, 100–3
    Cairo Declaration on Human Rights
        in Islam, 102, 103
    UN, Universal Declaration of Human
        Rights, 101, 102
Husayn b. Ali, 51, 54, 111, 172, 173, 177
hybridity, 11, 12

ibadat (religious duties/worship), 107–8,
    127, 136, 165, 185
Iblis/Satan, 34, 66, 128, 192–3
Ibn Arabi, Muhyi al-Din, 153
Ibn Ishaq, Muhammad, 37, 40, 42, 44,
    67, 137
Ibn al-Kalbi, Hisham: *Book of Idols*, 35
Ibn Taymiyya, Taqi al-Din Ahmad, 91,
    152, 223, 224
Ibn 'Umar, Abd Allah, 141
identity, 1, 13, 15
    Muslim identity, 10, 13, 129, 199, 211
    see also belonging
idolatry, 35, 202–3
    see also shirk
ihsan (virtue), 20, 187
ijtihad (legal reasoning), 68–9, 88, 117,
    176, 222

ijtihad (legal reasoning) *cont.*
  mujtahid, 88
imam, 3, 10, 139, 142–4
  role of, 142–3
  Sunni/Shi'i distinction, 172
  see also authority
iman (belief), 20, 24, 187
  fundamental beliefs, 20, 188
India, 2, 5, 54, 168
innovation (*bida*), 91, 152, 221–2
integration, 3
intention (*niyya*), 19, 117, 127, 140, 166,
  188
Iran, 1, 2, 55
  Iranian Revolution, 180–1, 183
  Shi'ism, 55, 168, 180–1
Iraq, 168, 181–2
Irwin, Robert: *For the Lust of Knowing*, 5
Islam, 14–26, 189
  din, 16–17
  din al-fitra, 23, 229
  diversity, 1, 9, 20, 26
  final message, 15, 20, 23, 25, 41
  five pillars of Islam, 18–19, 20, 24–5,
  134
  monotheism, 17, 20, 22, 25, 34
  public aspects of religious life, 135–6
  Qur'an, 16
  studies on, 239 n.2
  transformation, 1, 3–4, 5, 104, 237
  universal claims, 15
Islam, history of, 5, 14, 16, 29–58
  early expansion of Islam, 51–5, *52*
  military expansion of Islam, 49–50
  see also pre-Islamic world
Islamic anthropology, 23, 186, 188,
  195
Islamic ethics, 185–212
  akhlaq, 25, 86, 186
  central concepts of, 186–9, 211
  free human will, 188
  gender relations, 206–7
  and Greek philosophy, 186
  ilm al-akhlaq, 185–6, 191
  normative sources of, 189–93
  sharia, 185, 189, 191, 209, 211

  see also aesthetics; economy; *halal*;
    haram; *hudud*; sin
Islamism, 217, 219–36
  colonialism, reaction to, 219, 220,
    225, 226, 236
  definition, 213, 215–16, 221
  founders of, 222–36
  ideology, 216, 220–2, 225–6, 228,
    229, 231, 236
  jihad, 215, 227–8, 231, 234
  jihadists, 214, 215, 230
  martyrdom, 215, 227, 228, 230
  media, 216, 226, 231, 232, 234
  origins, 219–20, 230, 236
  radical Islam, 10, 24, 214–17, 221, 230
  recruitment, 230–1, 232
  revivalism, 215, 226, 228, 236
  Shi'i Islamism, 181–2
  see also Deobandis; Hamas; Hizbullah;
    Muslim Brotherhood; *salafi/*
    salafiyya; the Taliban; terrorism;
    violence; *wahhabism*
Ismael, 49, 128
Ismail, Salwa: *Rethinking Islamist Politics*,
  216

Jafar al-Sadiq, 175
jahiliyya, 35, 47–8, 229, 230
Jami, Mawlana Abd al-Rahman, 150
Jesus, 30, 57, 61, 70, 138, 205
  the Gospel, 61–2
jihad (effort), 215
  greater *jihad*, 188, 215
  holy war, 213
  Islamism, 215, 227–8, 231, 234
  lesser *jihad*, 188, 215
jinn (demon), 23, 34–5, 44, 78, 192
Judaism, 5, 7, 15–16, 47, 62–3, 136, 192
justice (*adl*), 87, 187

Kaaba, 32–3, *34*, 35–6, 49, 128
  black stone, 33, 50, 128
  circumambulation of, 33, 50, 128, 129
  haram, 33, 50
  kiswa, 128
  see also hajj

kafir (apostate/infidel), 24, 99, 187, 228
kalam, 74–6, 86, 107
    Islamic theology, 14, 17, 20–1, 53, 63, 69
Khadija, Muhammad's wife, 40, 43, 46, 51, 137, 172
Khaled, Amr 234
Khomeini, Ruhollah, Ayatollah, 181, 182
knowledge (*ilm*), 84, 86, 163
kufr (apostasy/infidelity), 88, 101, 187

Lebanon, 183
legitimacy, 69, 95, 158, 218
lifecycle rituals, 107–9, 117–26, 129
    birth and naming, 118–20
    coming of age rituals, 120–1
    ritual participation, 108–109
    see also death and funerals; marriage
Lincoln, Bruce: *Holy Terrors*, 220–1

madrasa, 77, 85, 92, 142, 143, 225, 241
Manger, Leif: *Muslim Diversity*, 5
marriage, 94–100
    agreement of, 121
    impediments to, 98–9
    mahr, 96–7
    marriage contract, 95, 96, *96*, 99
    nikah, 95
    sahih, 95
    as social institution, 95, 241 n.12
    wedding, 95, 97–8
martyrdom, 54, 111, 170, 171, 177–80, 184
    Islamism, 215, 227, 228, 230
Mary, mother of Jesus, 29, 70
Mawdudi, Sayyid Abul al-Ala, 225–6, 229
    Jamaat-i Islami, 226
Mecca, 32–3, 44
media, 92–3, 129, 133–4, 205–6
    Islamism, 216, 226, 231, 232, 234
    Muhammad's life on film, 39
    social media, 9, 14, 93, 237, 240
Medina, 26, 46–8, 49
    Medina model, 48, 190, 191, 221, 222, 236

migration, 9, 10, 237
    see also diaspora; *hijra*
minority, 8
    Muslim minority, 168, 176, 211–12, 239 n.1
Mongols, 54, 174
monotheism, 7, 8, 15
    Islam, 17, 20, 22, 25, 34
Moses, 46, 138, 185, 205
mosque, 3–4, 49, 144–8, *147*
    communal prayer, 14, 49, 144, 146
    Grand Mosque in Mecca, 128
    jami, 146
    masjid, 146
    mihrab, 146–7
    minaret, 138, 145, 146
    minbar, 146, 147
    Mosque of the Prophet, 48, 50, 55, 129
    networking, 3, 144
    women, 4, 147–8
    see also Friday prayer; *qibla*; *salat*
muamalat (social/ritual activities), 107, 108, 136, 185
Muhammad, 15, 23, 25, 29–31, 35
    devotion of, 29, 31, 39, 55–6, 150, 224
    mantle of Muhammad, 12, 113
    al-nabi, 20, 30
    Night Journey, 22, 43, 44–6, 113, 138, 158, 205
    nur muhammadi, 23, 56
    Opening of the Breast, 44, 57
    qualities, 55–6
    Qur'an, revelation to Muhammad, 25, 29, 30, 41–3, 57–8, 66–7
    al-rasul, 20, 30
    seal of the prophets, 30, 57
    Splitting of the Moon, 44, 57
Muhammad, historical person, 36–48, 57
    birth of, 56, 112
    death, 50
    early life, 38–40
    public activities, 40–7
    religious, communal and military leader, 47–8

Muhammad, historical person *cont.*
wives, 40
Muhammad Abduh, 219, 226
multiculturalism, 8, 199, 204, 237
Muslim, 1, 25–6, 48
definition, 19–20, 25
population, 1, 2
social and ritual obligations, 43
Muslim b. al-Hajjaj, 73
Sahih Muslim, 173, 188
Muslim Brotherhood, 226–30
Muslim calendar, 109, 110–17
Dhu al-Hijja, 111, 116–17, 127
hijra calendar, 47
Muharram, 109, 110, 111–12, 178–9, 184
New Year's Day, 112
Rabi Al-Awwal, 112–13
Rajab, 110, 113
Shaban, 110, 113–14
Shawwal, 109, 111, 116
see also festivals; Ramadan
Muslim community, *see umma*
Muslim/non-Muslim relations, 1–2, 6–7, 15, 190, 209
non-Muslims and sharia, 92
Mutazilites, 69, 90, 186

Orientalism, 3, 4–5
Ottoman Empire, 55, 211
millet system, 8

pagan, 7, 33, 34, 195, 230
pilgrimage, 5, 149, 177, 184
umra, 127
see also hajj; visit to graves and shrines
poetry, 35, 150, 203
political Islam, 35, 214
civil society betterment, 217, 233
Islamic liberals, 235–6
political mobilization, 3, 218
takfir as political strategy, 24
women's leadership, 218, 232–3
see also Islamism
polytheism, *see shirk*
prayer, 3, 6, 15, 148–51

communal prayer, 14, 49, 144, 146
dua, 149–50, 151
funeral prayer, 125
istighfar, 150–1
retreat, 115
voluntary additional prayers, 115, 141
see also Friday prayer; *salat*
pre-Islamic world, 31–6
gods and goddesses, 33, 34, 35–6, 193, 239 n.5
predestination, 20, 23, 34, 188, 193
providence, 20, 34, 189
Psalms, 61–2
punishment, 193, 194, 207
purification, 19, 25, 137, 166
after childbirth, 120, 140
ghusl, 124, 140
ihram, 127
tahara, 108, 136, 139
washing of the corpse, 124
wudu, 125, 139, 140

qadi (judge), 89, 90, 97
al-Qaradawi, Yusuf, 234
qibla, 32, 43, 49, 136–7, 140, 146, *148*
qibla compass, *53*
Qur'an, 1, 19, 20, 30, 59–69, *61*, 80
ajza, 76
Arabic language, 6, 59, 62, 66, 76, 81
editions, 68, 240 n.8
as foundation for juridical and theological arguments, 60
hafiz, 77
as holy artefact, 60, 78, 81
Islam, 16
Islamic ethics, 189–90
Laylat al-Qadr, 41, 111, 115, 189
poetry, 35, 63
recitation of, 41, 59, 60, 76–8, 81, 133
redaction of, 67–9
revelation of, 24, 25, 29, 30, 41–3, 57–8, 66–7
as source of sharia, 86–7
structure of, 63–7
tanzil, 20, 41, 64

translations of, 240 n.8, 10
see also tafsir
Qur'an, suras and verses, 63–7
abrogation, 65–6
The Elephant, 38
al-Falaq, 119
al-Fatiha, 17–18, 19, 20, 59, 98, 141
from Mecca, 41, 43, 64
from Medina, 41, 64, 65
al-Ikhlas, 20, 21
al-Nas, 23
The Night Journey, 44, 45
Throne Verse, 17, 141
Ya Sin, 122–3
see also basmala
Quraysh clan, 31–2, 33, 38, 50, 51
Qutb, Sayyid, 228–30

radicalism, see Islamism
Ramadan, 24, 109, 111, 114–16
fasting, 14, 19, 25, 114, 116, 198
Laylat al-Qadr, 41, 111, 115, 189
Qur'an, recitation of, 76, 77, 133
refugee, 5, 10, 12
religion, 13–25, 26
din al-fitra, 23, 187, 229
role in personal and public life, 221
see also Islam
repentance (tawba), 187, 188
resurrection, 20, 121, 124, 126
Rumi, Jalal al-Din, 158–60

al-Sadr, Muhammad Sadeq, 182–3
Safavids, 55, 174, 180
Said, Edward: Orientalism, 4–5, 16
saints, veneration of, 134–5, 154, 165
controversy on, 150, 152, 224
see also visit to graves and shrines
salafi/salafiyya, 91, 223, 226, 229, 232
common features, 221–2, 224
salat (canonical prayers), 18, 19, 25, 43,
55, 108, 136–42, 242
ablution, 137, 139, 140
bodily movements, 138, 141
call to prayer, 138, 145–6
prayer leader, 139
prayer rug, 145

requirements, 139–41
timing, 109, 138–9, 140
see also mosque; prayer; purification;
qibla
Saudi Arabia, 91, 127, 177, 224–5
schools of law, 20, 90, 104, 211
Hanafi school, 91, 235
Hanbali school, 75, 91, 223, 224–5
Jafari school, 91, 175
Maliki school, 91
Shafii school, 91
shahada (witnessing of faith), 19, 20–1,
118, 122, 136, 140, 141, 215
sharia, 14, 17, 19, 58, 83–104, 185
definition, 83–4
five sharia values, 88
implementation, 90–4, 104
in Islamic ethics, 185, 189, 191, 209,
211
in Islamic history, 84–6
methods, 87–9
sources of, 86–7, 104
see also divorce; economy; human
rights; marriage
shaykh, 90, 151, 153–4, 156, 160,
161–3
functions of, 161, 162
marabout, 162–3
see also Sufism
Shi'i Islam, 13–14, 167–84
aesthetic expressions, 171, 179, 203–
205
history of, 173–4
imamate, 172, 175–6, 184
Iran, 55, 168, 180–1
mahdi, 114, 175, 176, 181, 182
martyrdom, 54, 111, 170, 171, 177–
80, 184, 204
Muharram, 111, 178–9, 184
Muslim minority, 168, 176
population, 168, 169, 241 n.19
quest for legitimate leadership, 168–
73, 183, 213
Sevener/Twelver Shi'ism, 174, 175,
184
Shi'i Islamism, 181–2

Shi'i Islam *cont.*
  Shi'i theology, 69, 174–6, 184
  Sunni/Shi'i conflict, 39, 53–4, 167,
    171–2, 181–4
  taqiyya, 176
  turbah, 179, *180*
  see also Ali b. Abu Talib
shirk (polytheism), 7, 8, 24, 34, 35, 50,
    152, 158, 187, 224
sin, 176, 187, 188, 192, 208
  original sin, 186, 211
sira:
  conduct, 37
  sira literature, 36–8
SIS (Sisters in Islam), 232–3
  Anwar, Zainah, 233
  Wadud, Amina, 233
slavery, 190
Sufism, 22, 69, 149, 151–65, 166
  aesthetic expressions, 154, 203
  criticism of, 152–3, 158, 166, 223–4
  definition, 151, 156
  dervish, 156, 160
  dhikr, 158, 160, 164–5, 193
  history of, 157–60
  Mevlevi order of whirling dervishes,
    160, *161*
  prayer beads, 150, 158, 164
  rituals, 151, 154, 156, 164–5
  Sufi order, 151, 160–4
  Sufi theology, 91, 149, 153, 157–8,
    160, 163
  zawiya/tekke, 154, *155*, 156, 166
  see also shaykh
sunna, 25, 36, 37, 51, 57
  Islamic ethics, 191
  as source of sharia, 87
Sunni Islam, 13–14, 53
  aesthetic expressions, 205
  Sunni/Shi'i conflict, 39, 53–4, 167,
    171–2, 181–4
  taqlid, 88

al-Tabari, Muhammad, 75
tafsir (Qur'an exegesis), 60, 68, 81, 86,
    225, 229, 230

contemporary Qur'an interpretation,
    78–9
Taji-Farouki, Suha: *Modern Muslim
    Intellectuals and the Qur'an*, 79
takbir, 22, 141, 142, 150
Taliban, the, 234–5
taqlid (imitation), 88, 104, 222
taqwa (piety), 21–2, 163, 187, 231
tawhid (God's unity), 20, 22, 81, 185,
    188, 239
tax, 7, 48
temptation (*fitna*), 23, 187, 193
terrorism, 214–15, 235, 236
theft, 101, 193, 194
Torah, 61–2
tradition/custom (*ada/urf*), 5, 85, 107,
    191, 211, 223
  umma, 12–13
Turkey, 1, 2, 54, 236
  Diyanet, 93, 143

ulama (Islamic scholars), 13, 68, 76, 89–
    90, 176, 237
Umar b. al-Khattab, second caliph, 51,
    53, 54, 208
Umayyads, 53, 54, 170, 173–4, 177
umma (Muslim community), 6, 8–13, 17,
    43, 48–51, 81
  early *umma*, 37, 47, 48–9, 239
  excommunication from, 24
  meanings, 8–9
  Medina model, 48, 190, 191, 221,
    222, 236
  tradition, 12–13
usury (*riba*), 208–10
Uthman b. Affan, third caliph, 43–4, 53,
    54, 68

violence, 213, 214, 216, 230, 235
  see also terrorism
visit to graves and shrines, 5, 10–11, 49,
    149, 154, 165, 178, 223
  Karbala, 176, 177, 178, 184
  Najaf, 171, 176, 178, 184
  see also saints, veneration of

al-Wahhab, Muhammad b. Abd, 223,
224–5
wahhabism, 50, 55, 177, 215, 222, 224–5
definition, 224
the West, 3, 5, 182
wine, 193, 196–7, 199
see also alcohol
women:
dress code/*hijab*, 121, 200–1, *200*
education, 13, 142
endowment, 100
hajj, 126–7
leadership, 218, 232–3

public ritual life, 4, 77, 113, 133, 134,
135, 147–8
widow, 126
see also gender issues
worship *see ibada*; mosque; prayer

zakat (alms), 19, 25, 48, 108, 116, 136,
210
zamzam well, 129
Zaynab, Muhammad's granddaughter,
10–11, *11*, 172, 177
Zoroastrianism, 7, 8, 31, 47, 180

I.B.TAURIS INTRODUCTIONS TO RELIGION

Daoism: An Introduction – Ronnie L Littlejohn
HB 9781845116385
PB 9781845116392

Jainism: An Introduction – Jeffery D Long
HB 9781845116255
PB 9781845116262

Judaism: An Introduction – Oliver Leaman
HB 9781848853942
PB 9781848853959

Zoroastrianism: An Introduction – Jenny Rose
HB 9781848850873
PB 9781848850880

Confucianism: An Introduction – Ronnie L Littlejohn
HB 9781848851733
PB 9781848851740

Sikhism: An Introduction – Nikky-Guninder Kaur Singh
HB 9781848853201
PB 9781848853218

Islam: An Introduction – Catharina Raudvere
HB 9781848850835
PB 9781848850842

Christianity: An Introduction – Philip Kennedy
HB 9781848853829
PB 9781848853836

Hinduism: An Introduction – Will Sweetman
HB 9781848853270
PB 9781848853287

Buddhism: An Introduction – Alexander Wynne
HB 9781848853966
PB 9781848853973

Mormonism: An Introduction – Malise Ruthven
HB 9781780760100
PB 9781780760117